Cutting Edge Gardening
in the Intermountain West

Cutting Edge

Gardening

in the Intermountain

West

Marcia Tatroe

Photographs *by* Charles Mann

JOHNSON BOOKS • *Boulder*

Portions of this text were first published in the *Colorado Gardener*, *The Denver Post*, the *Rock Garden Quarterly*, and the *Saximontana* (the newsletter of the Rocky Mountain Chapter of the North American Rock Garden Society).

Published by Johnson Books, a Big Earth Publishing company:
3005 Center Green Drive, Suite 220
Boulder, Colorado 80301
E-mail: books@bigearthpublishing.com
www.johnsonbooks.com

Cover design, text design, and composition: Pauline Christensen

10 9 8 7 6 5 4 3 2 1

Library of Congress Cataloging-in-Publication Data

Tatroe, Marcia.
  Cutting edge gardening in the Intermountain West / by Marcia Tatroe ; photography by Charles Mann.
   p. cm.
  Includes index.
ISBN 978-1-55566-387-2
  1. Alpine gardens—Great Basin. 2. Alpine garden plants—Great Basin. 3. Rock gardens—Great Basin. I. Mann, Charles, 1951– II. Title.
  SB459.T38 2007
  635.9'528—dc22
                        2006034857

Printed in Singapore

CONTENTS

PREFACE

ONCE, WHEN A RADIO INTERVIEWER asked why I garden, I told him that he might as well ask me why I breathe, so important is gardening to my life. Even so, I'm not one of those gardeners who built my first garden at the tender age of six, and I never really planned to take up gardening as a profession. I just presumed that gardening was something that everyone did. My mother gardened and taught me to garden, but she never actually called herself a "gardener."

My earliest interests extended to anything that was out of doors—animals, insects, rocks, and plants got equal attention. As a child, my pockets were always full of any bits of nature I could catch, from sand dabs and frogs to pinecones and seashells. I grew sweet potatoes and carrot tops on sunny windowsills. I also hatched chicks, allowed three white rats to reproduce into dozens, and trapped caterpillars in jalousie windows to witness their transformation into butterflies.

Born in Wisconsin, I grew up in such diverse places as Key West, Florida, and Monterey, California. When Randy and I married in 1970, my itinerant lifestyle continued as we moved to the Pacific Northwest, then back to California, and eventually on to Holland and England. Because I never stayed in one place for more than a few years, I never had the opportunity to build an extensive garden until coming to Colorado in 1987.

Before that, the gardens I built resided in my fantasies—while I tended actual gardens attached to rentals. Landlords frown on having their property dug up and reordered, so instead, I spent countless hours contemplating the garden I would eventually build. Over the years, this became more and more of an obsession. By the time we arrived in Colorado, I was ready to hit the ground running. The garden I had in mind then was going to rival anything we had seen in England.

My personal piece of real estate in Centennial, Colorado, seemed huge when we chose it. In reality, it's only a scant quarter acre, with a typical suburban house consuming much of the space (both lot and house are large compared with England and Holland, where residential properties are quite small). At the time we moved here, there were no mature shade trees anywhere in our fairly new neighborhood. The soil tested a daunting pH of 8.4—every garden book I consulted said this was too high to grow much of anything. But back then, water was still plentiful and cheap.

A neighbor directed me to the only other gardener in our neighborhood. Diane Byers, who lived just a couple of blocks up the street, became a fast friend and the first of many mentors. I drew up plans, visited area nurseries, and with the help of our two sons, Kevin and Keith, and Diane's husband, Bob (he and Randy got a kick out of running the sod stripper), started removing sod and building flowerbeds. Fortuitously, that winter I also attended a series of lectures on xeriscaping by renowned landscape architect and author Jim Knopf, sponsored through Denver Water.

I was instantly hooked by Jim's brand of xeriscape. Among my strongest childhood memories are the rugged coastline of Central California and the snowcapped mountains of the West. The grandeur of Zion National Park, the deserts of the

Southwest, and the badlands of my father's childhood home in South Dakota are forever embedded in my soul. Forests and trees never had the same impact as the dramatic beauty of deserts and rocks. I'm always puzzled when I hear folks complain about crossing Nevada or Wyoming, calling the high steppes nothing but "miles and miles of miles and miles."

To me, the very vastness of these wild open basins, each hosting a unique plant community and geography, is haunting and seductive. I thrill to the roller-coaster drive through this mountain and basin topography. It's not that I don't understand the appeal of the shaded glen—it's just that I prefer more excitement in my scenery. Texture, soaring rock faces, every color in the artist's palette, and horizons that go forever are what I crave. The Intermountain West was love at first sight.

As infatuation gave way to a lifelong commitment to my first real home, I realized that this cloudless, dramatic, and dynamic landscape demanded a different sort of garden, one that reflects the unparalleled natural beauty that surrounds us. Drought and ongoing water shortages are forcing all of us in this region to rethink long-held garden and landscape conventions. This isn't all bad. Learning to garden with less water has become the catalyst for creating a new garden aesthetic—one where gardens speak strongly about where we live and who we are.

Prickly blue spheres of globe thistle *Echinops ritro* add texture and drama to the Intermountain West garden.

ACKNOWLEDGMENTS

ANYONE WHO HAS MET HIM knows that, as well as being an accomplished and sensitive photographer, Charles Mann is also an extraordinary wit and a philosopher. He and I have worked together frequently for the past ten years. Because shoots involve an inordinate amount of waiting around for perfect light conditions, we've had lots of time to chat. This book grew out of our many conversations, as we struggled to make sense of gardening in a place where conventional wisdom too often fails us. For his inspiration, encouragement, and support, I am eternally indebted.

A special thanks goes to friends who proofread the manuscript, wading through typos and punctuation errors (and always apologetic when pointing them out). Sally Boyson, Diana Capen, Rebecca Day-Skowron, Panayoti Kelaidis, and Hugh Mac Millan were invaluable for their help and advice. John Starnes provided expert advice on roses, and Deb Golanty of the Helen Fowler Library at Denver Botanic Gardens gave us insights into the publishing process. For help in identifying plants: Bill Adams of Sunscapes, Pueblo, Colorado; Mikl Brawner of Harlequin Gardens, Boulder, Colorado; Bob Pennington of Agua Fria Nursery in Santa Fe, New Mexico; and the catalog from Plants of the Southwest in Santa Fe, New Mexico.

This book would not have been possible but for all the generous gardeners who opened their gardens to us—in many cases, repeatedly, as we waited for the light to cooperate or a particular flower to open. Heartfelt thanks go to: Ann and Larry Andersen, Belinda Arbogast, Joan Brink, Jan Davis, Rebecca Day-Skowron, Rochelle Eliason, Kelly Grummons of Timberline Gardens, Karen Haataja, Barbara and Marc Horowitz, Laurie Jennings, Dan Johnson, Gwen and Panayoti Kelaidis, Mary Ellen Keskimaki, Gerry Krueger, Eileen and Patrick Mangan, Harlyn and Jerry Mlynck, Diane and Tom Peace, David Salman of Santa Fe Greenhouses, John Smith, Laura and Tim Spear, Sandy Snyder, Mary Ellen Tonsing, Andrew and Gay Ungerleider, Susan Yetter, and Denver Botanic Gardens. Also invaluable were the skills of editor Marlene Blessing, designer Polly Christensen, and publisher Mira Perrizo, who patiently made hundreds of plant list edits with never one word of complaint.

My ever-patient husband, Randy, once again, typed the whole darned book with only the occasional complaint. Rock gardening may be my passion, but Randy is my rock.

Introduction:
Developing a Regional Aesthetic

_W_e live in a magical place, but, for the most part, gardeners in the Intermountain West have not yet learned to make magical gardens. It's not that we are unaware of the grandeur that surrounds us. Tourism is one of our most profitable enterprises and outdoor recreation is a huge draw for visitors and residents alike. A home with a view commands a premium price. But, when we make landscapes and gardens, few of us acknowledge what is unique about this land or what distinguishes it from other parts of the country. Too many of us ignore a basic tenet of landscape design—that a sensitive landscape reflects the _genius loci,_ the sense of place that defines the spirit and the underlying character of the local environs.

Overleaf: Local rock and colorful flowers in the Butterfly Garden at Yampa River Botanic Park, Steamboat Springs, Colorado.

Left: A cobalt blue garage wall makes a brilliant backdrop for hollyhocks and golden columbine. Ann and Larry Andersen's garden, Denver.

IN THIS RESPECT, we are not alone. Most of America settles for a one-size-fits-all mentality that has been dubbed "the American national landscape." As in other parts of the country, the landscaping norm for Denver, Boise, Salt Lake City, and Cheyenne is lawn, foundation plantings of shrubs, and one or two shade trees. Our monotonous landscapes might be, at least in part, due to our country's diverse heritage. Immigrants brought colorful ancestral customs to America, which subsequent generations hastily jettisoned in a determined attempt to fit in. We've been engaged in the social equivalent of the color exercise required of every art student in which all of the pure colors in the spectrum are mixed together. The result is neutral gray. In much the same way, the pedestrian American landscape appears to be the unintended consequence of our melting-pot culture. Beyond the occasional flower bed, really bright colors in the landscape make Americans uncomfortable—and are often discouraged or forbidden by community covenants. (When I painted my front door cobalt blue, one of my neighbors complained that it was "awfully bright.")

A notable exception lies within our region. In Santa Fe, New Mexico, the entire community embraces both its cultural history and natural character. Artwork and adobe pay tribute to longstanding traditions, and landscapes and gardens reflect the drama of the desert through native plants, local stone, and "coyote fences" built of rough-hewn juniper poles. Gates, walls, and mosaics wear strong colors that stand up to a brilliant planting palette of orange poppies, yellow rabbitbrush, and purple clematis, all playing off the dazzling blue sky that is the trademark of this region. Rather than manicured bluegrass, lawns are more often textural carpets of drought-tolerant blue grama or buffalo grass. Widely recognized and revered, the Santa Fe aesthetic has been an unqualified success. Even so, few other places have followed suit.

The southwestern style of this garden reflects both its cultural and natural character with adobe construction, accented by brightly painted woodwork and hollyhocks, sunflowers, and cosmos against a coyote fence of weathered wood. Joan Brink garden in Santa Fe, New Mexico.

Several years ago, I was discussing America's lack of regional identity with Randy when he responded, "Oh, I get it. It's like the difference between national brands and microbrews." Seeing my puzzled look, he explained that national brands appeal to a homogenous nationwide market, whereas microbrews are aimed at a local or niche market. Over the past couple of decades, microbreweries have emerged all across the country, each reflecting local nuances and brewmasters' personal idiosyncracies. As a result, you get unlikely ingredients, such as chocolate-raspberry or pumpkin—no one has ever accused a microbrewer of making a boring beer. The popularity of microbrews suggests changing attitudes toward regionalism. So, why do we in the Intermountain West continue to make landscapes that look so much like those in Peoria?

Teaching Beatles Songs to a Parrot

If our landscapes are as unexciting as a national brand of beer, our garden aesthetics tend to be inappropriate to our climate and water availability. For inspiration, we look primarily to England. Few places on earth are less like the Intermountain West than the pastoral, green rolling hills of England. Yet doggedly, many of us attempt to turn our personal piece of real estate into an English garden. While it might be possible to approximate an English garden using adapted stand-ins for traditional plants, our gardens can never be more than a faint imitation of the real thing. It's like teaching a parrot to sing Beatles songs. You might recognize the tune (and David Letterman might be interested), but no one is going to mistake the parrot for John Lennon.

To add to the confusion, most of us have no idea what an English garden actually looks like. We conjure up a floriferous image of the nostalgic, but idealized cottage gardens popularized by Victorian artist Helen Allingham or the monumental flower borders of Gertrude Jekyll. The long border, a vestige of the Victorian era when labor was cheap and any impracticality possible, is as rare

Nothing better represents the Intermountain West than a garden filled with flowers. Eilene and Patrick Mangan's Bear Creek garden in Lakewood, Colorado, in summer with yellow rudbeckias in foreground.

today in England as it is in America. Even in its heyday, the long border existed within the larger context of the estate garden, which concentrated on architecture and plants used as architecture, not flowers. My memories from four years of living in England and visiting dozens of gardens are of monumental hedges and stately old trees. Flowers were always of secondary importance.

Flower gardens actually represent our region more accurately than they do the English countryside, where nearly every square inch of real estate has been domesticated for the past several centuries. In the Intermountain West, wildflowers abound. A visitor to Denver Botanic Gardens once asked me who maintained the prairie flowers east of Denver. I'm certain she expected to hear about some local effort similar to Ladybird Johnson's Texas wildflower program. But the miles and miles of wildflowers along the interstate are completely natural.

It's further irony that, while we attempt to create what we perceive as English gardens, the English have great awe and admiration for our native flora, which we too often dismiss as "weeds." When the great English plantsman Christopher Lloyd visited Colorado in 2003, he was ecstatic to find prickly pear cactus blooming in the foothills south of Boulder. (Those who emulate the English aesthetic are unlikely to admit this plant to their gardens.) Mr. Lloyd declared that the last thing he wanted to see in Denver was an English-style garden. When he visited the gardens of Dan Johnson and Gwen and Panayoti Kelaidis, three of Colorado's leading horticulturalists, he was thrilled to see cacti, agaves, and yuccas intermingled with myriad dryland plants.

A mix of cacti and dryland flowers in the Tatroe garden in June, with pink spikes of Sunset Crater penstemon *Penstemon clutei*.

Above left: Tropical cannas and elephant's ears ramp up the drama in Dan Johnson's Englewood, Colorado, garden.

Above right: Crocosmias and dahlias are appropriate choices for oasis zones.

American gardeners have always borrowed heavily from other gardening cultures. However, relying exclusively on garden styles developed in other places handicaps our potential, not to mention dooms us to failure. No matter how much we wish otherwise, delphiniums grown in a Denver garden never will achieve the majesty of those that grew in an alleyway, untended, near my home in England. Trying to be something we are not has led to the widely held belief that gardening in the Intermountain West is extremely difficult. And it is, if you're trying to garden as if you lived in Oxford, England, Seattle, Washington, or Pennsylvania.

All gardeners, myself included, can be forgiven for wanting to grow at least a few plants that are considered "difficult." (These plants are actually maladapted to our growing conditions.) Our impulse to do so might be rooted in nostalgia for another time or place or it might be sparked by something that caught our fancy in a catalog or magazine. While this is perfectly understandable, gardeners who are sensitive to their site's possibilities and limitations will not devote their entire garden to such plants. Xeriscape principles recommend treating heavily watered zones as oases within the larger landscape. An oasis zone can be as unnatural as tropical cannas and coleus growing in a container filled with potting soil, fertilized weekly with Miracid to counteract alkalinity in the water, and watered daily.

My garden contains a number of such oasis zones, including dozens of containers. There is also a pond, a small rock garden, and a vegetable garden that all get water two or three times a

week. To increase the likelihood of success, I use a potting medium that has a high water-holding capacity in the containers. I also carefully considered the microclimates before siting the rock garden and the vegetable garden.

One-third of my garden is essentially unirrigated and relies on regional natives and plants from similar environments from around the world. Equating to xeriscape's dry zone, these areas are arguably the most compatible with the natural environment. The rest of my garden is a compromise. Mixed borders and beds, with flowering shrubs, roses, and a host of traditional perennials live shoulder to shoulder with native plants that require weekly irrigation during the growing season (sixteen times a year—about one-third of the water bluegrass requires). Most of the plants I grow are familiar. But you know you are not in England when the path that bisects the borders is a dry streambed. Or that native waxflower *Jamesia americana* is planted among the hollyhocks.

What I am advocating is a hybrid garden, one that brings together the best of all worlds. The resulting garden embraces whatever gardening traditions we bring to it, but also celebrates the attributes and qualities of our region. Going to the extreme measures necessary to grow azaleas where the pH is 8.4 may not be folly. Trying to recreate an azalea and rhododendron garden on the scale of the historic collection of Exbury in England is. Despite a few such limitations, gardeners in the Intermountain West actually have more choices than gardeners anywhere else.

Barbara and Marc Horovitz have created a hybrid garden in Denver, Colorado, with a mix of adapted natives and introduced plants, artwork, and garden trains (tracks just visible at upper right).

Clues to Our Unique Sense of Place

Our region got the big box of crayons. Purple verbena, gold California poppies, and petunias in several colors.

It is our good fortune to live in a region where, other than the bluegrass lawn (which is still routinely prescribed by municipalities, developers, and home-owner associations), there is no clearly recognized mature garden aesthetic. This leaves us free to explore all of the new possibilities that are opening up as water shortages force the "taste police" to rethink their public policies. Drought, depleting aquifers, and population pressures are starting to change attitudes in most communities. Xeriscape is not the dirty word it once was in the 1990s, when covenants of several new housing developments in the Denver metro area forbade its use (as if saving water was a recognizable style rather than a method of landscaping). But xeriscape, with its main emphasis on conserving water, does not always go far enough. More

often than not, xeriscapes simply reinterpret the "national landscape" with drought-tolerant plants. We can do better than that.

In addition to the Santa Fe style, there have always been a few creative individuals in the Intermountain West who have ignored convention and built gardens and landscapes that have a regional complexion. Some of these designs are an abstraction of the natural landscape. In others, native plants or historical references are what give the garden its character. In most cases, it's a combination of clues that tells us that a particular garden or landscape belongs here. Because each individual gardener emphasizes different parts of the formula, the Intermountain West aesthetic does not risk becoming a cliché. There is no one right way to skin this particular cat.

With few exceptions, all of us in the Intermountain West garden in an arid or a semi-arid environment.

The more we acknowledge this fact, the more our gardens reflect our natural character. Anyone who has driven through a rural area in this region has undoubtedly come across a ranch house surrounded by an emerald-green expanse of lawn. The owners take great pride in their accomplishment. However, the effect is as incongruent as a penguin sitting on a lily pad. Urban landscapes are equally out of place, but on a much grander scale. From the air, our cities and suburbs are like very large penguins sitting on very large lily pads. No attempt has been made to dialogue with the larger environment. Green lawns and urban forests are completely artificial constructs that could not exist without huge amounts of supplemental water, a resource that is fast becoming scarce.

Our natural landscapes are embellished with every color in the artist's palette. Green does not dominate as it does in wetter regions—bright color is representative of our colorful landscape, where even the soils are polychromatic. We got the big box of crayons, so why do we continue to surround our homes with a monochrome of green? The greener our gardens and landscapes, the less appropriate they are to the Intermountain West. And consider this: while we make landscapes greener than our natural paradigm, trendsetters in other parts of the country covet plants with colored and variegated foliage, their goal to bring more color into their gardens and break up the monotony of green.

Diversity is almost always missing from the "national landscape." Although the Intermountain West is highly diverse and complex, the typical landscape here also displays a very limited plant palette. Count the number of species in the average front yard in your neighborhood and you might be surprised to learn the number seldom

Above left: The natural landscape that surrounds us is diverse and complex, with geographic irregularities and extreme juxtapositions. City of Rock, Idaho.

Above right: When a garden is broken into smaller spaces, it reflects the natural diversity—and plant choices expand commensurately. Tatroe garden.

Splashing water adds movement and life to Jan Davis's garden south of Denver.

exceeds five or six. A landscape with so little variation is mind-numbingly dull and uninteresting. This lack of diversity is also disturbing from an ecological standpoint. For example, in dramatic contrast to our landscapes, the foothills west of Denver host over 1500 species of vascular plants. Every one of these species supports a network of creatures that are displaced when we build subdivisions and lay sod over former prairie or scrubland. Bluegrass lawn provides food and habitat for webworms and June bugs, but little else.

Our region's natural environment is filled with irregularities and extreme juxtapositions within short distances. Ecosystems such as the shortgrass prairie may appear uniform and featureless, but they are actually mosaics of microclimates where slight changes in geography have huge consequences for plant life. Buttes or gullies accommodate entirely different plant communities than the prevailing vegetation. Gardeners, who emphasize and create microclimates in their gardens by breaking their properties into a series of smaller spaces with diverse plant choices, reflect this natural pattern.

Water has a profound effect on our natural landscapes, sculpting the topography and creating some of our most spectacular scenery. While this is a dry region, ponds, lakes, streams, waterfalls, and rivers do crisscross the landscape, occasionally as permanent features, but more frequently as only an imprint of where water once shaped the land. Dry washes and gullies have as great an impact on the local ecology as a perennial mountain stream, both responsible for microclimates where opportunistic plant life takes advantage of the altered circumstances. Replicating such elements in the garden, whether they contain water or not, has a similar effect, expanding the number of microclimates and types of plants that can be grown.

Nearly always associated with water is the rock it lays bare. Few things are as uniquely iconic as the dry streambed. Rock has a strong influence on regional character throughout the Intermountain West and the inclusion of rock in gardens and landscapes connects us to the mountains and the desert—places where rock and stone dominate. Indigenous rock

and stone literally tie our gardens and landscapes to the natural landscape, whether as complex as an engineered wall or as simple as a single prominently placed boulder. Flagstone quarried from red sandstone along the Front Range of Colorado, long the primary material of choice for Denver and its environs, has a strong local connotation. Dark gray shale called rundlestone plays a similar role in gardens in Alberta, Canada. Every locale within our region has one or more distinctive types of rock that can be used to create such a local signature.

Another shortcoming of the "national landscape" is that it changes very little from one season to the next. When I moved to Centennial, my brother, Bill, who has lived in Colorado most of his adult life, teased that there are only two seasons here—summer and winter. I have since discovered that this misconception is widely believed, no doubt strengthened by the bluegrass lawn's two-season growing cycle.

When the grass greens up in May, it is time to garden. When the grass turns brown in autumn, the gardening season is officially over. Only our devotion to the seasonal rhythms of the bluegrass lawn can explain the nearly universal acceptance of dreary gardens and landscapes from October through May. While we content ourselves with brown lawn, the natural landscape is at its finest in winter, both plains and steppes assuming a mantle of silver and gold, accented with rusty reds, chocolate browns, in addition to every shade of green.

Few things define our sense of place as well as our native flora. Certain signature plants are universally recognized as symbolic of this region. To readers of Zane Grey, sagebrush brings to mind the steppes of the Great Basin and the high plains east of the Rockies. Plant one in your garden and you'll undoubtedly find yourself humming cowboy campfire tunes. Throw in rabbitbrush, Indian paintbrush, and

Above left: Old prison walls provide historical context at the Idaho Botanical Garden in Boise.

Above right: Sidewalks in older parts of Denver inspired the author to replace a utilitarian concrete walk with red flagstone slabs. Tatroe garden.

Susan Yetter's Denver garden features a terrazzo basin that started life as an elementary school drinking fountain.

purple penstemon and the scene could be nowhere else. While I'm not advocating gardening exclusively with native plants, including them is essential to the creation of a regional identity.

Cultural and historic character is not always as distinctive in our region as in many other parts of the country. In most of our large cities, architectural influences are clearly European, but they represent a mishmash of styles. A strong influence on regional character is the "well-planned city" philosophy that emerged in the early part of the twentieth century, at a time when miner's camps and trading posts matured into cities. Typical of this are Denver's and Salt Lake City's tree-lined boulevards, wide-open parks, and expansive lawns. Even though our historic character is not always well defined, studying older parts of our cities yields some inspiration, if only in materials used. The brick and stone architecture that predominates in older neighborhoods readily translates into appropriate garden or landscape metaphors. For example, the historic red flagstone sidewalks in the Washington Park neighborhood in Denver inspired me to replace the utilitarian concrete sidewalk between my front door and driveway with similar red flagstone slabs. Custom-cut in the town of Lyons, the flagstone capital of Colorado, my version is on a slightly smaller scale than the public sidewalks, but still retains the character of the original.

Brick patterns reproduced in walls, patios, and stairs can also pay homage to historic buildings. Additionally, remnants from the past, available from architectural salvage yards, can be worked into the structure of a garden. In her Denver garden, dumpster diva Susan Yetter outlined flower beds with sandstone lintels from a demolished elementary school, supported a pergola with old stone columns, and laid patios and walks with hand-chiseled feldspar cobblestones that once paved the street behind Denver's Union Station. A terrazzo basin, originally a drinking fountain at a local elementary school, got new life as a water feature. An old Coors porcelain insulator holds a sundial. The privacy fences separating the Yetter garden from neighbors on either side are a patchwork of salvaged items as well. An old wagon wheel at the top of one section supports a climbing rose. A wrought-iron basement guard fastened atop another section sports Virginia creeper. Old screen doors interweave with open latticework, wooden slats, and chain-link sections.

The basic building blocks of garden design are essentially the same, no matter where you live. The balance and relationship among the various fundamentals, including mass, form, line, color, texture, and scale, are what gives the garden its distinctive flavor. Whether formal or informal, or any other recognizable style, what gives a garden a regional inflection is translating each component into a local context. By manipulating all of these elements—color, diversity, and the effects of water, rock, cultural and historic references, and seasonal beauty—we can define our regional identity.

There is also the people factor. We in the Intermountain West have always taken pride in our rugged individualism. It is not surprising then that when we do break with tradition, interesting things happen. Some of the most innovative, quirky, and exciting trends in gardens and garden art today are occurring in our region as old ideas about how things should be done are discarded and new horizons explored.

Art and Personal Expression in the Garden

Whatever the motivation, most of us enjoy embellishing our gardens with something other than plants. Nothing could be more appropriate. Gardens are, after all, expressions of personal taste. Never ones to overlook such a marketing opportunity, garden centers and home improvement stores currently carry a bonanza of garden kitsch. These include genuine resin stones, plastic daisies that twirl on the slightest breeze, and windmills with optional little Dutch girls. These are not my taste—but then garden art is highly personal. I admit to real pride of ownership over a resin pink flamingo's head on a spike that some of you might consider tacky. And, I can't deny it. A purple and gold shovel-bird looks quite fetching with purple and gold crocuses in spring. A faux stone at the entrance to my vegetable garden proclaims "Welcome to My Garden" (it was a gift from my mother).

Garden art can be anything you deem artful. Somber or playful, purchased specifically as garden art or improvised, the only requirement is that the object you choose either withstand the elements—or disintegrate with charisma or attitude. Whimsy in the garden announces to the world that this gardener doesn't take gardening too seriously. Quirkiness creates a sense of surprise and playfulness. Familiar objects turn up in unfamiliar roles. After they took out the last of their lawn, friends Myrna Wyndecker and Vicki Danielson parked an old rusted push lawn mower in their garden where it started life over as a trellis for morning glories. Another friend pokes golf balls into appropriately sized holes in a boulder next to her pond. Dan Johnson of Englewood, Colorado, creates mobiles from sticks and seashells and places weathered pieces of bone in his garden. Anything that appeals to you is worth a try.

My own interest in embellishing the garden goes back a few years to a lecture in Denver. A local garden designer decreed that, unless its cost exceeds a certain dollar amount, garden art is tacky. I had, at that point, only one piece of sculpture, a bronze rabbit that Randy and I had splurged on to celebrate our twenty-fifth wedding anniversary. My rabbit met the speaker's criterion for "tasteful." But I viewed his pronouncement as a challenge. Things have been pretty well running amok ever since. Looking back, I don't remember what came next— it might have been the abstract bat made out of rusted sheet steel and ball bearings from a local garden boutique. Or it might have been the terra-cotta garden goddess from the Santa Fe flea market.

All of my gardens now feature a magpie's collection of objects, spanning the entire spectrum from tasteful to tasteless. Mosaics of marbles, sea glass, polished pebbles, broken bricks, washers, bolts, and

Above: A life mask made by artist Barbara Horovitz gives her garden a touch of whimsy.

Top right: Carved desert driftwood reveals the face within. Ungerleider garden, Santa Fe, New Mexico, designed by Julie Berman.

Bottom right: Artist Jeannie Schlump transformed a warehouse wall into a scene of the Veedavoo rock formation near her home in Laramie, Wyoming.

brass keys accessorize the rock lawn in the front yard. There are watering basins for snakes and toads, birdbaths and birdhouses, sculptures, wind chimes, trellises, and fossils. Bright, iridescent marbles and large glass beads liven up birdbaths (a splash of chlorine bleach in the water once a week keeps things shiny). At first glance, it is not obvious how much ephemera is out there. All of these items are woven into the fabric of the garden as unobtrusively as possible. My goal is to provide little surprises here and there, not the clutter of a rummage sale.

At some point, there began an invasion of spheres that continues to this day. Gazing globes are quite fashionable in smart gardening circles, but my taste runs more to rocks and minerals fashioned into spheres. The first ones that found their way into my garden were crafted of relatively inexpensive sandstone. Then, hallelujah! Import stores, craft stores, and candle shops started offering spheres made of granite and marble. So far, a dozen, from golf ball- to basketball-sized, have followed me home. Spheres sitting at path intersections, singly or in groups, or huddled next to troughs or pots, provide contrast to naturally shaped stones. Along the dry streambed, they collect in the curves, as if deposited as flotsam from a flood. A set of shiny metal bocce balls are arrayed in a small rock garden, where they provide a touch of effervescence, especially in the winter months when the plants are dormant and the reflective spheres are clearly visible.

And then I discovered rock shops. Many of their spheres are carved from semi-precious stone, making them too pricey for the garden, but occasionally I find one of sandstone, quartz, or copper that is affordable. I also acquired naturally occurring concretions called moqui marbles. These resemble small cannonballs and are an interesting addition to another one of my rock gardens. I have taken a fancy to engraved river rocks as well. Some of these are decorated with Asian characters; others proclaim "Love" or "Peace." The ones I prefer have carvings of stylized insects and small animals. These are camouflaged, mixed in with other river rocks in the dry

streambed, where visitors to the garden—especially children—get a kick out of seeing a frog or a grasshopper on what is otherwise an ordinary-looking rock. Hidden in the river rock downstream are stone faces of Malaysian fertility gods, called *Otaks,* from a local import store.

When I was a kid, I littered my mother's garden with plastic farm animals. Now I clutter my own garden with lifelike sculptures of animals that might conceivably be found in a garden. This is a peaceable kingdom—rabbits, waterfowl, and foxes made from pottery, bronze, and concrete don't eat the plants or each other. I'm partial to creatures that I wish would move into my garden, but don't, such as toads, frogs, lizards, and horned toads. A roadrunner in the xeric garden reminds me of my former home in southern California. (Perhaps cast concrete alligators partially buried in the lawn remind other homesick gardeners of Florida—somebody must buy those things.)

Books, magazines, lectures, and television shows are all good places to gather ideas for the garden, but nothing beats visiting gardens in person on a garden tour. The year that Randy and I attended the Garden Conservancy tour in Colorado Springs, we came away with a newfound obsession for birdbaths. The gardens we visited were all very different from one another, but there was one common element—every garden had a unique birdbath. Most were handcrafted, a few were clearly works of art. Our dime-store birdbaths seemed tacky by comparison.

So began a quest that was to last the better part of that summer. The first place we hunted was on the Internet, where we discovered some very nice birdbaths with copper dishes and a couple made of stone. The copper ones were not exactly what we had in mind, and those made of stone completely exceeded our budget. A few weeks later, on another garden tour in the Black Forest north of Colorado Springs, there it was—the perfect birdbath basin. Randy Bowen, a local potter, had displayed a dozen of his stoneware basins in the garden and every one was a treasure. The only difficulty was choosing our

A Garden Conservancy–worthy birdbath surrounded by pink and blue phlox, yellow mountain basket-of-gold, and blue veronica in May.

favorite. Now we had a basin but no stand. Our quest continued for another few weeks—this time we carried a heavy pottery birdbath basin everywhere we shopped. A Mexican furniture store yielded the perfect fit—a wrought-iron table stand. Two months of searching had finally resulted in one very beautiful birdbath.

The second birdbath was more problematic. A catalog offered a handsome birdbath carved from granite, but I couldn't afford the shipping let alone the birdbath. A plan emerged. Randy and I visited a quarry in Lyons, picture in hand, where a very patient saleswoman helped us find a column of red sandstone. We ordered cut pieces for the base and the

neck and two weeks later—with the help of liquid nails—we had a stone birdbath stand that, although it looked little like the one in the catalog, was quite attractive in its own right. The search for a basin ensued—this time with a stone column in the trunk of our car. Stores that sell Middle Eastern products carry large copper basins, and these were a possibility. Then we hit the jackpot at Smith and Hawkins, where another very patient salesclerk lugged out every birdbath top in the store to the parking lot until we found a match—a hammered, double-hulled copper bowl. We were now the proud owners of two Garden Conservancy-worthy birdbaths.

Gardening Is Different Here

ardens are created within the context of the natural environment. Only by understanding the complex interactions between the two can we hope to make intelligent gardening decisions—or figure out what went wrong when problems arise. Of course, this is easier said than done. For much of the last century, the gardening industry has further confused the issue by adopting an approach that overlooks the great differences from one region to the next. Only fairly recently have national gardening publications acknowledged that making uniform recommendations for places where conditions are as dissimilar as Atlanta and Salt Lake City is as futile as trying to cram the stepsisters' feet into Cinderella's glass slipper.

IN THIS RESPECT, gardeners in the Intermountain West have a rougher time of it than most. The bulk of our garden lore comes from the more heavily populated east and west coasts, and from England. Much of this advice is not only inappropriate, but also frequently detrimental to our gardens, whether concerning soils, disease problems, or plant culture. Seasoned gardeners learn through trial and error to adapt—but what works is not always obvious. Even apparently local information may be ill advised. Gardeners in the high desert environment around Redmond, Oregon, have more in common with those in Denver, Salt Lake City, or Boise, than they do with fellow Oregonians in Portland, only a hundred miles west. One January, when I flew into Oregon on my way to give a talk in Redmond, this disjunction was quite obvious from the air. Even in winter, Portland is emerald green, damp, and cloudy. In sharp contrast, the area around Redmond, on the east side of the Cascades, is a sunny landscape of golden rabbitbrush and green pine trees that is hardly distinguishable from the foothills on the eastern slope of the Colorado Rockies, the high plains of northern New Mexico, or the cold steppes of southern Wyoming.

Geography, Weather, and Ecology

The Intermountain West is a vast area that encompasses all parts of the interior western United States where winters are cold, summers hot, and precipitation less than 15 inches per annum. This includes the Intermountain Desert (also called the Great Basin Desert), a high-elevation desert that experiences cold, snowy winters and an annual precipitation of a fairly generous (for a desert) 7 to 12 inches, most of which falls as snow in winter. Bracketed by the Cascades and the Sierra Nevadas to the west and the Rocky Mountains to the east, the Intermountain Desert stretches from southeastern Washington,

'Lilac Wonder' tulips do well in our region, where winter provides the chilling they require.

central and southeastern Oregon, southern Idaho, through most of Nevada and Utah, the extreme western edge of Colorado, northern Arizona, and northwestern New Mexico. The Intermountain West also includes the mesas and canyonlands of the Colorado Plateau in western Colorado, southern Utah, northern Arizona, and northern New Mexico, as well as the cold steppes and prairies of Montana, Wyoming, southern Alberta, and southern Saskatchewan. To the east of the Rockies, this region extends to the cold and semiarid high plains of eastern Colorado, western Kansas and Nebraska, and North and South Dakota.

Regardless of where you live within this region, one constant is incomparable natural beauty. This is big sky country where horizons are so vast poets have claimed they can see the actual curvature of the earth. Everything about this landscape is larger than life. This is also a land of topographical extremes. The majestic Rocky Mountain chain dominates. Smaller mountain ranges spread like ripples east and west from the Continental Divide. These are young mountains, steep, jagged, and . . . well, rocky. From a distance, they appear solid and uniform, but traveling into the mountains reveals a dizzying geographic complexity.

Our region has a continental climate, where, as described by Mutel and Emerick in *From Grassland to Glacier* (Johnson Books, 1992), "The weather is marked by extreme variations in temperature and precipitation from year to year, season to season, day to night, and even hour to hour." It's not at all unusual for it to snow at my house, while at the same moment, Denver, only fifteen miles away, basks in sunshine—or vice versa. On more than one occasion, I've observed rain falling on my side of the street but not on the other.

In general, this is a sunny climate with bragging rights to more sunny days than San Diego or Miami. Summers are hot, often brutally so, and winters are commensurately cold. In many areas, low temperatures dip well below zero in winter, occasionally for extended periods. Solar radiation is much greater here than in most other parts of the United States and increases with elevation. Ultraviolet light is 90 percent higher at 10,000 feet than at sea level. In any season, winds can be fierce, occasionally knocking over fences and sending anything that isn't tied down into the next county. The Front Range of Colorado (the easternmost ranges of the Rocky Mountains) and north to Cheyenne is the hail capital of the world, where damaging hailstorms are a regular occurrence, hitting some unlucky gardens every year. Atmospheric humidity is extremely low at all seasons—prompting a friend to tease that you don't need a towel to dry off when you get out of the shower. (He claims that all you have to do is spin around a couple of times.)

From one locale to the next, precipitation patterns can vary dramatically, often within improbably short distances. Alamosa (elevation 7,455 feet), in southern Colorado, with an average of 7 inches of annual precipitation, is only fifty miles distant from Wolf Creek Pass (elevation 10,850 feet), which receives a generous 45.4 inches. Mountain peaks often block Pacific moisture, leaving their eastern flanks dry, in what are called rain shadows. Or as one Denver weather forecaster put it, "The Rocky Mountains act as a giant snow fence." Precipitation increases with altitude, which explains why forests mostly occur at higher elevations. Where trees do grow, different species populate different exposures. Dense stands of spruce or fir dominate north- or east-facing slopes, where they are afforded some protection from drying wind and sun. More often, pine forests are restricted to drier, more exposed south- and west-facing exposures, where sunlight melts snow more rapidly.

Very few places in the Intermountain West record precipitation totals that compare with those in the eastern half of the United States. A physical map underscores this reality. With the exception of coastal areas and mountain peaks, the East is green, and the West is brown. In our region, most of us live in the plains and plateaus where the climate is semiarid. Billings, Montana, Salt Lake City, Utah, Denver, Colorado, and Sheridan, Wyoming all average around 15 inches of annual precipitation. Many communities are considerably drier. Boise, Idaho, averages only 11.7 inches. Mountain communities can be substantially wetter, but no large cities in our region approach the average annual precipitation of Boston (44), Atlanta (49), New York (43), or New Orleans (60).

Soils can be as extreme as our weather. Topsoil is a rarity, seldom more than a couple of inches deep. Organic matter, a major component of topsoil, is also nearly nonexistent, especially in the more arid parts of the Intermountain West. Vegetation is relatively sparse and organic matter desiccates, "burning off" (sometimes literally), before it can be incorporated into the soil. Alkalinity is the norm at lower elevations, acidity more commonplace where conifer forests prevail in mountain communities. Maladapted plants can have a rough time of it in either case. Salts and other minerals toxic to plant life are a frequent problem because there is not enough precipitation to rinse them out of the soil.

But the news is not all bad. Because of our low humidity and cool nights, gardens here experience a fraction of the disease problems that are commonplace in other parts of the United States. Fungal and bacterial diseases such as fusarium, phytophora, and verticillium wilt, words that strike fear in the hearts of gardeners in other regions, are almost unheard of. Every place I visit, including the deserts of the Southwest, seems buggy by comparison. We do have our pest problems, but many insects that plague gardeners in other regions cannot cope with our capricious weather. Pest nematodes, microscopic worms that damage plants, are the bane of gardeners where conditions are more moderate. As a rule, nematodes don't tolerate our clay soils, dry soils, or cold winters, making them a rarity in the Intermountain West.

USDA Zone Maps

A look at the USDA Zone Map illustrates the difficulties in making generalizations about our climate. This map, developed by the American Horticultural Society (AHS) and distributed by the United States Department of Agriculture, broadly divides the country into eleven hardiness zones, according to the lowest expected minimum temperatures in each—zone 1 has the lowest (below -50°F) and zone 11 has the highest (over 40°F). The zone numbers represent a 10°F range in temperature. So, for example, zone 4 has an expected winter low no less than -30°F, zone 5 has an expected winter low of no less than -20°F, and so on. (For the USDA zone map, see http://www.usna.usda.gov/Hardzone/ushzmap.html.)

A crabapple might be listed for zones 4 through 8, zone 4 representing the minimum temperature

the tree can withstand and zone 8 indicating that it won't flower unless winter temperatures drop down to 10° or 20°F. The latter isn't much of a consideration in our region—it's cold enough here for any plant that requires winter chilling—but it does explain why lilacs, peonies, tulips, and the like, will not bloom in gardens in the Deep South. Sunset Books has developed their own climate zone map for the western United States that divides the West into twenty-four zones. The Sunset climate zones take into account other factors such as humidity, geographic and seasonal characteristics, so they tend to be more locally accurate. (For the Sunset zone map, see http://www.sunset.com.)

The American Horticultural Society (AHS) has produced a second climate zone map—the Plant Heat-Zone Map—based on expected maximum high temperature in summer. Quite a number of plants are intolerant of heat, particularly when combined with high humidity. This new zone map charts the number of days the temperature exceeds 85°F. Plants are then rated by their heat tolerance for each of the climate zones across the country. If the AHS heat map gains wide acceptance, you can expect to see a crabapple listed as 4–8, 8–1(the first pair of zone numbers indicates cold hardiness and the second pair indicates heat tolerance). This code indicates that the crabapple is not cold hardy below zone 4, will not perform well where winters are warmer than zone 8, and can't tolerate heat beyond zone 8. Cool summers through heat zone 1 (where temperatures never rise above 85°F) won't affect the crabapple's performance. There is no relationship between heat zone numbers and cold zone numbers. (For the AHS plant heat-zone map, see http://www.ahs.org/publications/heat_zone_map.htm.)

East of the 100th meridian, an imaginary line that bisects the country from North Dakota through the western third of Texas, zone borderlines generally run in gently undulating horizontal bands, the zones getting warmer as they become more southerly. Transition from one area to the next is gradual. Eastern states have at most two to

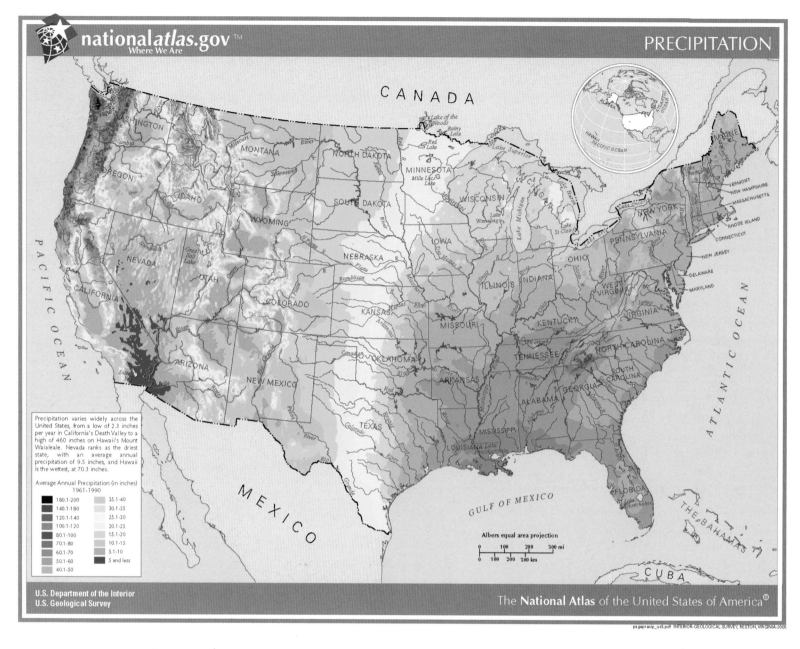

nationalatlas.gov ™
Where We Are

Precipitation varies widely across the United States, from a low of 2.3 inches per year in California's Death Valley to a high of 460 inches on Hawaii's Mount Waialeale. Nevada ranks as the driest state, with an average annual precipitation of 9.5 inches, and Hawaii is the wettest, at 70.3 inches.

Average Annual Precipitation (in inches)
1961-1990

180.1-200	35.1-40
140.1-180	30.1-35
120.1-140	25.1-30
100.1-120	20.1-25
80.1-100	15.1-20
70.1-80	10.1-15
60.1-70	5.1-10
50.1-60	5 and less
40.1-50	

Albers equal area projection

0   100   200   300 mi
0   100   200   300 km

U.S. Department of the Interior
U.S. Geological Survey

The **National Atlas** of the United States of America®

pageprecip_us3.pdf INTERIOR-GEOLOGICAL SURVEY, RESTON, VIRGINIA-2005

three zones. Kansas, just east of Colorado, for instance, is cut roughly into two broad northern and southern bands, much like a layer cake.

The Intermountain West is an entirely different story. Colorado and Utah each encompass eight different climate zones, reflecting their capricious topographic diversity. In these states, zones twist and swirl like colored oils in a lava lamp as they conform to mountain ranges and river valleys. Transitions can be quite abrupt. Anyone who has traveled

across this region has experienced the phenomenon of being cold one minute and hot the next. We dress in layers and carry coats in the trunks of our vehicles—summer and winter. Throughout the year, temperatures are significantly cooler at higher elevations. The result is dramatic differences in ambient temperature within short distances. As related by Mutel and Emerick, the 35-degree temperature difference between the summit of Pikes Peak and Las Animas, Colorado, 115 miles away, is equivalent to the average annual temperature difference between south Florida and Iceland.

So, what does all this mean to the gardener? Zone ratings provide only one part of the equation you need to consider to make an informed decision. The only thing the zone number tells us is whether the plant has a reasonable chance of surviving winter in our region. For instance, you might assume that if you live in zone 5 Denver and choose a zone 5 rhododendron, success is assured. Unfortunately, it's not that simple. The rhododendron may indeed be cold hardy to -20°F as the zone 5 rating suggests, but winter hardiness is only part of the story. Rhododendrons also require neutral to acid, well-drained but moist soil, plus bright, indirect sunlight—all conditions difficult to replicate in sunny, dry Colorado. Plants must have all of their cultural demands met. Relative humidity, winds, overnight temperatures in summer, hours of sunlight, length of growing season, and winter moisture are just a few of the variables that can affect a plant's performance. Zone numbers do not provide any of this information.

More than once I've heard the phrase "hardy in Denver" used to disparage reports of the large number of plants that survive cold winters here but not in other areas with the same or milder zone ratings. This is particularly true when compared with places where winters are wet. English lavender survives here but not in zone 5 Boston. The explanation, in this case, is our relatively dry winters. We can add water to assist those things that require it, but it's nearly impossible for gardeners in wetter regions to exclude rain and snow. The combination of cold and wet soil is deadly to many plants. A gardener I visited in northwestern Oregon put his rock garden in an old freezer so he could close the lid if it rained too often for his plants. Countless plants that survive dry winters in the Intermountain West cannot be easily grown in plant meccas like Seattle or Portland.

Because we experience dry heat and cool nights in summer, gardeners can either ignore the heat zone ratings entirely or use them to help determine

English lavender is intolerant of winter wet.

Late snowfalls may freeze buds or flowers.

which plants might prefer afternoon shade. Anything rated for a heat zone warmer than your own will likely accept full sun in the Intermountain West. Plants rated for cooler regions usually need protection from sun during the hottest part of the day. Monkshood is a good example. It dislikes heat and will not survive under any circumstances in the southern United States. But monkshood grows strong and healthy against a north-facing wall in my heat zone 7 garden.

Keep in mind that all of the zone maps were compiled using average temperatures. Record-breaking lows—or highs—can occasionally kill otherwise suitable plants. The timing and duration of a cold spell and the presence or absence of snow cover (which protects plants buried beneath) may also affect winter hardiness. Plants are more susceptible to freeze damage in early fall before they've had a chance to harden off, and any time after they've broken dormancy in late winter or spring. Briefly hitting a record low does less harm than a long stretch of arctic temperatures. One way you can hedge your bets for winter hardiness is to choose plants rated for one or two zones colder than where you live.

A word of caution: plant hardiness ratings are based solely on gardener's experiences around the country. Ratings often discount genetic variability

Thunder showers too often bring damaging hail.

within a single species. Because gardeners experiment with new plants, this information is continually changing. If, in our region, gardeners never defied accepted zone ratings, we would not be growing the amazing range of plants from vastly dissimilar climates that thrive here. Let zone ratings be guidelines for your plant choices, not hard-and-fast rules.

Coping with the Weather

Gardeners who wish to keep their sanity intact learn to adopt a fatalistic attitude toward the weather. In other regions, garden achievements may be about stewardship or vigilance, but here it often comes down to luck. Doing everything right is no guarantee of success. An untimely cold front sneaks down from Canada and no amount of spraying, watering, or fertilizing can forestall the damage. Fifteen minutes of hail can wipe out several months of hard work and leave the garden in tatters.

What we can do is protect new buds and tender foliage in spring, or flowers when they are at their peak in late summer, by covering them with an arsenal of low-tech plant protection devices, including cardboard boxes, bushel baskets, and garbage cans. The dilemma is deciding whether to go to the trouble. If a Pacific front is poised to drop only an inch or two of snow, this exercise is usually unnecessary. These snowstorms are relatively warm and a small accumulation of snow won't do much damage. More than a couple of inches is another matter entirely. Unseasonable wet, heavy snow crushes flowers, snaps tree branches, and, all too frequently, demolishes full-grown trees.

Arctic storms can also do a great deal of mischief. Bitterly cold temperatures not only destroy buds and flowers, but may kill otherwise winter-hardy perennials and shrubs that have broken dormancy in the false springs of late winter that are commonplace in our region (particularly in March). When they first leaf out, many plants are extremely sensitive to cold temperatures. This time around, snow cover of at least several inches is what gardeners hope for, because a blanket of snow is good insulation against the cold. But, if you trust the forecast and snow doesn't materialize, damage can be severe and extensive.

The mere possibility of an arctic front in spring or autumn sends me into a panic. More than once I've run outside into falling snow or freezing rain to throw evergreen boughs over low-growing flowers and to cover taller plants with five-gallon nursery pots. (A plant stake speared through one of the drainage holes and into the ground holds the pots in place.) Large containers filled with annual flowers get a tomato cage pushed into the soil and a sheet thrown over the top. Even a wet sheet will blow away in a gale, so I attach the sheet to the wire cage with clothespins and wrap a bungee cord around the container. There's really no easy way to cover a mature fruit tree, so I leave these to fate. (Some gardeners string Christmas lights on their fruit trees to keep them a bit warmer.) Small shrubs and flowers are manageable. The most valuable plants get the tomato cage treatment. A card table can protect a fairly good-sized shrub.

The morning after a spring snowstorm, I wake to an unnerving sight, one that reminds me of the Masterpiece Theater drawing room scene where the family is returning from an extended absence. Boxy shapes draped in white sheets and studded with clothespins are interspersed with dozens of overturned plastic nursery pots. Faced with the reality of cleanup without the accompanying adrenalin rush, I'm left wondering at my sanity in trying to outwit the weather.

Hail is a threat that comes with every passing thunderstorm. Front Range gardeners in Colorado and Wyoming are regularly pummeled with chunks of ice the size of marbles, golf balls, and even, occasionally, tennis balls. When dropped accidentally, ice cubes have made dents in my oak floor—the garden doesn't stand a chance. (I'm told that gun-shy gardeners in Cheyenne resort to growing vegetables under cover to protect them from the seven hailstorms this city averages every growing season.) The same conditions that precede hail often mean a tornado is imminent. When the sky turns yellow and green, you'd better take shelter rather than try to protect the garden.

After hail trounces your garden, there are a few things you can do. Let things dry out, and then rake up all of the debris and toss it into the compost bin. If the storm hits early in the year, cut down damaged or broken stems. In late summer, it is best to leave things alone, where safe and practical. Severe pruning at this point may stimulate new growth that is susceptible to frost damage. In this case it is safer to wait until after the first hard frost. Severely damaged vegetables and annuals are usually a complete loss. Replant these only if it is early enough in the season to ripen another crop. Later in the year, if there is enough time left in the growing season, replace damaged plants with cool-season vegetables and flowers. Some experts recommend spraying plants that are only lightly damaged with a foliar fertilizer and a sulphur-based fungicide to prevent disease. Or try a spray or drench of immune-boosting aspirin (three aspirin dissolved in four gallons of water) and/or the protein "Messenger." Water regularly so the plants don't have to deal with drought-stress on top of injury.

It is imperative to remove debris and damaged plants from ponds to avoid toxic build-up in the water. Unfortunately, a sudden drop in water temperature also can kill goldfish and koi. Other than removing fish from the pond temporarily every time a storm threatens, there isn't much you can do to prevent this. A fish kill, mercifully, is a rare event. It has only happened to me twice in two decades.

Weather in the Intermountain West is always a hit-or-miss affair. One minute the garden is suffering from heat and drought, the next it's under a foot of water. So what can you do to rescue your treasures from drowning when the monsoons flood the garden? If the water has receded by the next day, your troubles are over. Just leave the irrigation system off for a few days to allow the soil to dry out. Your plants will be thankful for the thorough soaking the brief flooding provided. But when water remains standing for more than twenty-four hours, it's time for action—many flowers rot if kept that wet for more than a short period of time. Dig a small trench from the highest to the lowest point in the garden to help drain off the water. Other than vowing to raise the soil level and improve drainage when you rebuild the garden, there isn't much else you can do at this point. Most plants will survive a flood. If annuals turn brown and decay, pull them out and replace them. Damaged shrubs and perennial flowers may need a couple of months to recover.

The Power of Microclimates

The complex topography in the Intermountain West creates an infinite number of microclimates. These are places where the number of hours of sunlight, the amount of water, ambient temperature, and/or soil type differs, sometimes radically, from the generally prevailing conditions. Naturally occurring microclimates can be as small as the shadow of a rock on the tundra or as large as a cliff face in the desert. The lesson of microclimates is that wherever they occur, plant life takes advantage of the atypical habitat and diversity expands correspondingly. The extra protection afforded by a pile of boulders above treeline accounts for the relatively large two-foot tall Rocky Mountain columbine *Aquilegia caerulea* on the tundra,

where the preponderance of plants have evolved to be short and compact in response to harsh conditions there. Water that accumulates in depressions on the western edge of the shortgrass prairie supports the grass big bluestem *Andropogon gerardii* and other plants generally found in the wetter, eastern tall grass prairies. Reduced competition on the shale barrens of the northern Front Range of Colorado, a habitat too restrictive for other plant life, results in some of our most treasured wildflowers, such as Bells' twinpod *Physaria bellii*.

The number and intricacy of microclimates in our region is directly responsible for the wide variety of plants we can grow. The impact on gardens can hardly be overstated. It accounts for a tree fern surviving the winter in a Denver garden and the amazing *Hesperaloe funifera* by the entrance to the Education Building at Denver Botanic Gardens. The difference in microclimates nearly always explains why you can grow a particular plant and your neighbor cannot, even when conditions appear to be nearly identical. In other regions distinctions are not so marked. Charles tells of walking around his parent's house in Arkansas and realizing the intensity of sunlight was essentially the same on all four sides. The prevailing light in Arkansas, like much of the eastern United States, is misty and filtered. In our region, where temperatures and conditions vary profoundly from one exposure to the next, we can accommodate the needs of a greater number of plants. For example, siting fruit trees on the colder east or north side of a structure helps prevent them from breaking dormancy until later in the season when their blossoms are less likely to be damaged by a late frost. Warm southern exposures and areas where the soil never freezes are good places to try slightly tender perennial flowers such as crocosmia, agapanthus, and alstroemeria.

The overriding climate in my front yard, a space forty by forty feet, is created by the house itself, which faces northeast, its bulk casting a large shadow over much of the area. Within this space there are also dozens of microclimates. Some are not

Golden columbines and variegated zebra iris in a small microclimate (18 inches by 6 feet), with morning sun and afternoon shade. Tatroe garden.

readily apparent. Many different types of soils are distributed throughout this area, where they were dumped one truckload at a time. During the cut and fill process used to terrace my development, foreign soil was brought in and the native soil redistributed. In some cases, sterile subsoil from basement excavations ended up on the surface. Each pocket of soil supports a different group of plants.

Hardscape elements, including the sidewalks, a stacked stone wall, the driveway, and other paving materials create additional microclimates. Concrete is notorious for reflecting heat and drying out adjacent plants, which explains why lawn can have a difficult time growing next to sidewalks and driveways. Conversely, nonporous hardscape, like

concrete and asphalt, concentrates water, a phenomenon you might have noticed when driving along desert highways, where the lushest vegetation grows at the edge of the road. Similarly, a patch of ajuga has entrenched itself next to the sidewalk in my driveway garden, creating the odd juxtaposition of xeric opuntia and desert holly with moisture-loving ajuga growing at their feet.

Where plantings cast shadows, microclimates may be either permanent or seasonal. A ponderosa pine next to my driveway casts shade year round, making an ideal habitat for true shade-loving plants. A monumental hardy pampas grass, standing ten to fourteen feet tall, casts a dense shadow only from late summer through early spring. After the grass's annual shearing in April, this area experiences full sun until the grass grows tall again by late summer. My solution here is to plant spring-blooming ephemerals and bulbs, flowers that need sun in spring and then go dormant in summer when the grass shades the bed.

Other microclimates are of my own making, as for example, when I dug out the soil in one section of the flagstone terrace and replaced it with sand to accommodate plants that require faster drainage. Whenever I elect to water one section of the garden more frequently than another, this also creates a microclimate where the soil is wetter than in neighboring beds. On a larger scale, the entire front yard is dramatically different from the back, which faces southwest, or either of the side yards. This is especially apparent on a winter day when a thick covering of snow persists in the north front yard while at the same time all of the snow has melted on the south-facing backyard. It is also unmistakable on a hot summer day when the backyard is unbearably hot but the side yard is cool and comfortable in the shade of a large chokecherry.

A few plants are so adaptable that they will thrive nearly anywhere (dandelions come to mind), but most plants have a set of conditions that must be met to ensure their success. When I bring a new plant home, the first thing I do is check the tag for clues to its cultural requirements. "Moist soil" gives me some information but not the whole story. There's a vast difference between the anaerobic conditions in clay that never dries out and the oxygen-rich soil along a streambed. In this case, it's helpful to discover the plant's native habitat. Does it come from a wet meadow in Tennessee or from a stream bank in Utah? Googling a plant name on the Internet is one of the easiest ways to learn a plant's origins.

Occasionally the only option is trying out different microclimates in the garden until happening upon the correct fit. This was true of a chartreuse-leafed *Campanula portenschlagiana* 'Aurea' that I was determined to grow. The only clue on the tag was "part shade." I killed several of these plants

Some microclimates are of our own creation. A sand bed in the flagstone terrace. Tatroe garden.

Above left: The right combination of circumstances for Dalmatian bellflower *Campanula portenschlagiana* **'Aurea'. (Photo by R. Tatroe)**

Above right: Blue poppies are nearly impossible to grow at lower elevations in our region, but they come back year after year in Rebecca Day-Skowron's garden in Franktown, Colorado.

until I hit on the right combination of sunlight (dappled), soil type (well-drained clay loam), moisture (moderate), and protection (rocks on all sides) at the edge of stone stairs beneath a small grove of pines and aspens in the backyard. The same plant that I had been starting to think was ungrowable is robust now that it has what it needs. This experimentation is not unlike the natural process of plants sending out thousands of seeds. Only those that land where conditions are suitable actually germinate.

Most of us on the Front Range of Colorado, myself included, would be doomed to failure if we tried to grow Himalayan blue poppies. Rebecca Day-Skowron's success with these provides a couple of lessons for the rest of us. Although she says she was bent on growing this ethereal beauty the first time she saw a picture it in a seed catalog, in Rebecca's case, conditions in her garden made this goal achievable. The Himalayan blue poppy, as its name suggests, is a mountain dweller, at home along forest edges, at elevations from 10,000–13,000 feet. It occurs where soils are acid to neutral, where monsoons provide consistent summer moisture, and where snow protects the dormant plants from extreme winter cold. The blue poppies' very presence in English gardens, where conditions differ considerably from its natural habitat (though it has a reputation for being difficult to grow there, too), suggests that the plant is at least somewhat amenable to cultivation. Greater success in the north of England, and in parts of America where winters are cold and summers cool, is a further clue that coolish summer temperatures might be a non-negotiable part of the equation.

At 1,000 feet higher in elevation, Rebecca lives where summer temperatures are indeed slightly chillier than in other parts of metro Denver. Most years, she can harvest cool-season vegetables such as peas and lettuce all summer long, but her tomatoes ripen poorly. Rebecca chose to try the blue poppies first in the coolest part of her property, an area beneath ponderosa pines and Gambel oak that is shaded during the hottest part of the day. Her neutral and well-drained soil is similar to that found in the poppies' natural habitat. A thick accumulation of pine needles acts as a substitute for winter snow cover. Rebecca provides the one missing ingredient, consistent summer moisture, with supplemental irrigation.

Not surprisingly, gardeners who live in Breckenridge, Colorado, at nearly 10,000 feet in elevation, where conditions are even more like those found in the Himalayas, have no trouble growing blue poppies. Again, the trick to growing any plant is to meet its cultural requirements. It sounds obvious, but throughout our region pines are routinely planted in heavy clay soil, surrounded with bluegrass, and then killed by the three times weekly irrigation the lawn needs to stay green. The entire time I've lived in Colorado, I've watched a neighboring development with

"pine" in its name do just that in a futile attempt to have both pines and bluegrass growing together. If the planners better understood their site, they might switch to buffalograss, a native grass that is culturally compatible with Ponderosa pines—and save a lot of water, and pines, in the process.

Rethinking the Bluegrass Lawn

For the last fifty years, lawn has been the defining feature of the American landscape, even in our arid and semiarid region where water is a scarce resource. There may no longer be enough water to sustain lush, green lawns at every home, business park, and median strip in every community in the Intermountain West. Since lawns are responsible for the largest percentage of our household water consumption, this might be a good time to rethink bluegrass as a landscape institution. Not long after my elderly parents moved from California to Colorado in the 1990s, my father made a telling comment before the drought struck, even more so as the days of cheap and abundant water have slipped away. "What's with the lawns?" he demanded, completely mystified. "I've lived all over this country and I've never seen lawn so green or so perfect."

I blame the late S. R. DeBoer, a landscape architect whose views on native plants and rock gardens I enthusiastically share. We part company, however, when it comes to bluegrass lawn. In 1948, in his book Around the Seasons, DeBoer called the lawn the "pride of Denver's summer season, the glory of the gardens of the plains and the valleys in the mountains, greener than any other green in nature . . . the envy of neighboring cities, for nothing elsewhere can equal the velvety irrigated bluegrass in the mile-high sections of the Denver region. Not in emerald Ireland, not in beautiful Holland, not in the East nor in the Pacific West are the greens as green. Set in the grays and browns of the dry prairies, and on the arid slopes of the foothills, here they are, kept by man's effort, maintained in the very face of nature's laws."

DeBoer was a man of his time. No longer do we rejoice in violating nature's laws. And yet the highly

A mosaic of ground covers in front of Mary Ellen Keskimaki's home in Golden, Colorado, makes better sense than a hillside of unusable turf.

manicured and artificial lawn still reigns supreme in the Intermountain West. Despite DeBoer's enthusiasm, anything this unnatural has to be an acquired taste. Throughout the twentieth century, Americans were sold the desirability of the lawn, both with good intentions to "beautify" the community and to market a whole new variety of chemical products for lawn care. Garden designers still regularly pronounce the greensward an essential ingredient of the well-designed garden, arguing that no surface better provides counterpoint to flower beds. It just isn't so. Any flat surface serves the same function as a lawn. Materials such as brick or stone do it with more style and flair.

Xeriscape! Colorado has always recommended that homeowners take a hard look at how they use lawns in landscapes. One of the fundamentals of

xeriscaping is locating lawns where they have a practical purpose, rather than carpeting the entire yard in turfgrass. A lawn for children and pets to play on makes sense. Lawn on steep hillsides and other unusable areas does not. But faced with recommendations to use turf alternatives whenever appropriate, most of us don't know where to start. Because we are more comfortable choosing materials for the inside of our homes, it might help to think of horizontal surfaces in the landscape as "floors" and consider what other "floor coverings" could replace bluegrass lawns. The lawn is the perfect place to break out of our green-on-green mindset. Not many of us would choose green carpet, green walls, green furniture, and green accessories for the inside of our homes. Here's an opportunity for us to experiment with the same range of styles in our land-

scapes as we do in our interiors. And at the same time conserve precious water.

One alternative is gravel. Not those Sun City–style zero-scapes (color-matched to the house paint) of wall-to-wall gravel. When gravel replaces lawn, but is surrounded by shrubs, trees, and flowers, it then provides a neutral contrast to the green backdrop. Gravel is a perfect "floor" for outdoor living and offers all of the practicalities of lawn without the ongoing maintenance and water it requires. You can add color to gravel by scattering the seeds of self-sowing wildflowers like California bluebells or California poppies. Or put weed barrier under the gravel for an essentially no-maintenance surface.

You might also consider replacing large areas of lawn with pavement or decking. Bricks and flagstone are good paving options, but any material that can withstand our climate is a possibility. One homeowner in Denver made a freeform "lawn" of brick that ebbs and flows throughout her entire backyard. Similarly, broken chunks of concrete can be arranged in the manner of randomly cut

Above left: In the Horovitz garden, gravel offers all of the practicalities of lawn with none of the water lawn requires.

Above right: Treat level areas as "flooring" and choose material that best suits its use. In the Tatroe garden, a brick terrace stands in for lawn.

Top: Charles Mann's Santa Fe garden features an elegant "lawn" of blue-flowered woolly veronica *Veronica pectinata* and square-cut flagstone pavers.

Bottom: Yellow candelabras of self-sowing biennial mullein *Verbascum bombyciferum* in Diane and Tom Peace's front yard cottage garden in Denver.

flagstone for an attractive effect. An artist in Calgary, Canada, made "tiles" of concrete in Styrofoam molds and then pressed two contrasting colors of river stones onto the surface to create a patio inspired by the Chinese garden style. Two friends in Fort Collins replaced their front lawn with a formal design of square flagstone pavers interplanted with gray-green woolly thyme. The result is a serene outdoor room that requires very little irrigation.

Ground covers are also a workable solution for low-use areas. Snow-in-summer *Cerastium tomentosum* quickly covers the ground in silver, as does pussytoes *Antennaria* sp. If you want green, evergreen winter creeper *Euonymus fortunei* will do the trick, sun or shade. Hardy yellow iceplant *Delosperma nubigenum* is green all summer but blushes burgundy red in winter. Any ground cover will do: The more persistent and fast spreading, the better it will knit together to form a solid carpet. Choose low-growing woolly thyme for a lawn that blooms in late spring and smells heavenly when trod upon.

Flower gardens are usurping lawn in many older neighborhoods. Cottage gardens, with their quaint and colorful jumble of grandmother's flowers, have always been fashionable. The prairie style, a blend of native grasses and flowers, is also becoming increasingly popular. In Golden, Colorado, Mary Ellen Keskimaki has developed a unique approach, covering a steep hillside in her front yard with a medley of tough ground covers arranged in large patches to form blocks of color.

Many neighborhood covenants mandate lawns, at least in the front yard. Before making changes, talk to the homeowner's association about your plans. If what you have in mind is reasonable and well thought out, most associations will grant a variance. For those that require an actual lawn, ask if you can switch to a more drought-tolerant alternative to bluegrass. Three of the most readily available are buffalograss (not only tolerates but thrives on clay), blue grama (prefers sandy soil),

and turf-type tall fescue (forms a dense green sod and greens up early in the spring).

My garden is so tiny I forego lawn entirely, but I do have open, level areas that stand in for lawn. In design terms, these are called "negative spaces," which are essential in preventing the garden from being overwhelmed by the bulk of plantings. (Negative spaces also echo the vast openness of basin and plain topography.) To enjoy your handiwork, you need places to stand back, not to mention room for strolling, sitting, eating, and relaxing. A 440-square-foot brick terrace in my backyard is ideal for entertaining. The first level is mortared onto the existing patio slab. A second terrace, one step down from the first, is dry-laid on sand. Admittedly, we can no longer host large weddings or a game of croquet in the backyard, but four or five card tables and chairs

fit comfortably. The setting, surrounded by gardens, is much more inviting and intimate than the expanse of lawn we replaced.

Replacing Bluegrass with a Rock Lawn

When Randy and I moved into our home, the front yard was a typical suburban landscape of lawn, a couple of trees, and borders of junipers mulched with several truckloads of red and black lava rock. We removed the junipers and a fireblight-ridden crabapple but left a ponderosa pine. It was, after all, the only green thing left in the front yard besides the bluegrass. The lawn was divided exactly in half and into two levels by a low rock wall of dry-stacked local sandstone parallel to the house. To improve the proportions, we moved the rock wall back several feet toward the house. At the same time, we

A flagstone terrace with self-sown red lupine is a water-conserving alternative to the bluegrass lawn it replaced. Tatroe garden.

widened the existing borders and dug in various types of compost along with all the volcanic rock mulch, reasoning that it would make a respectable soil amendment. The plan was to make the front garden a conventional one of lawn surrounded by mixed borders of flowers, shrubs, and trees.

For several years we were content with the way things transpired. But, since neither of us is a lawn fancier, we eventually found ourselves looking for an alternative. Recalling my friend Diane Byers' flagstone patio, where woolly thyme planted between the pavers forms a nearly solid mat of gray-green, we decided a similar treatment would give us the look of lawn without the water and fuss a lawn demands. Since the front of our house faces north, this side is more comfortable on a summer afternoon than our hot backyard. I imagined a café table and chairs where we could sit, cool drink in hand, and enjoy the heady aroma of thyme perfuming a warm, summer evening.

Constructing the terrace was an easy weekend's work for three people. We chose red flagstone to complement the used red brick on the front of our house, and figured a two-inch thickness would be sturdy enough for our purpose. At the stoneyard, we picked out pallets with at least a few pieces that were several feet across. The stones went directly onto our previously pampered bluegrass lawn (prompting an astonished neighbor to slam on her brakes and demand an explanation). We reasoned that the in the heat of summer, the stones would smother and rot the grass underneath. To facilitate planting and weeding, we left fairly wide spaces of two to five inches between the stones and used a single application of glyphosate to kill the exposed grass. (Several thicknesses of newspaper layered under the stones would have killed the lawn just as effectively and eliminated the need for an herbicide, but it would have taken much longer.)

Laying flagstone is like working a giant jigsaw puzzle. My son, Keith, a teenager at the time, loves puzzles, so we enlisted his help. The largest pieces went down first, somewhat randomly throughout the terrace. Next, we built the perimeter, leaving the edges quite uneven to allow the flower borders to intrude into the terrace and to soften the margins. With the perimeter in place, we laid the smaller stones, repositioning them until we were pleased with their arrangement. Lastly, we filled all the joints with pink and gray pea gravel and built a bench of cut red flagstone in one corner. Our intent was to leave the terrace alone until the following spring to be quite certain the lawn was dead before planting the thyme. (It was at this point that one of my son's friends commented that our creation had all of the charm of "a direct nuclear hit.")

That same summer I decided that what the terrace needed to make it more interesting was a few planting pockets. When I removed a few medium-sized slabs I found, much to my relief, that the sod was indeed dead. I filled these areas with taller plants. Our original idea to plant thyme might still have had a chance if it hadn't been for all of my visits to garden centers and plant sales. There were dozens of new plants that needed a home, nowhere obvious to put them, and a big, empty expanse of stone and gravel—before too long the woolly thyme idea was abandoned entirely.

My biggest concern was the heavy soil, not what most rock garden plants prefer. Because the dead sod formed a six-inch layer of decent humus-enriched topsoil, and the whole area slopes gently toward the street, drainage was not the problem I had feared. Another concern was that the heat of the stone on a summer day, hot enough to blister bare feet, would cook the plants. As it turns out, the flagstone makes ideal mulch, keeping the soil beneath cool and evenly moist. The northern orientation also limits the number of hours that this side of the house really bakes.

Placing the stones over live sod was successful despite a few early misgivings. It is unnerving to have any surface wobble underfoot, so we were worried about some rocking that occurred the first summer. As the soil compacted and settled under the weight of the stones, the unsteadiness disappeared. Since that time, the surface of a few stones has flaked, but no piece has actually cracked. A real advantage dead sod has over the more traditional sand and gravel subsurface is that it is not as attractive to ants. (Parts of the brick-on-sand patio in the backyard sink as much as an inch a year as ants undermine it.) Weeds have not been troublesome either—with the sod left undisturbed, most of the weed seeds stayed buried too deep to germinate.

When planting amid the flagstones, I strove for strong texture by varying leaf form, size, and color, as well giving some thought to attractive color combinations. To my eye, plants look more natural arranged in groups with uneven spacing but allowed to mingle at the edges with neighboring groups. A few larger, bolder, or vertical plants scattered throughout the paving provide accents to stop the eye, acting much like punctuation on a written page. Because they are easy to walk over, low mounds, mats, and ground covers that spread out over the stone are the best forms for the majority of the plants between the flagstones. I did include thymes after all, since they are the ideal paving plant, creeping about and following the contours of the rocks. But rather than using woolly thyme exclusively, I tucked a half-dozen different varieties here and there.

Hen and chicks is another obvious choice for planting between flagstones, the red and blue varieties especially lovely against the red stone. Each rosette has rapidly expanded into a large colony. (Do use care when siting these and other succulents. When walked on, they smash and become slippery.) A dozen species of dianthus dot the paving, some quite tight and prickly to the touch, creating perfect little mounds, while others are lax and floppy. Foliage ranges from silvery blues through soft greens. All sport cheerful star-shaped flowers in shades of pinks and whites, many smelling sweetly of cloves.

The flagstone is the perfect place to enjoy plants whose flowers are so small that they are best viewed on hands and knees but whose growth is too vigorous for the confines of a trough. (This also eliminates the need to balance precariously on a rock while trying to get really, really close up on

a berm.) *Stachys chrysantha* and *Nepeta phyllochlamys* are just two examples. Both have outstanding silver, textural foliage and they might reasonably be grown for that alone. But their tiny and subtle flowers are among the prettiest in the garden and it would be a shame to overlook them. Sitting on the flagstone, I can fully appreciate these diminutive blossoms in complete safety and relative comfort.

In 2001, I removed an area of flagstone approximately 6 x 6 feet, dug out the soil to a depth of one foot, and replaced it with coarse sand. All this because I was determined to grow *Raoulia australis* and was convinced a sand bed would do the trick. It died, as did the sand penstemon *Penstemon ambiguus* that I figured would be right at home in a sand bed. I have no explanation for either failure. However, other sand-loving plants thrive here, including *Anacampseros rufescens, Arabis androsacea, Arenaria drypidea, A. hookeri,* sea thrift *Armeria setosa, Dianthus myrtinervius, D. squarosus, Gypsophila bungeana, Penstemon cyanocaulis, Scutellaria resinosa,* and *Stomatium beaufortense.*

Winter—Unparalleled Beauty

When was the last time you came across a book extolling the virtues of the winter garden in, say, Jackson, Wyoming, or Edmonton, Canada? Books on this subject always seem to originate in climates milder than our own—and not without good reason. Filling an entire volume with plants that look their best in winter, where temperatures routinely dip to -20°F and below would be a stretch. Still, something has to be done. Winter lasts a very long time in these parts. You can't very well avert your eyes every time you walk outside for six months of the year. A modest amount of planning promises to set things right. Some of our most glorious garden scenes occur in winter. Bare branches encrusted with hoarfrost, red berries against crystalline snow, snow irises and crocuses defiantly polychromatic in an otherwise gray and brown world—few things rival these images.

Once in early January, Randy and I were driving along a major thoroughfare north of our house when he exclaimed, "Those probably aren't real." For a second I couldn't figure out what he was talking about, and then I saw it—a median planting full of blue and purple flowers. They looked like daffodils, but the color was wrong. Some enterprising landscaper had decided to defy winter's gloom by "planting" silk or plastic flowers. The effect was about as convincing—and unnerving—as a flock of pink flamingoes lined up in a snowbank. Fortunately, it isn't necessary to go to such extremes to have flowers in winter in our region. Many of the little bulbs, those that top out at around 4 to 6 inches,

start blooming in January. Plant enough of them and by late winter you are guaranteed to have sheets of color where there would otherwise be nothing but bare dirt. It is only a matter of choosing the right bulbs. Until recently these bulbs belonged almost exclusively to the realm of the rock gardener. The more unusual bulbs still require a search, but every nursery and home improvement store features a handful of crocuses, scillas, snow iris, and those little early tulips that cause the uninitiated to ask why their tulips are so short this year.

The selection improves every season. One spring I was amazed to find *Crocus ancyrensis* 'Golden Bunch', a very early yellow crocus that

I had could previously only get by mail, included in the Martha Stewart collection at K-Mart. Garden centers are an even better bet—most have increased their inventory in recent years to include hundreds of varieties of little bulbs. Not all of these are early bloomers. Look for "late winter" or "early spring" on the label. In most years, this translates to sometime in February or March—April at the latest—depending on the weather. For the most part, these bulbs are downright cheap, so buy lots, never fewer than twenty-five of one type. A hundred will make a bigger impact. You really can't have too many.

Despite winter flowers, the main emphasis at this season is on earthtones and texture. Take notice of the many different types of bark on trees and shrubs and make sure your garden has a good variety. The bark on some trees is rough and craggy, like the bur oak *Quercus macrocarpa* with its deep fissures and silvery gray patina. Smell the similarly coarse bark of the Ponderosa pine, and on warm days you might detect a scent of vanilla. In marked contrast, the bark of the native river birch *Betula occidentalis* is smooth and shiny, embellished with short horizontal white lines. Bark on young stems is a rusty red. The shaggy bark of beautybush *Kolkwitzia amabilis* peels into long strips of gold and gray that loosely curl around mature branches and resemble the deteriorating nest of a paper wasp. The bark of aspens is green-tinged and feels waxy to the touch. You could be excused for branding the red twig dogwood cliché because it shows up so many regional landscapes. Even so, I would miss its familiar red silhouette in the winter garden.

Some years fruit and berry set is damaged by a late freeze, but generally we can rely on an abundance of red, orange, yellow, purple, and blue berries on various trees and shrubs. The Russian hawthorn *Crataegus ambigua* outside my kitchen windows provides months of cheer, its cherry-red fruits gradually deepening to claret and hanging on until late winter when birds returning from their migrations strip the branches bare. Gardeners with

room to let a large suckering shrub take over one corner of their property could include one of the sumacs, either the Rocky Mountain sumac *Rhus glabra* or the similar staghorn sumac *R. typhina*. Both produce cones of fuzzy red fruit held aloft like flaming torches. Cotoneasters are Cinderella shrubs, often scorned by serious gardeners as too common. But, in winter they become the belle of the ball, their brilliant scarlet fruits breathtaking against gray branches with or without snow.

Likewise, many roses dress in winter finery, wearing hips like red, orange, or black jewels. Redleafed rose *Rosa glauca* makes up for ho-hum flowers with one of the finest displays of scarlet hips on purplish stems. Cultivars of *Rosa rugosa* bear huge vermilion hips, some the size of shooter marbles. Rosarian John Starnes recommends *Rosa spinosissima* with black hips that "gleam like obsidian beads," *R. canina* with "bright red, sweet-tart hips," and 'Mr. Nash', an old-fashioned shrub rose that produces "pendulous clusters of hundreds of plump, yellow-orange hips the size of large olives."

Ornamental grasses add life and movement to the winter garden, many every bit as attractive in dormancy as in summer's fullness. The maiden grasses, the miscanthus kin, are among the latest to bloom. In many years, early frosts and snow put a stop to their potential display, but when snow doesn't knock them over, the plumes are magnificent, at the same time wispy and graceful. The bottlebrush grass *Hystrix patula*, its seedheads stiff and angular, becomes ever more golden as winter advances. The seedheads of the blue avena grass *Helictotrichon sempervirens* don't last the entire summer, let alone into winter, but the clump itself is this grass's claim to fame. It maintains an evergreen steely blue cast until an arctic cold front freeze-dries the clump, transforming it into a gold and pewter pompon for the rest of the winter.

Xeriscapes and native plant gardens put the conventional bluegrass and juniper landscape to shame in this, the "off" season. Most of our native grasses age to golden flax, while clumps of little and tall bluestem become so red they appear to be on fire.

Seedheads of clematis brighten the winter garden.

Fluffy seedheads of rabbitbrush *Chrysothamnus nauseosus* stand unbending on stiff, gray-green stems. Sagebrush is lustrous silver. Yellow and rusty red fruits on prickly pear cactus *Opuntia* spp. stand out in sharp contrast to frosty skies. Stark outlines of yucca poke up through freshly fallen snow. Seedheads of yarrow, butterfly weed, dotted gayfeather, coneflowers, and prairie clover each add textural character to the blend as well as providing food for overwintering birds.

Plants are not the only things that make the winter garden satisfying. By late autumn, trellising, stones, brickwork, and sculpture reemerge from camouflaging greenery, reminding us that more than plants are necessary to create a garden that holds our interest all year round. Winter is a good time to reassess the structural content of the garden. Winter is also often a good time to work in

the garden. But, unlike gardeners in milder climates, for us gardening in winter is optional. Other than watering occasionally, we really can leave the garden to its own devices. But why would you want to?

Due to our association with the ski industry, Denver, Boise, and Salt Lake City have a reputation for colder and snowier winters than we actually experience. While cold and snowy winters do define our region, what sets us apart from other cold places in the country is that, except at higher elevations, snow does not stay long on the ground. There is enough snow for the occasional calendar-photo moment—but not so much that it becomes a nuisance. We hardly ever have to endure what Randy calls "snirt," that mix of snow, ice, and dirt that coats every surface for weeks on end following snowstorms in places where snow sticks

around. Between snowfalls, there are plenty of warm days, even in the dead of winter. You really can garden here year round if you choose.

Spring—The Frenzied Season

Every day in spring there is something new to behold. Here, the tiny blue flowers of *Veronica peduncularis* 'Georgia Blue', there, a flurry of white from *Arabis caucasica* 'Variegata'. The dry rock garden is filled with Easter daisies, the *Townsendia* clan, and various early bulbs. The first primroses poking up through the latest snowfall cheer the woodland garden. Any flower is welcome at this time of year when the calendar says spring, but the weather is all too often still wintry. However, of all the April flowers, none tugs at my heart like the pasqueflowers, so named for their arrival near

Easter. The Lakota Sioux call our native pasqueflower *Pulsatilla patens* "twinflower," and believe that it sings a song that awakens other slumbering flowers, thus initiating the new season.

In late spring, flowering trees and shrubs join the floral chorus. Frost routinely destroys the flowers of forsythia and crabapples, but fortunately there are shrubs that are almost never damaged by untimely freezes. One of them shades the west side of my house. The chokecherry *Prunus virginiana* 'Canada Red' has honey-scented chains of delicate white blossoms. When the wind blows and a blizzard of petals swirls beneath the tree, it is like being inside a snow globe on a warm spring day. The fruit that follows makes wonderful jelly and pancake syrup. (If friends didn't share their bounty with us, I wouldn't know this. Robins strip my tree before I get a single fruit.) In my front yard,

Snow crocus come up early, but close tightly on stormy days.

Pasqueflowers *Pulsatilla vulgaris* announce the arrival of spring.

clove currant *Ribes aureum*, a 6-foot shrub with miniature yellow trumpet-shaped flowers, scents the whole block with its exotic perfume. This is an adaptable shrub, content wherever it is sited—sun, shade, irrigated, or dry. Mine puts up with some of the worst soil in my garden, a patch of heavy, sticky clay along the front fenceline that is alternately too wet or too dry for most things. The clove currant also produces edible berries. (The robins get those, too.)

Unfortunately, the white pompons of the wayfaring tree *Viburnum lantana*, though pretty, smell like three-day-old fish. Once when we walked through the garden, Randy asked, "What's that smell?" I'm sure he thought I was using some new, stinky organic fertilizer. (You might as well spread chicken manure or milorganite, commercially available recycled sewage sludge, the week these blossoms come out and get the olfactory assault over all at once.) Also reliable for flowers in May are barberries *Berberis* spp. (tiny flowers, but worthy of close scrutiny), the Russian hawthorn *Crataegus ambigua* (it also smells faintly of fish, but with sweet overtones), brooms *Cytisus* spp. (yellow flowers that smell faintly of gasoline), bridal veil spirea *Spirea* x *vanhouttei* (no scent), and boulder raspberry *Rubus deliciosus* (finally, another winner in the fragrance department, this one smells like the white roses it resembles).

Spring is a busy time for gardeners everywhere, but in our region this is a hyper-season, when time moves at warp speed. Even if you spend every warm day from February on out working in the garden, spring chores remain unfinished. The end of May, unfortunately, is the drop-dead date. The seasonal clock runs out on many garden tasks. According to the experts, perennial flowers, shrubs, and trees can be safely transplanted at any season when the ground is not frozen. But cool weather makes success more likely. It is also a whole lot less work for the gardener who must monitor hot-weather transplants with the attention of an intensive-care nurse.

Planting and transplanting are not the only activities that keep us busy in spring. The list of chores seems endless. If you have not pruned roses and clematis by now, they will shortly be blooming in rat's nest of winterkilled brown stems. Weeds must be removed before they begin to multiply. Yellow-foliaged plants require fertilizer posthaste. Mums need pinching. Flowers that bloom in early spring and are finished require deadheading. There are never enough hours in a day. Adding to the chaos of spring, weather at this season can be hot enough to melt nursery pots one day, and a chilly 22°F the next. I've never purchased even one lottery ticket or put a single quarter in a slot machine, but I do participate in a game of chance every spring,

betting on when the last frost date will arrive. Even though the last frost date for my area is supposed to arrive in mid-May, more than once it has snowed on my garden in June. The last frost date is like a baby's due date: Neither ever arrives as predicted. Waiting until summer to set out frost tender flowers is not an option, so every spring we wager that this year it will not freeze in June.

By the time the average last frost date gets here, I have been preparing for this day for a couple of months. As summer bulbs become available in March, I pot up lilies, dahlias, begonias, and the like, some newly purchased, some saved from the previous year. They all get a head start on a windowsill or under grow lights in the basement for a

Spring in full swing at El Zaguan in Santa Fe, with pink roses, peonies, and beautybush.

few weeks before it is time to get them outdoors. At the same time, I start seeds of those annual flowers that are not readily available from local nurseries. Buying trips begin in earnest the minute flowers appear at local retailers, signaling that spring is imminent.

Watching me unload the car one day, a neighbor asked just how many plants I buy in a year. With more than fifty containers to fill with annuals, it is a bunch. During the first couple of weeks of May, my back patio resembles a small nursery. With its cover of shade cloth, this is a good place to shelter greenhouse-grown plants as they acclimate to sunlight, wind, and fluctuating temperatures. When frost threatens, they get covered with a fabric frost blanket (available from garden centers). If a hard freeze looks likely, I hustle the whole lot indoors for the night.

Getting even sun-worshippers that have been started under artificial light accustomed to the real thing is a gradual process, much as we did when natural tans were the height of fashion. To prevent sunburn, we lay out in the sun for a few minutes each day, gradually increasing our sun exposure. Doing the same thing with plants helps them adjust or "harden off." Like our tanning regimen, this involves actual cellular changes. Some plants make it regardless—witness the number of survivors in any home improvement store parking lot. When buying plants from these places, I pick from the lower, shaded levels of the carts and hedge my bets by pampering the transplants. Anything grown outdoors in nurseries on the relatively misty West Coast also benefits from a period of hardening off.

Midsummer Doldrums

Admittedly, it is difficult for someone who dislikes heat as much as I do to work up much enthusiasm for gardening when daytime temperatures average in the nineties and mosquitoes reach plague proportions. But July and August bring some of our most spectacular flowers. On any day in July and August, I can count more than thirty different kinds of flowers in bloom in the driest parts of my garden. Included in this inventory are all of the usual suspects from every list of xeriscape flowers—butterfly weed, prairie clover, winecups, prairie coneflower, Russian sage, and gaillardia. Also blooming in midsummer are a few native wildflowers whose continued anonymity mystifies me. Boulder landscape architect and author Jim Knopf introduced Mexican campion, *Silene laciniata*, years ago in his book *Xeriscape Flower Garden* (still the best guide for starting a xeriscape flower garden in our region), but I can only find plants and seeds from sources in New Mexico. This is a pretty little flower with orange stars. Maybe its orange color holds this plant back from wider popularity. In any case, Mexican campion is striking alongside the more commonplace orange butterfly weed.

Blazing heat can take a toll on irrigated flower beds. If it gets too hot, many perennials generally reliable in midsummer drop their flower buds before they have had a chance to open. But even during a spell of record-breaking temperatures, some perennials stand out for their unflagging heat endurance. On these, not a leaf wilts, not a petal drops, even when the mercury tops 100°F. This hardy group promises a good show every year and will, without a doubt, perk up the midsummer doldrums. Among these are the exquisitely fragrant butterfly bush *Buddleia davidii*, globe thistle *Echinops ritro*, the gayfeather *Liatris spicata*, and torch lilies *Kniphofia* spp. Also standing up to midsummer heat are some lesser-known perennials. Crocosmias are a bulb that every gardener transplanted from California knows well. The variety 'Lucifer' is hardy here, though it never reaches the size it attains in milder climates. The flowers are a scorching red-orange, appropriate for the hellishly hot days of August. On a cooler note is the lavender-blue wild petunia *Ruellia humilis*, a sprawler that is great at the feet of other taller perennials. This completely hardy petunia look-alike is as floriferous as its namesake.

It's never too hot for daisies. When temperatures are so high that even mosquitoes take shelter, summer-blooming daisies make their debut. With origins as diverse as alpine meadows, the high plains, and eastern swamplands, there is a daisy for every sunny place in the garden. Probably the most well known of the summer-blooming daisies is the gleaming white Shasta daisy, a flower that has been in cultivation since the late nineteenth century. Short-lived in much of the United States, Shasta daisies can live for decades in the Mountain West, where summer days are hot but nighttime temperatures relatively cool. Three-foot-tall 'Alaska' is the most cold hardy, surviving winter lows of -50°F, making it a good choice for colder parts of our region. Dwarf Shastas 'Little Miss Muffet', 'Silver Princess', and 'Snowcap' form tidy mounds 1 to 2 feet tall and don't require staking. Other variations of Shasta daisies include those with double and semidouble flowers and creamy yellow 'Cobham Gold' (which, because of its color, looks more like a florist's chrysanthemum than a Shasta daisy).

The rudbeckias, sometimes called coneflowers, but also known as black-eyed Susans, are golden yellow with dark brown or black centers. The one that appears in every municipal planting across the country is 'Goldsturm', a large-flowered selection that blooms from midsummer through hard frost. Equally long-blooming, but with flowers that are more prim and proper, is the dwarf rudbeckia 'Viette's Little Suzy'. Six-foot-tall 'Golden Glow' is too invasive for many situations, but perfect for naturalistic gardens where it can travel about without making a nuisance of itself.

Don't limit yourself to the commonplace. Very few gardeners try the perennial sunflower *Heliopsis helianthoides*. Native to the eastern United States, this sunflower is short-lived in other parts of the country but solidly perennial here. Golden yellow 'Summer Sun' is the standard at 2 to 3 feet tall, but there are larger cultivars available, such as 'Karat' and semidouble 'Golden Plume', both 4 feet tall. For foliage every bit as attractive as the flowers, look for 'Loraine Sunshine'. Its green-

Globe thistle *Echinops ritro* stands up to July's heat in the Ungerleider garden.

It's never too hot for purple coneflower *Echinacea purpurea*. Barbara Duno garden, Santa Fe.

veined white leaves resemble those of coleus. Shasta daisies, rudbeckias, and heliopsis can survive some drought, but bloom continuously from midsummer until hard frost with regular watering. Water will also affect their ultimate height as drought stunts their growth. All prefer full sun and soil well amended with organic matter.

There are also daisies for drier parts of the garden. If there is one plant that is a common denominator for the Intermountain West, goldenaster *Heterotheca villosa* is it. This wildflower is found throughout in our region. Every pasture and vacant lot in the Denver metro area is covered with these low mounds of yellow daisies, growing without one drop of supplemental irrigation. This is one of the few wildflowers that continued to bloom and thrive even during the extreme drought of 2001–3. Flowering from midsummer through hard frost, goldenaster looks better if *un*irrigated, becoming lax and seeding invasively when overwatered. Also tough and highly drought-tolerant are thrift-leaf perky Sue *Hymenoxys scaposa* and chocolate-scented chocolate flower *Berlandieria lyrata*, both golden-yellow daisies, and Blackfoot daisy *Melampodium leucanthum*, which has small white flowers. All three top out at 6 to 8 inches tall and bloom the entire summer and into autumn.

As to drought-tolerance, the echinaceas are a mixed bag. Golden-flowered Ozark coneflower *Echinacea paradoxa* is not even remotely xeric. Slightly more so is the purple (it's really pink) coneflower *E. purpurea*, but drought-stressed plants are short and miserable-looking compared to those receiving regular water. Pale coneflower *E. pallida*, also pink, is fairly drought-tolerant. Prairie purple (also pink) coneflower *E. angustifolia* withstands drier conditions better than the rest of the group, but when grown too dry its petals appear singed.

Gaillardia, another daisy that can withstand some drought, is more robust and floriferous with regular watering. 'Goblin' is a compact variety that has burgundy red flowers with yellow edges. 'Baby Cole' is nearly identical but shorter yet at 6

to 8 inches tall. 'Burgundy' is 2 to 3 feet tall with flowers a solid rusty red, 'Golden Goblin' soft gold. Coreopsis are heat- and drought-tolerant daisies that come in every shade of yellow. Named cultivars are all similar, with varying petal arrangements and heights. 'Early Sunrise' is a particularly intricate form with several overlapping rows of petals that create a sunburst effect.

By the end of August, even daisies look downright tired. Summer's flowers are well into their scruffy stage. Asters and mums are fully budded but not quite ready for their turn in the sun. It becomes all too evident that, in the throes of the heady spring rush, we forgot that it might also be nice to have a

few flowers after Labor Day. If we all heeded garden design tenets and planned for a third of the garden to peak at each season, we would not find ourselves facing this end-of-summer slump. Unfortunately, some of us do not exercise the self-discipline required. In spring we pack every empty space with new purchases, leaving no room for late summer booty. There is a solution. Rip out anything that did not, for any reason, meet your expectations earlier in the year. Then head off to the local nursery to find replacements that look spectacular right now to fill holes you have created. You will be surprised at the selection. To add to the appeal, many nurseries have "end of season" sales in late summer.

In late summer, aster, liatris, chocolate flower, and gaillardia create a symphony of lavender and yellow in the Howard garden.

Autumn's Potential

For fall color, bigtooth maples in Utah rival sugar maples in the Northeast.

Unpredictability is the rule at any season in these parts, but autumn's potential seems to be the most fragile. Not infrequently, exceptional color is ruined by an early blast of cold air from the arctic. When this happens, our gardens go into Indian summer blackened and flattened. The occasional autumn, though, makes us forget past disappointments. Then the world is dressed in gold, burgundy, scarlet, and burnished copper tones—the rich hues of arts and crafts fabrics and Persian carpets. Trees glow in colors as iridescent as carnival glass, variously reflecting and refracting sun-

light, or burn with the intensity of a ruby or a topaz. Fallen leaves scatter across the garden like so many jewels and shards of light, ready to come alive and scamper and skip away at the slightest breeze. They swirl and dance to catch and gather in corners, eliciting a satisfying crunch when trod upon. I carry the prettiest ones indoors to join gourds, pumpkins, Indian corn, witches and goblins, and then later, pilgrims and turkeys.

Some plants go down without a fight. One day they are full of vim and vigor, the next they are brown and withered, victims of even a light frost. Fall color depends on another sort of plant, those that go through a gradual decline toward winter.

A few of the best go out in a blaze of glory. In a good year, when the days are bright and warm and the nights cool but not frigid, autumn color can rival anything spring or summer offers.

Trees and shrubs that have purple leaves during the summer reliably turn brilliant shades of red most autumns. Maroon 'Schubert' (syn. 'Canada Red') chokecherry becomes a torch of crimson flames. The purpleleaf sandcherry *Prunus* x *cistina* and the purpleleaf plum *P. cerasifera* 'Newport' similarly catch fire. Also spectacular is the crabapple 'Thunderchild', its purple-tinged foliage briefly turning translucent garnet before dropping off to reveal deep purple-red fruit. The intense purple foliage of 'Royal Purple' smokebush blushes to reddish-purple. Red-leafed rose *Rosa glauca*, which has leaves that are more pewter than purple in summer, gradually changes to orange in October, made brighter yet by a profusion of shiny scarlet hips.

A large number of green-leaved trees and shrubs also turn brilliant shades of orange and red in the fall. Probably the best known are the maples. Of these, expect the brightest color from selected cultivars such as *Acer* x *freemanii* 'Autumn Blaze', red maple *A. rubrum* 'Red Scarlet', the sugar maple *A. saccharum* 'Legacy', and the box elder *A. negundo* 'Flame'. Most bigtooth maples *A. grandidentatum* have leaves that will turn red if the season is long

In autumn, the garden is dressed in tones of gold, burgundy, and burnished copper. Jan and Paul Barbo's garden, Espanola, New Mexico.

Long after the leaves have fallen, red fruit decorates the branches of Jade crabapple at Santa Fe Greenhouse's display garden.

enough, but some years frost kills the foliage before it has a chance to get past yellow. 'Autumn Brilliant' serviceberry rivals the reds of sugar maples. Many of the tough and drought-tolerant hawthorns also turn orange to red in fall, particularly striking against their red or black fruit. The burning bush *Euonymus alata* is as brash as a barroom floozy. When this otherwise plain-Jane green shrub puts on its Carmen-red finery, it always invites a great deal of comment.

'Autumn Purple' ash is another stunner that hardly commands a second look until autumn, and then it can stop you in your tracks. 'Skyline' ash also has reddish-purple fall color. 'Chanticleer' pear is

maroon. Of the oaks that do well in our area, the red oak and 'Crimson Spire' oak have the sort of fiery red foliage that finds its way into fall floral arrangements. Our native Gambel oak paints the foothills orange and crimson in October and can do the same for xeriscapes. Most viburnums indulge in red fall color, as do barberries, dogwoods, cotoneaster, chokeberries, sumacs, and spireas.

As aspen admirers know well, clear yellows and golden shades are the other colors of autumn. No tree turns yellow with more fanfare than aspens, but green ash, silver maple, Western hackberry, Eastern redbud, honey locust, golden rain tree, cottonwoods, locust, linden, river birch, and many cultivars of crabapples all end the season in these sunshine hues. In fact, almost any tree or shrub that doesn't turn orange or red will turn yellow before its leaves drop. After the leaves have fallen, fruits and berries will comprise the entire feast, but until then, they are the garden's garnish. Vermilion seedheads of sumacs resemble burning embers exploding from orange and crimson flames. Barberries go out in a blaze of color, ruddy red joining deepest burgundy and lustrous gold.

Shrubs and trees are responsible for the most obvious fall color, but many other types of plants also get into the act. The only reason to put up with Virginia creeper vine's invasive ways is to enjoy its scarlet fall foliage, bright red stems, and dark blue berries. Boston ivy is equally attractive and better behaved. Species and small-flowered types of clematis often produce yellow leaves, in addition to amazing feather-duster seedheads that are attractive well into the winter. Cooler temperatures and shorter days play host to a whole new gang of flowers. Most of these are tough characters, able to fend off whatever weird weather the season brings. Chrysanthemums and asters are autumn's staples with good reason. Planting a varied selection of these practically guarantees fall color. But don't stop there—fall can offer floral abundance that nearly matches spring's.

While there is nothing wrong with the chrysanthemums and asters of grocery-store fame, a search of your local garden center in late summer often turns up some unusual relatives you might otherwise never get to know. The New England aster *A. novae-angliae* and the New York aster *A. novi-belgii* are notorious for mildewed foliage. Other species are not so prone to this malady. *Aster pringlei* 'Monte Cassino' sends up thousands of tiny white daisies from September through October. *Aster laterifolius* 'Horizontalis', 'Lady in Black', and 'Prince' all feature foliage that starts out purple-black in spring and diminutive flowers with red centers that fade to pink as they age.

Annual flowers are often at their best in September and October. Many suffer heat in silence, refusing to bloom throughout the hottest summer months, perking up again as soon as more moderate temperatures return. In a good year, many annual flowers continue blooming past Halloween if they are not pulled in a frenzy of fall cleanup. Too many perennials to count continue blooming well into the fall. Others are spring performers that rebloom only if frost does not come early. For another group of perennials, fall is their season. Among these is the hybrid anemone, possibly the most elegant with large silken flowers shaped like old-fashioned single and semi-double roses. Much as I pamper them, I can hardly keep these beauties alive. However, where well-irrigated, they can be quite invasive.

More my speed is drought-tolerant azure sage, *Salvia azurea*, aka *S. pitcheri*. This is a floppy plant that defies staking. I just let it lounge. The flowers are deep cobalt blue. 'Grandiflora' is paler, the color of the sky in autumn. Similarly sky blue is another late bloomer, *Lobelia syphilitica*. This plant adores heavy, wet clay and will self-sow in such a site. White flowered forms are also available. Drought-tolerant Siberian sea lavender *Limonium latifolium* starts blooming in August and creates a purple-blue haze that lasts several months thereafter. This is the best of a notable family, its arching sprays of everlasting flowers equally valuable for flower arrangements or for playing off the daisies of autumn.

Perennials are not usually grown for their fall foliage color, but many do finish the year with a flourish, turning yellow or red as the season reaches its conclusion. Too seldom seen in area gardens is swamp milkweed, *Asclepias incarnata*, which becomes vivid yellow in fall, with the added charm of tarnished brown seed capsules bursting at the seams with white down. Foliage spikes of Kansas gayfeather *Liatris spicata* become burgundy red before they go over. The leaves of bloody cranesbill *Geranium sanguineum* turn as red as any maple. Silver-foliaged perennials generally keep their shimmering color until they freeze, making a strong impact that contrasts against the prevailing red and golden tones of the season.

Ornamental grasses shine in autumn. Turning brilliant golden yellow before going into winter dormancy, fall-blooming reed grass *Calamagrostis brachytricha* is an upright fountain that holds onto its seedheads well into winter. Delicate sand love grass *Eragrostis trichioides* sends up sprays of arrow-shaped purple seedheads, bringing to mind a school of darting minnows. Autumn moorgrass *Sesleria autumnalis* is unremarkable all summer—in fact, I have almost pulled it more than once, thinking a clump of bluegrass had invaded the front border. In fall, purplish black spikes are handsome with asters blooming nearby.

Late-blooming perennials can be counted on to continue sending up the occasional flower, sometimes through the end of November. The last flower of the year in my garden, signaling that winter is well upon us, is the autumn crocus *Crocus speciosus*. This true crocus has huge lavender-blue flowers with conspicuous veining that are as fragile as soap bubbles and will collapse under the weight of raindrops or a sprinkler's spray. These flowers come up solo without leaves, the foliage having made its subtle appearance in spring and then fading away. They are startling, popping up through the detritus of less intrepid, long-departed companions.

Orange horned poppies continue to bloom well into October most years.

The Essentials—
Soil, Water, and Garden
Maintenance

Thoughts on Soil

All three of the basic soil types—sand, loam, and clay—can be found in the
Intermountain West. Of these, the one most often cursed is clay, which has always been
considered the antithesis of good garden soil. Gardeners who find themselves thus
burdened feel like the fates have been unaccountably cruel. Their complaint? Wet clay
sticks to tools, gloves, shoes, and anything else it touches—making it nearly impossible
to work. But clay is not the only problematic soil.

In drier parts of our region, soils are generally highly alkaline (according to traditional gardening wisdom, too high for most traditional plants) and tend to contain ample potassium but deficient amounts of nitrogen, phosphorus, trace elements, and humus. The exception is in mountain gardens, where the gardener's complaint is extreme acidity or no soil whatsoever, only fractured rock. Sand drains well, but in water-deprived environs this can be a bigger drawback than sticky clay. In a few locations, such as the Black Forest of Colorado and the foothills west of Boulder, soil approaches the gardening ideal—neutral loam. If your site was ever used to grow crops, the soil is probably loam. Soils too poor for agricultural pursuits were generally left to grazing. Natural plant communities are also a good indication of soil type. Where soil supports healthy populations of ponderosa pine, the pH is generally moderate and drainage fast. Sagebrush scrub suggests slight alkalinity and moderate drainage. Rabbitbrush inhabits drier, sandier sites. Salt-tolerant atriplex and winterfat *Krascheninnikovia lanata* show up where salinity is too high for most other plants.

I have only minimal familiarity with pure sand. The former owners left a sandbox in one corner of the property. Rather than haul off the sand, I piled it up and made a rock garden. There are plants that populate sandy sites. But if you choose not to amend sand, your planting options are seriously limited. The trouble with sand is that it holds very little water. This is one time where mixing in a huge amount of compost (50 percent of the volume of the soil, or six inches to the top 12 inches of soil) can help improve the soil's water-holding capability. For more on dealing with sand see page 118 in the rock gardening chapter.

In my front garden, next to the sidewalk, is the worst kind of clay. This stuff resembles cookie

Shadscale *Atriplex confertifolia* and prickly pear cactus tolerate salty soils.

The gumbo lily *Oenothera caespitosa* is so called because it prefers "gumbo" clay soil. Tatroe garden.

dough when damp but crumbles into knuckle-bone-shaped chunks as it dries out. When I built the garden, I attempted to double-dig this bed to a depth of 15 inches. All these years later, whenever I plant something new, I still find large cheeseballs of intact clay studded with particles of unrotted humus. Dry clay is rock solid, impervious to digging. Garden writers, who apparently all garden with loam, warn us not to dig when the clay is wet or too dry. In our climate, where things go very quickly from one extreme to the other, we are left with a conundrum. Conceivably, there might never be a proper time to dig in clay. Nevertheless, I have come to value my clay soil. I can grow things here like hybrid lupines and English primroses that regional gardeners gifted with loam find difficult because their soil dries out too rapidly.

If I had any lingering doubts about clay, drought has dispelled them. Of the three soil types, clay is the clear winner for holding water. Clay can be difficult to moisten in the first place—water runs off when the surface is dry—but once moist, it stays moist for a longer time. The trick is to water in cycles. For example, if you want to apply $1/2$ inch of water and the sprinkler delivers that amount in fifteen minutes, let the sprinkler run five minutes, then turn it off for about fifteen minutes to allow the water to soak in. Repeat until the entire amount is supplied, experimenting with the intervals until there is no runoff.

One idiosyncrasy of soils in our region, regardless of composition, is that friability improves in winter and decreases over the summer. The action of frost opens air spaces. Occasionally the surface of the soil swells and cracks into lumps and furrows (called "popcorn" texture) in late winter. As temperatures moderate, the surface levels out again, and by late summer soil that was easy to dig in earlier in the season becomes as solid as concrete. If your soil is of this type, it's much easier to work in spring when a shovel can actually penetrate the soil. By fall, a pickax may be the only tool that will do the job.

Frost heaving, when the soil actually squeezes the plant right out of the ground, is a particular risk the first winter after planting. Roots exposed in this manner desiccate quickly, killing the plants. Vigilance is the only remedy. Because small transplants are the most vulnerable, check them often the first winter and get them back into the ground quickly. Transplanting in spring gives roots a chance to grow out into the surrounding soil and anchor themselves. Also helpful is shaking off most of the potting soil when planting. An intact block of roots and potting medium is guaranteed to frost heave. Winter mulch also helps prevent frost heaving.

The Value of Soil Analysis

Because the engineer's report that came with my house identified the underlying soil as a type of expansive clay called bentonite (this type of clay expands to twice its volume when wet and shrinks when dry), I had always assumed that the topsoil throughout my garden contained a large percentage of clay. It was not until after I had gardened here for seventeen years that I discovered that I had been mostly mistaken the entire time.

Charles was having difficulties with the soil in his garden in Santa Fe. I explained how he could do a low-tech soil test where you place one-third dirt and two-thirds water into a jar and add one teaspoon of non-sudsing laundry detergent or water softener. Then the jar is shaken and left where it can sit undisturbed for a few days. The soil settles out into three distinct layers, from heaviest to lightest. Sand comprises the bottom layer, silt is in the middle, and clay is on top (clay may stay in suspension indefinitely). Humus floats. You can figure out the percentage of each and refer to what soil engineers call a soil triangle, but a ballpark estimate will suffice. (To see a soil triangle, Google "soil analysis.")

It just so happened that at the time Charles and I were discussing soils, the electric company had been digging just beyond my property line and had left a pile of soil behind. This soil looked like what I find a foot beneath the amended layer in my garden. I was curious to know what it contained since my original soil tests had been done on soil that had been cultivated as landscape for seven years before I bought my home. This was a good opportunity to demonstrate to Charles the jar method. I was shocked to watch the soil in the jar immediately settle out in not three but two layers, sand and silt. After three days, there was still only a trace of clay. It turns out the bulk of the soil in my backyard is not clay at all, but one-third sand and two-thirds silt, technically a silt loam. This soil contains very little clay and no humus. A check of the USDA soil conservation service data confirmed that what they call loamy foothill sites do occur in my area.

This explains a lot. When I did a percolation test (to do this, dig a hole, fill it with water and observe how long it takes for the water to drain away), the drainage was fast (pure clay drains slowly). In clay there should also be a good amount of lateral movement. Water from my soaker hoses appears to go straight down. When dry, this "loam" is as dense as a brick. (Attempting to dig in it with a shovel produces a clanging sound.) I was telling my friend Kelly Grummons about my discovery and how my soil sometimes acts like quicksand. More than once I have stepped onto a wet patch and sunk up to my knees. He laughed and said that what I have *is* quicksand, and that on his parents' ranch in Wyoming cows frequently get stuck in this same stuff. Some plants are suited to silt loams, but the addition of several inches of compost has created a true loam and the best soil in the garden for a very wide range of plants.

A couple of lessons emerged from my misperception about my soil. Soil may occur in strata. The engineer is primarily concerned with what lies 10 feet beneath the surface, but the gardener deals with only the top couple of feet. So you know exactly what you've got, test the surface soil throughout the garden wherever it appears to be different, and the underlying layer as well, especially if they appear markedly dissimilar.

Pros and Cons of Soil Amendment

There are two schools of thought on soil amendment. The first advocates mixing in enough manure, compost, and fertilizer to achieve some sort of universal standard of good soil. The alternative is to use the soil *au naturel*, choosing plants that are compatible with existing conditions. Most gardeners, myself included, practice both. At one extreme is my vegetable garden, which I amended heavily in the first place and continue to amend at every opportunity. Tomatoes, peppers, beans, and other vegetables are heavy feeders and enjoy an organic-rich, crumbly soil mixture. The mix of 50 percent humus and 50 percent existing soil, fertilized several times a year, which vegetables prefer, is also not too rich for many traditional perennials such as daylilies or Siberian iris.

This same soil would spell death to many of the native plants in my xeric gardens. In these, I dug in a small amount of compost, mostly to improve drainage in compacted areas, but have added nothing since, other than broadcasting a light application of organic fertilizer pellets once a year. Penstemons, gaillardia, eriogonums, and most other xeric plants prefer a mineral-rich but organically poor soil.

In other parts of the garden, I'm aiming for something in between the two. Even though our soils lose organic matter rapidly in the heat of summer, I'm not about to dig up perennials, shrubs, and roses annually to add more soil amendment. These areas get an inch or two of compost as topdressing, broadcast on top of the mulch, once or twice a season. Earthworms undoubtedly drag some of that down into the soil. The plants seem able to make do, adapting to what may be slightly less than perfect conditions.

Some soils are so difficult to change that the best policy is to let the soil dictate plant choices. Pure sand and pure clay are good examples. As previously mentioned, clay can be difficult to amend. Even heavily amended sand loses organic matter and water, making it nearly impossible to grow plants that require a steady supply of either. When confronted with sand, it is helpful to look to nature's

model. The dunes in Great Sand Dunes National Park are covered with plants, as are the beaches of our coasts. Lavenders, sand phlox, and desert penstemons can all be difficult to grow in clay, but they adore the fast drainage sand affords. Look for "needs good drainage" on the label or go to the library and thumb through garden encyclopedias—most have lists of plants by soil type preferences.

In the strip along my front fenceline, a pocket of clay has the consistency of fudge. This soil could be amended—if only I had more determination and will power. But when initial attempts failed, it seemed prudent to admit defeat and instead look for compatible plants. Today, this part of the garden is as thick with flowers as any place on my property. Yarrow, asters, meadow rue, checkermallow, marsh mallow, clustered bellflowers, lysimachia, turtlehead, Joe Pye weed, ironweed, daylilies, and Siberian iris—all plants that thrive in heavy clay soil—fill this area with color for the entire growing season.

I have come to view soil amendment as a relative, rather than as an either/or proposition, a decision best made one bed at a time. If you are uncertain what to do, it is always safe to dig in a couple of inches of well-composted organic matter before planting. This creates a common denominator soil that is acceptable to the majority of plants. But consider the following before you amend your entire property: Doing so virtually eliminates soil microclimates and significantly limits the diversity of plants you can able to grow. Patchy environments, with a patch of clay here, a patch of sand there, accommodate a much wider range of plant possibilities.

Fertilizing Options

There are also no hard and fast rules when it comes to fertilizing, which is actually a form of ongoing soil amendment. Again, the choice is between growing what is naturally adapted to the conditions on your site and altering the conditions to suit the plants. (You're probably starting to notice a theme.) It cannot be denied that wildflowers

Above: Amending soils creates a common-denominator soil that is amenable to a wide range of plants. Mile High Border at Denver Botanic Gardens (DBG).

Left: Dryland plants prefer soil that is not overly rich. Chocolate flower and gaillardia in the WaterSmart Border at DBG.

Xeric plants such as rabbitbrush, sage, and zauschneria *(clockwise from top left)* need little or no fertilizer.

and weed patches alike prosper without benefit of fertilizer beyond what passing wildlife might contribute. A strict ecological interpretation advises the gardener to follow nature's model, growing only those plants that survive in this Darwinian scheme. While it sounds intriguing to let the site's conditions dictate what can be grown, this philosophy overlooks the reality of the average urban or suburban homeowner's plot of land. Nature would not choose to array the bentonite clay subsoil left over from the excavation for my house with the diversity of plant life that grows in the Front Range of Colorado. Were a natural calamity to cause such a massive upheaval, natural succession would

eventually reclaim the sterile subsoil, but it would take a very long time. In the meantime, most of the plants I want to grow would say "No thanks."

The wise gardener learns to compromise with nature, giving soil type, water availability, and microclimates a say in what will grow where. However, just because nature would not choose to grow tomatoes in Centennial, Colorado, does not make it hubristic for me to plant tomatoes. Working with nature means husbanding our resources with care and deliberation, not giving nature a line-item veto over every gardening decision. I choose to grow an unnaturally large diversity of plants and position them much closer together than natural conditions would allow. Because of this, I figure my plants can use a little assistance in the fertilizing department. My goal is to use only as much fertilizer as is necessary to maximize the potential for every plant in the garden. Xeric natives get a lot less fertilizer, far less frequently, than plants from meadow or woodland origins. Beyond that I watch the plants for clues—anything that turns yellow (that isn't supposed to be yellow) is crying out for some missing nutrient. As with every other facet of gardening, the best strategy is to watch your plants closely and let them be your guide to what they need for their well-being.

Some time ago I switched to using organic fertilizers, after reading that heavy salt concentrations in chemical fertilizers were hard on soil fauna, killing many microorganisms and prompting larger creatures like earthworms to leave. Another pressing concern was the effect chemical fertilizer has on plants when combined with our intense solar radiation and low precipitation. It is critical to keep the stuff off leaves or they will burn. There have been years when my garden appeared hail-damaged, but fertilizer was the real culprit. (I once killed a rose outright by dumping a cup of fertilizer at its feet and forgetting to water it in immediately and thoroughly.)

Organics seemed the sensible alternative. They are much lower in nutrients and so much less likely to burn leaves. (I've dumped a pile under every rosebush in the garden without watering it in and not a single rose has been harmed.) Besides, organic fertilizers made from manures and other natural materials contain micronutrients often missing in chemical fertilizers. With our alkaline soils, adding these micronutrients is often as critical to a plant's success as the big three—nitrogen, potassium, and phosphorus. Furthermore, the ingredients that these fertilizers contain—manure, blood meal, bone meal, fish emulsion, and the like—are mostly waste from agricultural and landscape pursuits that might otherwise get tossed into a landfill. Using these in the garden appeals to my environmentalist bent.

Large-flowered clematis prefers alkaline soils, but it also demands high fertility—fertilizer is a must for clematis to perform like these at Blue Lake Ranch in Durango, Colorado.

Rock mulch suits purple-flowered thymes and white Mt. Atlas daisies *Anacyclus depressus* growing in the pathway. Yellow foxgloves prefer organic mulch. Laurie Jennings' Boulder, Colorado, garden.

Imagine my horror one spring when everything in the garden emerged a sickly yellow. I quickly spread several bags of fertilizer, expecting things to green up directly. The yellow did not budge. I tried another brand of organic fertilizer, thinking the first batch must have been defective, but still there was no improvement. Finally, I resorted to using the soluble blue product that every celebrity who has ever gardened trumpets on TV. Things improved only slightly. It was not until July that the garden started to green up. About the same time, I figured out what was going on.

In spring I water very little. For any fertilizer to work, it needs water to wash it down into the soil. We had received very little precipitation that year and what we did get did not penetrate the soil very deeply. After two years of drought, there was no moisture below the top couple of inches anywhere in the garden. The fertilizer I had applied was sitting on top of the mulch, providing no benefit to the plants whatsoever. It was not until I started watering regularly in the heat of June that enough fertilizer got down to the roots to have any effect. In the future, when the soil is dry, any plant that turns yellow is getting a good soaking first before I add more fertilizer.

Malnourishment can cause flowers to communicate their distress by developing pale or yellowish foliage, becoming stunted, or failing to bloom. But too much fertilizer is equally unhealthy for your plants. Overfed flowers put all of their energy into growing leaves rather than blossoms. They also tend to become flabby and floppy and require remedial staking. Even worse, overly lush growth attracts insects and diseases. So think Jack LaLanne—you want your flowers fit and lean. But be aware that soil that is too wet can also cause an epidemic of jaundiced plants. Where the pH is over 7.5, saturated soils can prevent plants from getting the trace element, manganese. If the problem appears suddenly after a heavy rainfall, the yellowing can usually be reversed with a spray of a chelated iron product that contains manganese.

The goal is to work out a balance—providing just the right amount of fertilizer. Complicating things is the number of different types of flowers we crowd together into one flower bed. Each species has its own nutrient requirement, but it is only practical to deal with them as a group and strive for an average. Fortunately, most plants are not all that finicky. Soil provides for most of their needs and you only have to add those elements your soil is deficient in.

If you initially amended your flower beds with generous amounts of manure or commercial fertilizer, your plantings most likely will not require any additional feeding for the first season. Some organic amendments with large chunky pieces can tie up soil nutrients, particularly nitrogen, while they decompose. You might suspect this is the case if all of the plants in a new flower bed turn yellow in unison. Adding nitrogen will remedy this problem. If you crave scientific accuracy, buy an inexpensive soil test kit at a nursery or home improvement store, or you can send a sample to a soil-testing lab. A soil test tells you exactly how much of the fertilizers you need to use. Alternatively, you can employ the low-tech method of simply keeping an eye on your flowers and building a fertilizing routine based on their performance. Fertilizers are available in a large variety of formulations, but like toothpaste, the only real difference in products with the same ingredients is in marketing and personal preference. Nitrogen is nitrogen—the flowers really cannot tell the difference. Just follow label directions for whatever product you choose.

The Benefits of Mulch

I discovered the power of mulch one year quite by accident. I had planted annual flowers, the type that come in small six-packs, just before leaving town for a few days in late May. A neighbor offered to water the containers, but it didn't seem fair to ask her to lug a watering can several times a day to give those tiny seedlings a drink. Instead, I spread a three-inch thick collar of mulch around each plant and hoped for the best. In spite of searing heat while I was away, every one of those seedlings survived. Since then, I have made it a policy to mulch every new plant that goes into the garden. Mulch definitely helps retain soil moisture. Anything laid on the soil slows moisture loss in the same way a lid prevents evaporation of liquid from a container. (In rare cases, this can be problematic. Covering a low-lying, naturally wet area with mulch could conceivably keep the soil too wet for anything but bog plants—but this is not much of a consideration in our semiarid climate where overly wet soil is a rare complaint.)

Another consideration is purely aesthetic. When used correctly, mulch gives a garden or landscape a finished, unified look. The argument that planting closely solves this problem ignores the realities of spring when the garden is relatively threadbare, or, in times of drought, when gardens tend to be sparse the entire season. Bare dirt is hardly flattering to the garden. Moreover, nature abhors a vacuum. The proof is in how quickly an abandoned lot turns into a weed patch. Literally millions of weed seeds inhabit every patch of bare soil, just waiting for sunlight, water, and space enough to germinate. Every shovelful of soil turned over brings more of these interlopers to the surface, which explains why weeds are such holy terrors in new gardens. A thick layer of organic mulch inhibits seed germination. (Rock mulch, it should be noted, does not suppress weed germination.)

Mulch also slows soil erosion caused by both wind and water. Two inches of pea gravel spread on a steep slope behind my pond completely stopped the channels that had begun forming in the newly dug soil after every rainfall or watering. Just as important, gravel does not float. (The forest mulch I applied on a barely detectable slope elsewhere in the garden readily washes off onto the path.) Nor does gravel blow away. (All of the medium-sized bark mulch I used to cover the 80-foot long walk on the side of the house disappeared in a single storm—I have often wondered whether gardeners in Kansas buy mulch or just wait for it to blow in from Colorado.) Where gravel is not appropriate, the solution is to choose something heavy enough to withstand blowing or washing away, or fibrous enough to mat down. Use light-

Laura and Tim Spear's butterfly garden in Colorado Springs is heavily mulched with a mix of organic materials, including ground landscape waste, pine needles, and horse manure.

weight mulches only in level beds or where there is some sort of edging or a trench to contain them.

Organic mulch prevents rapid temperature fluctuations, which is a real benefit in our region. Soil beneath mulch is cooler in summer and remains warmer longer into the fall when roots are still actively growing. The soil also stays more evenly frozen in winter, which helps prevent plants from breaking dormancy early only to have their new growth frozen. Mulch also helps mitigate frost heaving in winter.

There is no one type of mulch appropriate for every plant. When deciding whether to use rock or organic mulch, consider the origins and needs of your plants. Forests and meadows create their own mulch. Leaf litter is rich in decaying matter, result-

ing in a soil underneath that teems with microorganisms and insect activity. Flora that evolved in similar life zones appreciate these conditions. Xerophytes, plants that originate in dry climates, generally do not. Plants from arid regions evolved in soils that are high in mineral content and low in organic matter. Rich, organic soils are counterproductive. Xeric plants grown in such a soil tend to either grow too quickly and die prematurely or succumb to disease and rot. Plants with arid and semiarid origins and plants that come from rocky places prefer a mulch of rock that more closely approximates their natural habitat.

You do not need to know a plant's geographic provenance, however, to decide which mulch is best. If a plant needs regular irrigation—once a week or more often—or if it requires a shady site, organic mulch is nearly always the better choice. It is imperative to group plants with like needs together in separate areas of the garden so they all can be mulched with the same material. It would be impractical, not to mention unacceptably unattractive, to have individual plants within a bed mulched with different materials.

When spreading rock mulch, a layer 1 to 2 inches deep is sufficient for small plants and a layer 3 to 4 inches for those a foot or taller. Unlike organic mulches, rock can go right up to the base of the plant, though do check to ensure that foliage is not buried in the process. If you absolutely, positively cannot stand the look of rock mulch, there is an alternative. Pine needles are open and airy enough to allow moisture to evaporate from the soil, and they don't decay readily, making them an acceptable alternative for newly planted xeric gardens. But, it's not safe to use this flammable material in wildfire-prone areas.

Landscape fabrics are designed for landscapes, not gardens. Landscapes are relatively permanent features, where, if all goes well, trees and shrubs stay in place for a decade or more. A garden, on the other hand, is a moveable feast, where plants are continually rearranged. Perennials need to be dug up and divided occasionally, and every annual that is added must have a hole dug for it through the mulch. For these reasons, landscape fabrics are unworkable in flower gardens. Landscape fabric does have its uses. It may be used to prevent weeds in unplanted areas such as walks and can limit suckering when applied around suckering shrubs such as the common lilac.

The ideal mulch for irrigated flower gardens is light and fluffy enough to allow water and air to permeate easily. You also want a material that decays readily so pieces incorporated into the bed add organic matter to the soil. The mulch should be fibrous and not too uniform in size and texture to help it stay put and not readily wash onto adjoining surfaces or blow off in a strong wind. Ideally, from an environmental standpoint, the mulch would also be locally produced and not trucked in from a great distance. Hay and straw are good choices for vegetable gardens, but for the flower garden, they do not pass the aesthetics test, looking far too agricultural. Pine needles run through a chipper-shredder are a good choice if you have a ready source of them. Forest mulch, a blend of forest duff and shredded bark, is probably the best of the commercial alternatives.

The scariest bugaboo in every mulch opponent's arsenal is the threat of nitrogen depletion. A study at University of California-Davis found no evidence of this occurring unless the mulch was mixed into the soil. Decomposing organic mulch actually improves soils, creating a passive soil amendment system. Smaller particles decompose more quickly than large. Wood decomposes faster than bark. (Chunks of redwood, in my compost bin for many years, have refused to decompose at all.) If nitrogen deficiency does develop, the simple solution is to add fertilizer.

Roots do grow up into organic mulch, but the Chicago Parks system found using an 18-inch-deep layer of mulch under mature trees did not adversely affect their health. It is important, however, to replenish mulch to ensure tree roots stay covered. To prevent rotting, it's also essential to keep the mulch away from the base of the tree. One real danger is sour mulch, which can be toxic to plants. Do not accept delivery of any mulch that smells of ammonia or vinegar. Mulch should have a pleasant earthy odor. Populations of voles can explode under mulch especially when used with fabric barriers. (Plant catnip or catmint to attract the neighborhood cats or set mousetraps.) Some really interesting fungal growths appear on organic mulches, including slime molds. Raking the surface of the mulch will discourage these harmless organisms if you object to their appearance. Do make sure that water can penetrate whatever mulch you use. It does no good to wet the mulch, leaving plant roots dying of thirst underneath. If the mulch you use becomes an impenetrable mat, loosen it occasionally with a rake or a three-prong fork.

Aside from a few weird materials (ground up tires come to mind), I must have tried every

Drought does not come as a shock to truly xeric shrubs such as yellow-flowered cliffrose *Cowania mexicana* in a demonstration garden at Santa Fe Greenhouses.

product on the market in my quest for the perfect mulch. The one I prefer? My own grindings of shrub, tree, and garden trimmings beat any commercial product I've tried. Pine needles, either left whole or run through a chipper-shredder are also ideal. Several inches of either, renewed annually, forms a loose mat that stays put but allows water to penetrate easily. For vegetables, I use 6 to 8 inches of hay or straw. My xeric gardens are mulched with 2 to 3 inches of pea gravel, also topped off annually.

Winter Mulch

Winter mulches (those used to protect plants over the winter) work best when applied after the ground is frozen. This may seem counterintuitive. However, the point is not to keep things warm, but rather to prevent soil temperatures from fluctuating as wildly as air temperatures. Plants fare better when soil cools down and warms up gradually from one season to the next. This is seldom the case in our region. Untimely warm spells can trick plants into breaking dormancy prematurely. Winter mulch helps prevent this by keeping the soil more evenly cold until spring truly arrives. Mulching in winter also helps moisture loss from the soil. A foot of snow is nature's best winter mulch, insulating the garden beneath like a down comforter. The temperature beneath deep snow stays a steady 32°F. Gardeners who live where snow lies on the ground all winter needn't worry themselves about winter protection.

It is not surprising to learn that there are also two schools of thought on winter protection. The first argues that nature should decide which plants are appropriate. Plants that cannot survive our winters without special coddling are allowed to expire—and good riddance to them. The nurturing gardener, who views every plant death as a personal failure, holds another perspective entirely. This gardener will go to great lengths to ensure a tender plant's survival, even if it means placing custom-built, temporary greenhouse structures over every vulnerable specimen. The garden will certainly look interesting in winter, much like a frozen lake littered with ice-fishing huts. But this isn't the winter interest that garden designers advocate.

Most gardeners fall somewhere between these two perspectives. The bulk of our plants must endure a sink-or-swim philosophy, with only a select few elevated to the status of pets. Winter mulch can provide that extra bit of insurance that borderline hardy varieties need to get through winter. Newly planted perennial gardens also appreciate some protection their first winter. A few inches of loose material insulates them without smothering the slumbering perennials. I personally draw the line at wrapping roses because there are so many completely hardy varieties to choose from. You may feel differently or live where winter gets colder than at my house. If so, by all means, wrap away. Plastic collars make this cheap and easy. Sold at garden centers, they snap into place around the rose to hold shredded leaves, other loose mulch, or compost. Cardboard boxes work just as well but then, of course, you'll be looking at cardboard boxes the rest of the winter. The handy gardener can construct elaborate lath and burlap houses for their pampered roses.

Autumn brings us plenty of free mulch—bags of raked leaves sit at curbsides in every community—free for the taking. (To avoid finding soiled diapers and chicken bones mixed in, I ask my neighbors to save their leaves for me.) I dump the leaves on top of flower beds and under shrubs and trees to a depth of 4 to 6 inches. Doing this when rain or snow is forecast helps prevent their blowing away. Some folks caution that large, waxy leaves, like those from cottonwoods, can mat down and smother plants, but this has not been my experience. If you are concerned, shred leaves—shredded leaves break down faster than those left whole. If you cannot get leaves, use hay, straw, shredded tree trimmings, or pine needles. Hay and straw would be ideal if they did not contain seeds that inevitably germinate come spring. Plus, you actually have to pay for hay and straw. Like leaves, used Christmas trees are free. Start

watching the curbside the day after Christmas for the annual bonanza of free mulch. Simply cut off the branches and lay them over the bed. In the spring, shred the boughs and either compost them or use the shreddings as mulch.

To hasten soil warming, you can remove winter mulch as soon as the danger of hard frost is past, stockpiling the material for compost or to put back in early summer. Because I am a lazy gardener, I leave winter mulches in place (with the exception of Christmas tree boughs) and allow the plants to grow up through them. I do rake the leaves in spring to break up clumps and mats to make it easier for emerging foliage to break through.

Coping with Drought

When I moved here in 1987, Colorado was in the middle of a thirty-year wet period. As with everything else in the Intermountain West, "wet" is a relative term. Except for a few isolated pockets where precipitation is more generous, this entire region is either arid or semiarid. Arid is generally defined in climatic terms as 8 inches or less of moisture annually and semiarid as 10 to 20 inches. For the first fifteen years, my garden was blessed with a generous 15 to 18 inches.

This is not to say moisture always arrived in welcome forms. Devastating hail has destroyed my garden more than once (along with the roof of the house), doing damage that would be hard to replicate except by a group of twelve-year-old boys playing with power tools. Floods have been a regular occurrence. Most years, several inches of the annual precipitation allotment falls in less than an hour, filling the flood control basin next to my house. More than once waves have temporarily lapped through the fenceline (and Randy proclaimed that we were now the proud owners of lakefront property). The occasional September snowstorm does as much damage as hail, crushing the garden under the weight of a foot or two of heavy, wet snow, and freezing an assortment of plants that weren't killed outright by the snow. Rather than soaking into the

A shallow basin beneath a mature bigtooth maple (at upper right) catches just enough extra moisture to keep this tree healthy in the drought of 2002. Tatroe garden.

soil, which is at its least permeable in late summer, snowmelt at this season quickly runs off into the storm drains, having provided great mischief but little compensation.

Even as historic drought worsened, no one was nostalgic for such water-producing events. But this is the reality of how water is most often delivered in the Intermountain West. The year 2002 brought us no bad hailstorms (there is always some hail at my house), no flood, no early or late heavy snowstorms. The price for this calm was drought. My rain gauge measured a scant 10 inches that year. Officially, Denver recorded less than 8 inches. Lawns dried up and died. Playing fields and golf courses were shut down. Water cops patrolled our

streets, enforcing water rationing, and concerned citizens turned in their neighbors. This was the drought that proponents of xeriscape had been preparing for all along.

I have been an advocate of xeriscape from the time I moved to Colorado. Back in the 1980s, Judith Phillips's *Southwestern Landscaping with Native Plants* was the only book available that addressed the subject of gardening with limited water. This excellent book and *Landscaping for Water Conservation in a Semi-Arid Environment*, published by the city of Aurora and Denver Water, were my introduction to gardening in Colorado. These, and a series of lectures by Jim Knopf for Denver Water, and later his book *The Xeriscape Flower Gardener*, reinforced my conclusion that xeriscaping was the only practical way to garden in a place where water was scarce, even in good years.

Although I had been practicing xeriscape principles all along, the drought came as a shock, to both my garden and to my sensibilities. Like most gardeners, I had been seduced by the seemingly plentiful supply of water and had too often ignored the admonition "moist soil" on plant labels. True, I had grouped these moisture-lovers together in high water "oasis" zones. But the oasis zones had gradually been getting larger. The drought of 2002 delivered a reality check and killed scads of these maladapted plants. That summer I decided to be water-frugal and cut irrigations to fewer than the three times weekly allowed at the time. No part of the garden received more than fifteen minutes once a week, which totaled one half-inch of water. I irrigated the xeric areas only two or three times the entire summer and let the vegetable gardens go fallow.

Several lessons emerged, some entirely predictable. In the xeric areas, shrubs were the clear winners. Rabbitbrush, fernbush, desert holly, saltbush, Apache plume, and other shrubs from parts of our region more arid than the Front Range of Colorado did not skip a beat. Even during the worst of the drought, precipitation totals provided as much moisture as these get at home in a really good year. The heat that accompanied the drought did not bother these shrubs a whit. In their opinion, life was still flush. Some native perennials, like Dakota vervain *Verbena bipinnatifolia* and prairie zinnia *Zinnia grandiflora*, though, stayed very small. They appeared to have been newly planted out from 2¼-inch pots, even though some had been in place for years. Conversely, shale columbine *Aquilegia barnebyi* had its best year ever, with blooms lasting a solid month. Other perennial flowers, like spotted gayfeather *Liatris punctata* and *Aster kumleinii* 'Dream of Beauty', looked the same; neither distressed nor encouraged by the heat and scant rainfall. The xeric area by the driveway stayed respectable throughout the drought.

The oasis zones, on the other hand, looked like the aftermath of a battle scene from the movie *Lord of the Rings*. Once or twice a week I would go on corpse patrol, walking through the garden, bucket in hand, pulling out the dead and the dying. By the end of summer, the flower beds were in a sorry state. A local store had gotten in dozens of flats of flowers that no one was buying. (In fact, a clerk scolded me for buying flowers during a drought.) These plants had not been watered and everything was crispy except the sweet Williams. I bought several six-packs of these intrepid flowers and used them to fill holes so that there would be something in bloom while I figured out what my next move would be.

One of the biggest surprises of the drought was the continued success of a mature bigtooth maple *Acer grandidentatum* in the xeric garden west of the driveway. This tree grows in riverbeds in Utah where it gets plenty of moisture. Had I seen it growing in the wild before I made the decision to plant it, I would have picked a more drought-tolerant tree for such a hot and dry location. Following the advice of Judith Phillips, I had planted this tree in the center of a depression, 10 feet across and six inches deep, to collect water. I had also dug a shallow trench to direct run-off from a drain spout downhill to the tree. Years of tampering with the garden have made the design less efficient, but I still credit the slight bit of extra moisture trapped in the basin for the tree's success. When Austrian and mugo pines were dying along the length of a boulevard near my home, there was not even a touch of scorch on the maple.

Permaculture— Putting Gravity to Work

The realization that the device of using a shallow basin to collect water was working coincided with a friend's recommendation that I read Toby Hemenway's *Gaia's Garden—A Guide to Home-Scale Permaculture,* which includes a chapter entitled "Catching, Conserving, and Using Water." Permaculture advocates working with natural laws to discover the simplest and most effective solution

A dry streambed in Charles Mann's garden carries roof water throughout the garden after a heavy rainfall.

to any gardening challenge. In a semiarid climate such as ours, where the primary concern is having enough water to grow a garden, the goal is to capture every drop of water that nature provides.

Some years ago, when Charles and I toured Denver gardens in the height of summer, he was appalled at how bad many of the unwatered areas of xeriscapes looked. Charles pointed out that local practices such as planting parking strips on soil raised higher than the surrounding concrete were counterproductive. Very little water, whether rain or irrigation, has a chance to penetrate the soil before it runs off. He wondered why we didn't employ the principles of permaculture. It would be more efficient to excavate the parking strips several inches lower than the surrounding concrete to give water a chance to puddle and soak into the soil Or, alternatively, a dry streambed (a shallow trench filled with river rock) could meander along the length of the strip, trapping water. He also mentioned how Arizonans often grade a level surface into a slight bowl shape to trap supplemental water for a lawn. At the time, I filed Charles's comments away without too much thought. His remarks came back to me during the drought of 2002, when most gardens on the Front Range resembled those crispy, unwatered xeriscapes he'd been complaining about.

At that point, I started looking for other ways to trap water. There were so many rumors flying around concerning water-use laws, it was impossible to know whom to believe. However, there did appear to be consensus on one thing—catching water in rain barrels definitely violates Colorado law. I'm not sure how such a rule could be enforced in a state where drivers ignore traffic laws with impunity: Still, it makes me uncomfortable to break the law. In any case, rain barrels may not be the answer to our prayers. I visited a rain barrel and cistern factory in Santa Fe in 2003 and fell in love with their refurbished vintage oak wine barrels (but couldn't figure out how to get it home in my Honda Accord without being overcome by alcohol fumes). One oak barrel would make a handsome garden ornament. But to provide room for enough barrels to make a dent

in my irrigation needs would consume a large portion of my small garden (and a forest of barrels wouldn't do much for the ambience of the garden either). The factory owner suggested running the excess water into a cistern, but I suspect the county might take an interest were I to bring in a backhoe. I'm told catching water in a cistern also violates Colorado water ordinances.

Both rain barrels and cisterns require some amount of energy to redistribute the water. What I was looking for was a system for collecting and diverting rainwater and snowmelt that didn't require pumps or any sort of plumbing. The solution I came up with is multifaceted, involving xeriscape, permaculture, and basic water engineering. Xeriscape principles provide some of the answers.

Mulching reduces evaporation and soil amendment improves the water-holding capacity of the soil. Choosing xeric plants and grouping them together in dry zones is another element in the xeriscape equation. But xeriscape's moderate and high-use zones rely on supplemental irrigation, which is no help whatsoever when communities ban outdoor water use entirely, as several did during the height of the drought.

In *Southwestern Landscaping with Native Plants*, Phillips discusses water-harvesting techniques, a few of which I had employed when building my gardens. As well as digging a depression for the bigtooth maple in the front yard, I also constructed a French drain on a steep hillside in the backyard to deal with an erosion problem. The

An infiltration trench, also called a wick, dug beneath an existing path and filled with scoria holds hundreds of gallons of water after every rainfall. Tatroe garden (photo by R. Tatroe).

two-foot deep trench is filled with scoria (that black and red lava rock that gardeners loathe), topped off with river rock and finished as a dry streambed. This trench carries water that overflows from the pond during heavy rains through the garden downhill. The drain also passes by and waters a small grove of aspens before it ends at a dry well (a pit 3 by 6 feet wide and 3 feet deep filled with more scoria and concrete rubble). No water runs off the property.

Not until I read *Gaia's Garden* on permaculture did I discover the added utility of contours in helping to trap water in the soil. I had long been puzzling over a group of plants by my driveway, not far from the bigtooth maple, that were significantly larger than the same plants a few feet away. The larger ones were growing on a berm (a low mound of soil), which I'd been assuming would dry out faster because the soil is better drained there. Intuition further suggested that a berm has more surface area exposed to evaporation. But oddly, the purple coneflowers on top of the berm, were 2 1/2 feet tall, those on the side of the berm 18 inches, and a clump on the adjoining flat area only 8 inches tall.

And then it hit me. The berm is next to and downhill from a walk of river rock that is essentially a rock-filled trench 6 inches deep and several feet wide. A downspout from the roof ends at this walk. Here was permaculture in action. An illustration in *Gaia's Garden* describes this process. A swale, a trench-shaped depression in the soil, holds runoff a little longer, giving it a chance to soak into the soil. If there is a berm located downhill from the swale, water collects under the berm. Plants on the berm have access to the water—hence the larger coneflowers on top of the berm. My walk had been acting as a swale to the low berm next to it.

This is where water engineering comes in. An article by engineer Richard Pinkham in the Winter 2002/03 issue of *WaterWise* addressed storm water management. He advocated directing runoff toward vegetated areas to "reduce requirements for supplemental irrigation" (and incidentally filter runoff to reduce pollution). Pinkham mentioned swales, but what really caught my attention was his description of infiltration trenches, actually swales filled with crushed stones. In other words: swales with storage capacity.

In *Gaia's Garden,* Hemenway discusses the optimal placement of swales and berms, which inspired me to build more infiltration trenches. It wasn't practical to dig up established areas of the garden, so I put a trench under an existing path that runs parallel to the slope and well away from the house walls. I used the excavated soil to build a new berm alongside the trench on the downhill side and filled the trench with scoria. This could have been any rock or rubble filler, but scoria is an ideal material because it holds weight well without settling. Then I covered the trench with landscape fabric. About three inches of pea gravel tops off the surface. You can't tell by looking which part of the walk passes over the trench. This one trench, 18 feet long, 2 feet wide and 1 1/2 feet deep, probably holds the equivalent of a half dozen rain barrels of water every time it rains. Better yet, it's stored right where the plants need it.

When our house was built, the goal of the engineers was to get water off the property as quickly as possible. To prevent damage to the foundation, the builder graded our property so it slopes away from the house. My goal is to foil the builder's original intent and to capture every drop of water that falls on my garden—but without damaging the house's foundation in the process. The infiltration trenches I built are far enough from the house—approximately 30 feet—so I don't anger the gods of expansive clay soil. Eventually I plan to construct several more of these trenches and corresponding berms in other parts of the garden. I am also eying every downspout and trying to determine the best method to direct roof water to where it will do the most good. It is just a matter of letting gravity do the work. And fortunately, exploiting gravity does not violate any of Colorado's water laws.

The Mysteries of Irrigation

It is always a shock to discover that parts of the garden are extremely dry the day after what appeared to be a generous amount of rain. Occasionally it's

Tree branches can block both natural precipitation and water from a sprinkler from reaching plantings beneath. Ungerleider garden.

the perception of generous that is the problem. A driving rain falls for 30 minutes, but the rain gauge measures barely a tenth of an inch—not even enough moisture to wet the mulch. When the rain gauge displays the magic number—one-half inch or more—that means a watering can be skipped, I feel like I've won the water lottery. That is, until I notice a dahlia lying in a heap on the ground. Even though one-half an inch of rain should have been sufficient, a probe reveals that there is no water whatsoever in the soil surrounding the dahlias.

How can that be? Sometimes it is fairly obvious. Tree branches effectively block rain from reaching the soil beneath their canopy, acting as aqueducts that carry water to the outer edges of the imaginary drip line where roots are more

actively growing. For this reason, it's almost always a good idea to water flowers growing under trees on a schedule rather than according to rainfall totals. (Unless, of course, the area beneath the tree is flooded with standing water for any length of time.) Other dry spots are a complete mystery. The soil on one side of a green ash in my front yard stays wet, the other dry. Gravity doesn't explain this disparity. Neither does soil composition nor prevailing winds. Perhaps the tree's roots are healthier and removing more water from the soil on the drier side of the tree. I really don't know, but just accept the fact and water that side of the bed more frequently.

In the spring of 2004, I installed hundreds of feet of soaker hoses made from recycled tires—in

Steep slopes present a handful of problems you don't have to deal with on level sites—gravity inevitably becomes an adversary. Slopes are difficult to irrigate effectively. Water runs off before it has a chance to soak in. Stopping soil erosion is another challenge—every gully washer cuts new and deeper channels until your garden starts to resemble a river delta. When you try to amend the soil, freshly loosened dirt slumps downhill. Mulch slides off hillsides. The steeper the grade, the more these conditions are exacerbated.

Terracing is one solution, but plants can help, if you choose those with roots that knit together quickly and hold the soil firmly in place. Eventually, the plants themselves trap water and allow it to soak in. The first plants you put in act as pioneers. They need to be tough enough to get by on spotty irrigation until they're established. You want fast spreaders, at least initially. (This is one instance where invasive can be an asset.) Once the slope is stabilized, the vigorous colonizers can be replaced.

I originally planted a very steep and hot hillside with dozens of tall bearded irises. Since they multiply so rapidly, someone is always giving irises away. I wasn't particular about color, just took all I could get and planted them evenly across the slope. Rather than amending the soil directly, I laid strips of dead sod upside down between the irises. The uneven surface immediately stopped severe erosion and helped retain water. (Someone is also always giving away sod but you might not want to tell them what you plan to do with it.) Once the hillside was stabilized, I gradually removed some of the irises and replaced them with a variety of other plants.

Planting steep slopes can be tricky. At Gwen and Panayoti Kelaidis' garden, mats of various types of ice plants help hold the soil in place.

spite of serious misgivings based on an earlier experience with these in the 1980s. (It's impossible to judge how much water is being applied without attaching a gauge or coiling the hoses into a 50-gallon garbage can and noting how long it takes to fill it. Soaker hoses also appear to apply water unevenly.) Carefully following the manufacturer's instructions, I laid them out in 100-foot sections throughout the garden and placed mulch over the hoses. Embarrassingly, my water use shot up 300

percent for a short time as I experimented with how long to run these hoses.

For years I'd been using sprinklers, which means stopping what I'm doing and changing their position every fifteen minutes (or about $1/2$ inch of water). With sprinklers, I was able to water more accurately, but it was not an efficient use of my time. Since one soaker hose covers the same area that four sprinkler cycles did, I only have to change the connection once an hour. Sprinklers do

have other drawbacks. Many of the airborne droplets blow away. The same thing that occurs with trees and rain happens on a smaller scale with shrubs and flowers. Taller plants block the spray from reaching shorter companions. Also, sprinkler-applied water, like rain, can knock flowers down. On the plus side, sprinklers help prevent mite infestations, which can become severe when foliage is continually dry. My compromise is to alternate the soaker hoses with a sprinkler, once in every two to four waterings.

Winter Water

Because precipitation from November through March is very low in the Intermountain West in most years, most authorities recommend winter watering. Humidity is also notoriously low, so moisture that does fall evaporates quickly. Parts of the Pacific Northwest and almost anywhere east of the 100th meridian get from two to four times more precipitation than we do. Plants from these wetter climates can get awfully thirsty waiting for spring rains. Prolonged winter drought can damage a large percentage of a plant's roots and weaken its vigor to the

Blue spruces benefit from irrigation in winter whenever snow has not fallen in recent weeks.

point that insects, disease, or extreme heat kill it later in the year. "Prolonged" is the key word. Dry spells of two or three months' duration do the most harm. Microclimates can exacerbate the situation. Plants growing along south or west sides of structures and on south- or west-facing slopes dry out more quickly than those in other areas.

Shade trees and broad leafed evergreens, like euonymus, Oregon grape, boxwood, and hollies, are highly susceptible to winter desiccation. Also vulnerable are Colorado blue spruce and junipers. Newly planted lawns and trees and shrubs planted in the fall are especially prone to damage. All of these benefit from periodic monitoring through the winter months.

Most horticultural experts advise watering at least once every three to four weeks. Does this mean you should set a sprinkler on top of the snow and let it rip? Well, no. You need to use some discretion. Quite a number of plants can be killed if kept sopping wet all winter. Even those that appreciate a drink once in a while do not need one if the soil is already wet.

Plants from arid regions often prefer to stay bone-dry all winter and should not be watered. Many western American and southern European natives are nearly impossible to grow in wet winter climates because they rot. Lavender, for instance, does not usually survive winter in warmer parts of the eastern United States, but is perfectly hardy in warmer parts of our region as long as you do not drown it. Before you drag out the hose, first take into account the needs of the plants. You can kill them equally dead with enthusiasm as with neglect.

My system is this. The first of each month between October and April I make a quick assessment of the garden. If a measurable amount of snow has fallen within the last week, or if there is snow on the ground, I do not water that month. When there is no snow cover, or I cannot recall a recent snowfall or rainfall (this is when garden journal entries come in handy), I tour the garden and look for dry spots. Finding any, I dig a hole with a trowel to see if the soil is dry below the sur-face. If the soil is dry several inches down, I set a sprinkler and let it run for thirty minutes or so. That's it until the following month. For maximum benefit, water at midday on a warm, fine day when temperatures are above freezing. Do not water frozen soil—the water either runs off or freezes into a sheet of ice. If the water does not soak into the soil, the plants cannot use it.

Too Much of a Good Thing

The irony of having too much water in a region where too little is the norm is all too commonplace. Newly laid bluegrass sod must be watered several times daily until the sod knits to the underlying soil. Some runoff is unavoidable. My friend Diane Byers had to deal with just such a situation when hers was the first house in a new development. When a new block of houses was built on the hillside behind hers, the daily flooding began. Diane, a landscape designer, had anticipated this and installed drainage ditches attractively disguised as dry streambeds of river rock. What she didn't anticipate was the magnitude of the problem.

While much of her garden rotted and died, a few flowers and shrubs reveled in the waterlogged soil. Diane is a daylily fancier and was amazed to see how much the daylilies enjoyed the swamp. Conventional wisdom warns that daylilies kept this wet develop fungal diseases—and they do in climates more humid than ours. Bluegrass wasn't an option—it won't tolerate this much water. If you have a spot like this in your own yard, flowers and shrubs are better choices. Daylilies excelled in her garden, but Diane also discovered many other flowers that happily accept these conditions and provide color at other seasons. She also found that water-loving trees and shrubs helped pull excess water out of the soil.

The downside to this solution is when your neighbor puts an end to the floods and you are stuck with a collection of water greedy plants. Fortunately, most of these, once established and

Common Name	Botanic Name
thinleaf alder	*Alnus tenuifolia*
bluestar	*Amsonia illustris*
big bluestem	*Andropogon gerardii*
swamp milkweed	*Asclepias incarnata*
New England aster	*Aster novae-angliae*
New York aster	*A. novi-belgii*
false indigo	*Baptisia australis*
river birch	*Betula occidentalis*
feather reed grass	*Calamagrostis x acutiflora*
fall-blooming reed grass	*C. brachytricha*
globe centaurea	*Centaurea macrocephala*
clematis	*Clematis integrifolia*
redtwig dogwood	*Cornus alba* or *C. stolonifera*
sea holly	*Eryngium planum*
rattlesnake master	*E. yuccifolium*
Joe Pye weed	*Eupatorium purpureum*
swamp spurge	*Euphorbia palustris*
queen-of-the-prairie	*Filipendula rubra*
daylily	*Hemerocallis* hybrids
water iris	*Iris laevigata*
Rocky Mountain iris	*I. missouriensis*
yellow flag	*I. pseudacorus*
seashore iris	*I. spuria*
red cardinal flower	*Lobelia cardinalis*
blue lobelia	*L. syphilitica*
Siberian catmint	*Nepeta siberica*
switchgrass	*Panicum virgatum*
nagoya	*Patrinia scabiosifolia*
prairie coneflower	*Ratibida pinnata*
little bluestem	*Schizachyrium scoparium*
autumn moor grass	*Sesleria autumnalis*
green moor grass	*S. heufleriana*
compassplant	*Silphium laciniatum*
goldenrod	*Solidago rigida*
Indian grass	*Sorghastrum nutans*
feverfew	*Tanacetum parthenium*
columbine meadow rue	*Thalictrum aquilegifolium*
dusty meadow rue	*T. flavum* ssp. *glaucum*
false lupine	*Thermopsis fabacea*
ironweed	*Vernonia noveboracensis*

Above: Feather reed grass tolerates occasional flooding. Aurora Water's Xeriscape Demonstration Garden.

Left: Columbine meadow rue *Thalictrum aquilegifolium* doesn't mind being wet one day, dry the next.

growing strongly, can get along with considerably less irrigation. For years, I had a similar situation in my front yard where a neighbor's sprinkler watered several feet beyond the fenceline every other day. Taking advantage of the extra water, I planted a native river birch, a redtwig dogwood, and a willow. After the neighbors sold their house, the new owner adjusted the sprinkler system and the free water ceased. These plants were mature at the time. Only the willow perished—the birch and the dogwood continue to thrive on one-fourth as much irrigation.

Water and the Suggestion of Water

The drier the surrounding landscape, the greater the role water plays in providing a sense of creature comfort to the garden. Water is not the first thing you picture in an English garden, but it is hard to imagine a sun-drenched Middle Eastern or Spanish courtyard without water splashing in a fountain. Water, in some form, is essential to conveying the image of the garden as an oasis. So in 1989, when son Keith mentioned he would like a pond, I offered to supply the materials if he would supply the labor. We chose a spot near our patio in the backyard where we could enjoy the sound of water from the patio. Pond authorities caution that naturalistic ponds should never be sited at the top of a hill where they make no sense from the standpoint of gravity. Our pond violates this directive, so we positioned it in front of an existing berm, reasoning that a natural spring might logically seep out of the hillside. Dirt from the excavation added elevation and bulk to the hillside behind the pond.

Our pond is small, 3 by 6 feet wide, 2 feet deep, and holds only 200 gallons of water. Keeping it filled adds very little to our household's water usage. The pond is an invaluable addition to the garden, the sound of even a small amount of splashing water refreshing and restorative. Originally a small stream of water seeped out over sandstone slabs to create a waterfall and splashed into the pond, reinforcing the natural spring image. (That is, until water restrictions banned waterfalls. At that point we switched to a bubbler.) A friend, who decided ponds were too much work, removed hers and provided the fish, the plants, and what should have been a forewarning. We lined our pond with heavy butyl rubber that was supposedly flexible (my memories are of trying to wrestle very stiff, unyielding material into the hole).

As advised, we built shelves for plants. No one mentioned that raccoons knock plants off shelves (to foil the raccoons we tied the plant containers to the side of the pond with wire). We installed a natural filtration system. No chemicals, not us. Nor did anyone tell me that leeches were part of a healthy pond ecosystem. We named our fish. Garter snakes swam in the water and picked off Goldie and Rudolf—we no longer name our fish. Water worked its way under the liner edges and caused the shelves to corrode. River rock fell into the pond every time a raccoon stepped on the rocks to get to the water and the fish.

After seventeen years, we decided to rebuild the pond and fix the edging. We also figured it was about time to replace the rubber lining (it was only guaranteed to last seven years) with a preformed shell guaranteed to last a lifetime. Having debated whether to fill in the hole, we concluded that we enjoy the sound of splashing water too much to get rid of the pond. And the pond did segue into what is one of our most successful ventures, a dry streambed that carries excess storm water from the pond.

Built over a French drain, the dry streambed follows an erosion channel that had meandered down the hillside during the construction phase (providing a valuable lesson: if you want a watercourse to appear natural, follow an erosion channel). The original path stopped at the top of the hill. The lower half was too rough and too steep to walk on. This created a dead end behind the pond, very much a design flaw. Some years later, I decided to remedy the situation. Converted to a path its entire length, the dry streambed hooked up with another path that came from the other direction that had

originally dead-ended at the bottom of the hill. This resulted in a more user-friendly, circular route.

Because this hillside was too steep to traverse safely without stairs, the streambed morphed into a dry waterfall. I moved the river rock aside, and Randy and I selected a dozen flat pieces of buff sandstone from a local stone yard. Then we waited until Mother's Day when my family was invited over for brunch. I told my son Keith what I really wanted for Mother's Day was for him to build me a set of stairs. The resulting staircase is both beautiful and solid. (You might wonder if family members view brunch invitations with trepidation.) To make the stairs resemble a dry waterfall, I reposi-

tioned the river rock on either side and planted the edges. The top, shadier section is the perfect microclimate for native ferns, plus other finicky plants like *Campanula portenschlagiana* 'Aurea' and the variegated *Symphytum* 'Goldsmith'.

Another dry streambed that doubles as a walk meanders from the driveway at the front of the house through the side yard and ends at the other side of the pond, creating the illusion of water traveling throughout the garden. This came about when the walk we had made of landscape timbers started to deteriorate. One of our first projects, this 77-foot walk connects the front yard to the back. The previous owner had outlined flower beds and a play area

Particularly in dry gardens, water is essential to creating the impression of the garden as an oasis. 'Raspberry Delight' autumn sage. Kelaidis garden, Denver, Colorado.

A small pond adds little to the household water use but provides water for birds and a host of other wildlife. Tatroe garden.

with chemically treated timbers. We recycled these into steps and edging for our path. From the beginning, it was apparent that the design had a few major faults. Every serious gully washer flooded the area and floated the timbers. Resetting steps was a thankless task and, over time, they became more and more uneven and difficult to walk on. The final straw was when we discovered the supposedly rot-resistant wood had, in fact, rotted. More disturbing still were the colonies of wood-eating insects that had taken up residence in the steps and edging. It was horrifying to think we were hosting a race of arsenic-immune super bugs.

Randy and I spent one entire Saturday pulling out and hauling rotten timbers to the dump. Then

we considered several options for our new path. Brick is too formal for my taste, but for a time I did contemplate a mosaic of broken brick and flagstone. Eventually practicality won out. We had used river rock as a mulch between the wooden steps and the thought of the backbreaking labor of removing it led to a river rock solution. Since it is easier to add to than to remove river rock, we built the walk in the form of a dry streambed.

Whether used as a path or as an infiltration trench to divert excess water, the second lesson to making a dry streambed appear realistic is to vary the size of the rock. For inspiration, Randy and I went to the mountains and studied a natural streambed, taking note of where larger rocks

Excess water from the pond runs through a French drain of rocks and rubble that lies beneath a stone staircase, built to resemble a dry waterfall. Tatroe garden.

A dry streambed on the west side of the house creates the impression that water runs from throughout the garden, and also slows runoff after a heavy rainfall. Tatroe garden.

collected. Our first step was hauling three large boulders home from the stone yard to place along the length of the path. These we muscled into position using an appliance dolly. The largest, at 480 pounds and slab-shaped, went into the shadiest spot where it serves as a seat. Next we placed two tons of 4-inch through 12-inch cobblestones along the edges to define the sides of the path and to hold the dirt back in the flower beds. These are distributed randomly and unevenly to look as if water had tumbled them there. We varied the width of the path from 3 to 4 feet, again aiming for the naturalistic effect of a mountain stream. To finish, we scattered a mix of $1/2$-inch and $1 1/2$-inch pebbles over the river rock down the length of the walk. The rough surface of this path slows runoff, giving excess water a chance to soak in. The side yard no longer floods.

What Makes a Weed?

A neighbor once accused me of growing weeds in my front yard. She's a tidy type who disapproved of the unmanicured nature of my garden, and also perhaps my taste in plants. My favorites are simple, informal flowers. Typical is Queen Anne's lace *Daucus carota*, a modest roadside beauty that appears on every weed list. It seems contradictory that I can also buy it in most flower shops. Sadder yet were the comments of a little boy who wanted to know why I was standing on the sidewalk looking out over the fall display of purple and gold in the field next to my home. When I told him I was admiring the wildflowers, he puzzled over this for a moment, then solemnly informed me that these were weeds and not wildflowers.

Since that day, I've given a lot of thought to just what makes a weed. *Weeds of the West* is helpful in identifying the real troublemakers, but is also a good source for plants with landscape potential. In the introduction, the authors admit that the term "weed" does not always indicate a plant that is completely without value, and that "some plants poisonous to livestock are considered desirable ornamental plants." Many beautiful native flowers included in this book—artemisias, rabbitbrush, Rocky Mountain beeplant, and prickly poppy—are classified as weeds just the same, simply because livestock can't or won't eat them.

Obviously it is a mistake to take weed lists too literally. Gardeners should certainly be aware of what plants threaten to overcome native populations in their area and not grow those. I pity the poor guy who conceived of the not-so-brilliant idea of introducing kudzu vine to the southern United States for erosion control. Today, whole states are being buried under its rampant growth. Fortunately, in the Mountain West, not very many ornamentals escape the garden. Our worst weeds are too unattractive to be mistaken for wildflowers and their spread is mostly due to overgrazing and poor land management. Native plant populations are lost, not because weeds have overrun them, but mainly because we build housing tracts on top of them.

Michael Pollan, in his book *Second Nature*, proposes a very sensible definition of weed as a "plant particularly well-adapted to man-made places," one that "evolved with just one end in view—the ability to thrive in ground that man has disturbed." Their evolution relies on centuries of farming and soil cultivation. They hitchhiked to this continent with European and Asian immigrants, spreading relentlessly. Whenever gardeners disturb the soil, these indisputable weeds will shortly arrive like uninvited guests to a party. The responsible gardener must be vigilant and toss them out. Leafy spurge, Russian knapweed, diffused knapweed, spotted knapweed, Canadian thistle, bindweed, and musk thistle are the worst offenders in the county where I live. Your local extension office can provide a list of the worst actors in your neighborhood.

Webster's defines a weed as "any undesired, uncultivated plant, esp., one growing in profusion, so as to crowd out a desired crop, disfigure a lawn, etc." The first half seems reasonable enough; but disfigure a lawn? That's where personal prejudice and social convention enter into the discussion. It wasn't so many years ago when clover in the lawn was considered a sign of good lawn management. Then nonselective broadleaf herbicides were introduced. It isn't possible to kill the dandelions without also eliminating the clover, so clover found itself redefined as a weed. Now, sadly, a whole generation of children is missing the pleasure of hunting for four-leaf clovers.

There are definitely plants I consider weeds. Weeds are freeloaders. They arrive uninvited and give nothing back. When my annual crop of *Malva neglecta* pops up by the thousands, I suffer no crisis of conscience pulling them out. I can't imagine looking fondly upon hell's bells *Campanula rapunculoides,* no matter how pretty its flowers, or smooth brome, two more thugs that are overrunning more polite occupants in my garden. I look forward to the year—hopefully in my lifetime—when these nuisances, and many others, are completely eradicated.

It is clear that each gardener defines his or her own weeds. But the gardener who is not overly tidy will be rewarded with some pleasant surprises. Birds bring me some of my favorite flowers. *Yucca glauca,* prickly poppy, and penstemons are among the many wildflowers that have appeared unbidden in my garden. My weed experiments (allowing unfamiliar plants to grow to partial maturity to identify them) have resulted in a profusion of yellow daisies, fall asters, and, admittedly, a few monstrosities that were hurriedly dispatched and composted. It is a good idea to learn to recognize the local nasties in the seedling state so you do not inadvertently start a patch of something truly awful (remember kudzu?).

So, how do you decide if a plant is a potential problem or a weed? In my opinion, a native plant (even if cattle won't eat it or if it is poisonous to humans or livestock) is not a weed. Although perhaps undesirable (like poison ivy), it does not seem fair to call it a weed. All of these plants are part of an ecosystem and some critter relies on each to survive. If it is not causing problems where it is, leave it

Those who are too quick to pull them might never get to enjoy "weeds" such as this showy milkweed *Asclepias speciosa* at the Mangan's Bear Creek garden.

Grabbing a bottle of weed killer is undoubtedly the quickest way to be rid of interlopers, but many of us are concerned about possible adverse health effects from herbicide use. Weeds in pavement cracks are remarkably easy to dispatch. Simply pour boiling water from a teakettle over their heads for instant annihilation. Smother large weed patches with overlapping thick layers of newspapers covered with several inches of organic mulch such as shredded tree trimmings. This treatment will kill even persistent perennial weeds.

If you prefer spraying, look for an organic fatty acid herbicide. Harmless to people and pets, they, unfortunately, may also be harmless to really noxious weeds like field bindweed and Canadian thistle. For these, several sprayings with a non-selective herbicide product containing glyphosate will do the trick. Glyphosate's safety is somewhat controversial so use it sparingly and only as a last resort. In weed wars, prevention makes more sense than trying to control the hordes after they've arrived. Spot treat dandelions with glyphosate if you absolutely must. Don't ever allow any weed to go to seed. If you don't have time to dig it out or spray it, at least pull off and discard the flowers. Otherwise, a single weed can produce thousands of offspring to bedevil you for years to come.

Though ubiquitous along highways in the Intermountain West, spectacular prickly poppies are too seldom seen in gardens.

alone. As to the question of whether or not poisonous plants should be grown as ornamentals, consider that some of the loveliest wildflowers can be quite deadly. Datura, delphiniums, and locoweed (not to mention tomato plants) all contain substances that are poisonous either to livestock or us. Although I would not grow them in a garden where small children play, I don't think it is right to call them weeds based simply on their potential toxicity.

Your experience will most likely be unique compared to other gardeners. Atlas daisy can be troublesome because of invasive seeding, but in my dry garden this is a well-behaved plant, providing me with only a handful of seedlings each year. On the other hand, one of my favorite flowers, the California poppy, is also one of my worst offenders, but only in irrigated parts of the garden. Beyond the really obvious noxious weeds, you will have to determine which plants qualify for weed status in your own garden. But do not be too free with the term. Do some weed experiments of your own, and you might be rewarded with some real treasures.

Composting with the Help of Zucchini

My composting system is as easy as it gets and it really does work. Randy made two compost bins, each three feet square and as tall, out of old fence rails and posts recycled from our original perimeter fence. These have removable gates, but are otherwise just crude wooden boxes. We paved the area next to the bins with bricks left over from our patio construction. The entire operation is tucked away in a side yard on the east side of the house behind a lattice screen.

I fill one bin at a time. Kitchen waste—minus meat scraps and anything salted—go straight into the bin as they accrue. Mostly this includes coffee grounds, vegetable peelings, and crushed eggshells. (As a bonus, you will find you no longer feel quite as guilty when fruits and vegetables spoil unused in the crisper—you can never have too much moldy or rotting food for your compost pile.) Small bits of yard waste also go straight into the bin. Larger, twiggy pieces go into the empty bin until there is enough stockpiled to justify getting out the chipper-shredder. Shredded materials decompose much more readily, plus a huge pile is quickly reduced to a couple of bucketfuls. The shreddings go on top of the kitchen scraps.

While you are still in the bin-filling stage, you can mix layers. This is where a removable gate comes in handy. Shovel all of the contents out of the bin and then shovel them back in again, giving things a good toss as you go. (You can skip this part if you like—I usually do.) Water the pile whenever you think about it. Eventually, you will have a bin full of partly decomposed bits and pieces. Now comes the coup de grâce. In spring, dig a bucket-sized hole into the top of the completed pile and fill it with garden soil. Plant two zucchinis in the soil. This is the only trick to making good compost.

In our dry climate, compost will not finish decaying without regular watering but it is difficult, at least for me, to remember to water a compost pile. The zucchini promise to nag you into watering them. (If you don't eat zucchini, plant a pumpkin, a cantaloupe, a gourd, or some other type of squash.) The amount of water required to grow zucchini is exactly what the compost needs in its final stages of decomposition. In the fall, after the zucchini are exhausted, the compost is ready to spread throughout the garden as topdressing or dug into new beds as a soil amendment. (Zucchini plants and all the overlooked baseball bat-sized zucchinis can go back into the bin.) Admittedly, there are more scientific and quicker compost-producing methods, but the zucchinis have never failed me.

Maintenance Issues

I'm often asked when is the best time to clean up the garden. I wish there was a simple answer, but there really isn't one that fits all situations. Every gardener has his or her own routine and strong opinions on this topic. However, "Whatever works best for you" is not a satisfactory answer. The debate about cleanup will undoubtedly continue as long as gardeners have a breath to disagree, but a few seasons experience will help you develop a feel for what works best in your own garden. Here are some things to consider.

Fully hardy perennials—those that can reliably survive severe winters here—can be cleaned up any time after their foliage turns brown in autumn. It's your call. If you like the shabby-chic look of golden brown stems, dried foliage, and seedheads, as I do, you'll want to leave things untrimmed until March or early April. If the order and tidiness of a newly plowed field is more to your liking, you can do your major cleanup in fall. Whenever you are uncertain about the hardiness of a particular perennial, or if it was transplanted into the garden earlier that same year, the conservative approach is to leave the old foliage and stems in place over winter to protect the crown of the plant. I also cover these plants with either a bucketful of pine needles or a couple of evergreen boughs from December through early April. The goal here is to keep the ground solidly frozen so the plant won't emerge prematurely during a February warm spell only to be damaged by the next hard frost.

A few perennials are prolific self-sowers. To prevent hundreds of seedlings from popping up all over the garden, remove seedheads from the following flowers in the fall, whether they are attractive or not: gaillardia, purple coneflower, asters, catmint, golden marguerite, and most of the mallow family. Another circumstance that necessitates fall cleanup is when a plant was affected by disease or a serious insect infestation earlier in the growing season. Disease spores and insect eggs spend the winter beneath the host plant, ready to jump into action the following spring. To mitigate ongoing problems, remove all debris and mulch and, if necessary, tuck fresh mulch around the base of the plant.

Fully hardy perennials like these coneflowers can be cleaned up in fall or left uncut so you—and birds—can enjoy their seedheads all winter.

The first flowers of the new season signal that it's time to start thinking about cleaning up the garden. (What good are crocus flowers if you can't see them beneath last autumn's litter?) Over the years, I've developed a ritual that resembles an archeological dig. Exposing the garden in February increases the likelihood of winter damage, so it's safest to remove the layers slowly and gradually.

I start with tall bearded iris. Hordes of aphids spend their winter tucked into iris fans. Pulling off withered foliage evicts these unwelcome lodgers, exposing them to hungry birds and the next round of cold temperatures. This activity also turns out ladybugs that have been sleeping in their larder, so to speak. When upended, they grumpily amble off to hibernate in the mulch for a few weeks longer. It usually takes me a week of working a couple of hours on each warm day to finish with the irises. By then, it's March and flowers are coming up fast and furiously, so it's time to pick up the pace. While it would be more efficient to clean out one entire bed before moving onto the next, that would lay everything bare to the elements all at once. I selectively cut back the hardiest stuff first. Anything planted the previous fall also gets to stay covered for a while longer.

Perennials rated hardy to a zone or two colder than my own Zone 5—yarrow, monkshood, columbine, goat's beard, asters, boltonia, campanulas, delphiniums, baby's breath, Helen's flower, daylily, Siberian iris, blazing star, lupine, plume poppy, beebalm, catmint, garden phlox, obedient plant, hardy sages, sedums, goldenrod, pincushion flower, lamb's ears, and veronicas—can be tended to in the first round in February. I break off brittle stems or use pruners or scissors to cut off the old foliage and trim stems down to ground level. If there is a layer of decaying, fallen leaves, I leave it in place on any bed that is mulched with organic mulch.

Rumpled helianthemums, phloxes, marrubiums, erodiums, basket-of-gold, sea thrift, veronicas, and teucriums all benefit from a short haircut in late winter or early spring to tidy them up for

Top: Leave the seedheads of marginally hardy perennials such as *Verbena bonariensis* in the garden over the winter to ensure seedlings the following season.

Bottom: Remove seedheads of any prolifically self-sowing flowers, like these Star of Persia onions, if they threaten to become a pest. Tatroe garden.

their spring show. They'll grow fresh new foliage and bloom a little later than if left unshorn and they're much more attractive with this treatment. Wait until mid or late March to cut back less reliably hardy perennials like hyssop, Japanese anemone, 'Powis Castle' artemisia, astrantia, fall chrysanthemums, coreopsis, gaillardia, kniphofia, and patrinia; and perennials with woody stems, such as lavender, tree mallow, and Russian sage. These plants need at least another month of protection from cold temperatures.

Ornamental grasses are usually grown at least in part for their winter presence, so these are customarily left alone until late in winter. If a storm knocks them akimbo, by all means cut down the resulting mess. The dilemma is that grasses need their annual shearing in late winter just when they are the most distinctive feature in the garden. My solution is to wait until spring bulbs are in flower to perform this operation. Colorful crocuses, snow iris, and early tulips act as a visual distraction until the grasses grow back.

Too often shrub and tree pruning is a rite of spring, done for no other reason than because guys with power tools have a strong urge to use them. Nothing else explains all of the poodle-cut junipers or the lilacs, cotoneasters, and barberries shaped, more or less, into balls. Although shrubs do need pruning periodically, doing it correctly takes no more time and only a bit more skill than turning out those unnatural shapes. Probably the main reason for mangling a shrub is that it outgrew its allotted space. Heeding the label regarding mature size can prevent this situation. With few exceptions, pruning should be undertaken only to shape and to improve the health, sturdiness or beauty of the plant, not just to limit overall size.

The cure to overgrown junipers is to take them out and start over. This time read the label to ensure that, when the replacement matures, it will not overgrow windows or block doorways and sidewalks. There is nothing wrong with creating living sculptures out of junipers if that is what you are aiming for. But I suspect most junipers are sheared into bizarre shapes more by accident than by design. You might be pleasantly surprised to learn that, left to their own devices, junipers can be very attractive shrubs.

There are genuine advantages to pruning in winter. When branches are bare, it is easier to see the what's what. Disease spores are dormant in winter, so it is safe to prune even fireblight-affected trees without going through the tedious process of sterilizing tools in a bucket of bleach water between cuts. Frozen soil is another plus. All of the trees and shrubs in my garden are planted in the middle of flower beds where I've gone to a lot of trouble to improve the soils. Compaction is the nemesis of good soil—each footstep smashes out air pockets and destroys the soil's structure. Working while the soil is frozen mitigates this damage. Standing on flowers is not good for them, either. In winter, flowers are, for the most part, safely tucked away beneath the frozen soil. Placing a tomato cage or a cardboard box over them while you are working can protect the few that stay above ground in winter.

Another considerable benefit of pruning in winter is that it keeps antsy gardeners occupied. It is far too easy to get up to all kinds of mischief on nice days in February. Pruning distracts us from prematurely tidying up perennial beds and poking around for signs of life. (Like all creatures, plants prefer to be left unmolested while they are sleeping.) There are plants that are not amenable to winter pruning. Leave roses alone until sometime in April. Pruning them any earlier may stimulate new growth, which is then vulnerable to late freezes. Most other trees and shrubs are more weather-wise, but treat all marginally hardy specimens like roses. Pruning spring-blooming shrubs such as lilacs and forsythias in winter will sacrifice some of this year's flowers. The buds of many early bloomers form the previous summer and, if cut off, the shrub will not flower again until the following year.

Do not remove more than one-third of a shrub or a tree at one go except for the few summer-blooming

Top: Sheer spring-blooming phloxes and basket-of-gold in late winter or early spring if they emerge from winter with a rat's nest of stems.

Bottom: Ornamental grasses are never more beautiful than when dusted with snow in winter.

Prune trees only to improve their natural structure. Ponderosa Border, DBG.

shrubs that may be treated like herbaceous perennials. Twiggy shrubs such as blue-mist spirea, butterfly bush, rabbitbrush, spirea, red-twig dogwood, and elderberry can be cut down to within a few inches of the ground in late winter to keep them compact. This treatment will not affect flowering, because all of these bloom on new wood.

Shrubs such as serviceberry, mountain mahogany, and viburnum are valued for their woody structure. Give these plenty of room to spread out. Late winter is a good time to remedy problems, regardless of whether it removes flower buds. First cut out broken branches, then branches that cross toward the center of the shrub. Also remove suckers from the base and water sprouts (the long shoots that grow straight up from large branches). Open up the center so that light can reach all parts of the plant. The overall goal is to make a vase shape. Many shrubs can be grown either as a thicket or in a tree shape. A chokecherry in my side yard is a good example. Initially I selected three sturdy stems to become the trunks and in subsequent springs removed all twigs and branches from the lower third of each. The chokecherry has grown into a large, graceful tree with branches that arch over the walk at the side of the house. (Visitors are surprised to learn that what they're seeing is a chokecherry, since the more common form for a chokecherry is a clump.)

Increasing the Likelihood of Transplant Success

Seasoned gardeners joke that stores sell plants in April so they can sell the same plants again in May—after late frosts have killed them. But early spring really is a good time to get most hardy things into the garden. Bareroot stock (dormant plants that look like dead sticks with their roots wrapped in plastic bags) can go out as soon as the soil is thawed. If no top growth is present, planting is a simple matter of digging a roomy hole, spreading the roots out and making sure the crown—the intersection where the roots and the top of the plant meet—is at ground level when the hole is refilled. Water well and success is virtually guaranteed (if the roots go down and the top is above ground).

If green leaves are evident, however, this new growth will be especially sensitive to frost or heat. One spring a home improvement store in my area had signs posted advising shoppers not to worry about the green growth on their bareroot plants. This is true, but only if you take a few cautionary measures. Follow the planting steps above, but this time cover the green parts until they have a chance to acclimate. Position an evergreen bough over short things. Throw an old sheet or a frost blanket (sold at garden centers for just this purpose) over

Wait until spring to cut back ornamental grasses and woody perennials such as autumn sage.

Indian paintbrush transplants establish more easily in fall. Pecos Compound—Julia Berman design.

large plantings, shrubs, and roses. Peg the material down with landscape pins (rocks also work) and leave it in place for several weeks. Don't let the soil dry out completely during this establishment period. If the top growth dies in spite of these measures, the plant will usually leaf out again but the energy expended can significantly set it back. Occasionally the plant does not recover.

Evergreen junipers, pines, and spruces are tough plants that put up with great abuse. But since these are almost always imported from nurseries on the balmy West Coast, they also benefit from being gradually introduced to our colder, drier conditions. Harden them off by leaving them outside where they can be sheltered from direct sunlight and wind for a few days before planting. Water every time the soil in the root ball dries out—before and after planting. If temperatures are forecast to go below 20°F, cover these plants, too, at least for the first few weeks.

Gardeners can be forgiven for overlooking fall's planting potential—the entire horticultural industry is geared up to support the spring rush. But fall weather is generally mild and cool and therefore easier on both the gardener and new plantings. There is also something undeniable in the air that brings the gardener alive again after the lethargic midsummer doldrums. When a gardener heeds an inner voice, it's usually with a shovel in hand and grand aspirations in mind. You don't have to be as vigilant with watering when the days are shorter and the soil doesn't dry out so quickly. Plus, plants are often temptingly inexpensive in the fall when nurseries clear out stock in preparation for winter.

In autumn, plants prepare themselves for winter dormancy by sending out new roots whenever the soil is not frozen solid. By the following spring, the plant is well on its way to being fully established and ready to leap into action. Dormant plants need much less water than they do during the growing season. They do need some water over the winter to prevent their roots from desiccating, so it is essential to remember to water new transplants

once or twice a month, whenever snow or rain has not fallen within the previous couple of weeks. This is a great deal less water than the every-hot-day regimen required to establish even xeric transplants in spring.

Spring weather in the Intermountain West can be frigid one day and broiling the next. Plants newly emerged from dormancy are particularly vulnerable to these fluctuations—they risk losing most or all of their top growth to an untimely frost. Or, one hot day dries out the rootball and kills the plant before you have had a chance to water it. A new tree planted in May might need watering twice a week the entire summer to prevent transplant shock. Conversely, the same tree, planted in September, when days are shorter and temperatures cooler, needs watering only five or

six times through the end of October and once a month during the winter. By the following spring, this tree will be fairly well established, requiring significantly less water when hot weather arrives.

I've lost an untold number of spring-planted trees, shrubs, and perennials to transplant shock, but I almost never lose plants set out in the fall. Indian paintbrush is just one example. One fall I planted three seedlings around the first of November. When these survived the winter, I purchased three more in April from the same nursery and added them to the same bed. In spite of a cool, mild June, every one of the latecomers perished. I had watered the November-planted paintbrushes only a handful of times from fall into summer. Those planted in spring got water every time they dried out, but the first hot day in July killed them

Plant marginally hardy variegated cooking sage in spring.

anyway. After ten weeks in the ground, they had never grown roots outside the original rootballs.

A few plants are not generally recommended for fall planting, zauschnerias and ornamental grasses among them. I've never heeded this warning because plants go on sale this time of year and I can never resist a bargain. My garden is full of fall-planted zauschnerias and grasses. The only trick is to water them infrequently but consistently throughout the winter. I've had equal success with every other type of tree, shrub, or perennial I've tried. The only things I don't plant in autumn are

those few perennials, like cooking sage and variegated thyme, that are rated for zones one or two warmer than my own. If a plant is somewhat iffy, I protect it with heavy mulch and a few evergreen boughs over the top. I try to get all plants in the ground at least six weeks before the soil freezes. For example, in the Denver metro area, because the soil freezes around the middle of December, the ideal cut-off date is November 1. I have to admit I violate this guideline, too, and usually get away with it. Planting in fall is much more forgiving than planting in spring.

Of Rocks and Rock Gardening

*J*t could be argued that the one element that best defines our regional character is rock. Rugged mountain ranges of rock dominate our natural landscapes, providing a stunning backdrop to communities throughout the Intermountain West. Although most of us reside on the relatively featureless plains and plateaus of our region, we are invariably drawn to places where rock prevails. Landscape architect Herb Schaal, designer of the rock alpine garden at Denver Botanic Gardens, contends that our "hearts are in the mountains" and the best landscapes "bring the mountains out onto the plains." Equally imprinted on our collective consciousness is the austerity of the desert landscape, from the grandeur of the canyonlands to the otherworldliness of hoodoo formations in the badlands. Along the foothills of the Front Range of Colorado, brightly colored sandstone hogbacks hint at the desert landscape beyond the mountains to the west. Unique to the Intermountain West is the juxtaposition and interconnectedness of two such dramatically different landscapes as desert and mountain. Using rock in our gardens represents both.

Overleaf: Rock in gardens represents the natural character of the Intermountain West. City of Rocks, Idaho.

Above: An arrangement of shaped stones and flowering pink thyme is a work of art in the Ungerleider garden.

WHETHER USED IN ITS NATURAL FORM, or quarried, cut, and shaped, rock and stone add texture, pattern, and contrast to gardens and landscapes. The effect can be naturalistic or highly formalized. A single boulder set into a garden hints at the grandeur of wilder places. A particularly beautiful stone can have the same effect on our senses as a work of art. Even unremarkable rock has a dramatic effect on the character of the garden as rocks and plants play off of one another's dissimilarities. Whereas rock is solid and permanent, plants are ephemeral and in constant flux. The disparate nature of the two elements creates tension and complexity in gardens and landscapes.

In purely practical terms, rock is relatively inexpensive and widely available in our region. Its durability makes it a good choice for building material. Nothing beats rock and stone for holding up to our

severe weather. Rock and stone can also have a profound effect on plant performance. It is said that if you kick a rock on the tundra, you kill a plant—so dependent is any plant on even the slight improvement in microclimate the rock represents. In the garden, as on the tundra, rock protects a plant's crown and roots from weather extremes. Siting a plant next to a boulder can sometimes moderate temperature fluctuations enough to increase its hardiness a zone or two. Moreover, water tends to collect and concentrate near rocks. When Diana Capen, of Perennial Favorites in Rye, Colorado, experimented with an unirrigated garden during the drought of 2001–3, she observed that individuals sited next to rocks were much more likely to survive than those nearby, but out in the open.

Long admired for its durability and attractiveness for steps, stairs, walls, and patios, rock and

Plants and rocks play off of one another's dissimilarities in the Kelaidis' rock gardens.

stone can also be used in unexpected ways. Slabs of flagstone made into benches or tables are widely available. On the prairie, stone columns called "Kansas fence posts," once stood in for scarce wood. Occasionally, they can still be found for sale in rock yards. One standing upright makes an interesting garden sculpture all by itself, but I've also seen them used for their original purpose with fence panels tied to the posts in the grooves that once held wire. Rochelle Eliason, of Arvada, Colorado, replaced a utilitarian drainspout with a

trough-shaped piece of lace rock. Inspired by her creativity, Randy occupied himself at garden centers for a full month one spring (while I shopped for plants), searching through piles of lace rock until he found a similarly shaped piece to replace the concrete drain spout by our driveway.

Conventional design wisdom dictates that rock should be kept in scale with the size of the garden so as not to overwhelm the space. But sometimes, surprising things happen when rules are bent or broken. A friend, the late Arun Das, unabashedly chose boulders the size of Yugos when he designed his small urban xeriscape in the historic Washington Park neighborhood of Denver. The result was anything but crowded. Large boulders had an unforeseen effect, visually expanding the small space.

From Gardening with Rock to Rock Gardening

Rock gardening has a long association with our region. In *Around the Seasons in Denver Parks and Gardens,* the late S. R. DeBoer claims to have built "the first garden of this type in Denver." Early in the twentieth century, he created a small rock garden in the city's Sunken Gardens, formerly on Eighth Avenue. Rock gardens, all the rage in England at the time, were also built at many private homes and at the original Elitch Gardens in Denver. DeBoer "made many trips to the mountains to study the way nature places her cliffs and rocks and . . . selected certain formations" for inspiration in an attempt to make his rock gardens as realistic as possible.

Our high elevations, sunny, dry atmosphere, and cold winters are exactly the conditions craved by alpine plants that are the stock-in-trade of rock gardeners. Some of the finest examples of traditional rock gardens are found here, what Charles calls "little jewelry cases of tiny and rare gems," filled with plants from high mountain environs as distant as Kyrgystan and the Chilean Andes. Anywhere else, it is nearly impossible to satisfy the cultural requirements of such treasures as alpine forget-me-not *Eritrichium aretioides* or alpine spring beauty *Claytonia megarhiza,* outside in the garden.

In recent years, a new style of rock garden that focuses on dryland plants has emerged in the Intermountain West. This, too, can be a collection of little gems. But these come to us from the "dryland tundra," a unique plant community of ground-hugging mats and cushions from plains and steppes where conditions are too extreme to support larger plant life. Gardeners in damper climates go to great lengths to prevent xeric acantholimons, astragalus, eriogonums, or townsendias from rotting. In other regions

Rock gardens allow us to display small treasures, such as Nevada bitterroot *Lewisia nevadensis* **'Rose Form.' (Photo by R. Tatroe)**

these plants are nearly always grown in specialized alpine houses, greenhouses where heat, cold, and aridity are artificially controlled. Satisfying the cultural requirements of xeric cushions and buns is relatively easy here, as long as drainage is good.

Before Randy and I moved to Colorado, I'm not certain that we recognized that there was such a thing as rock gardening as a style in its own right. When we lived in Holland and England many of the historic estate gardens that we visited did have "rock gardens." All too often the rockwork was on a monumental scale and there were very few plants. Their resemblance to abandoned quarries did not leave us with a positive impression.

The rock gardens we have now came about as a practical solution to issues we faced when we started to build our garden. To break ground for borders around the perimeter of the backyard, we rented a sod stripper and removed much of the lawn. Anyone who has stripped lawn knows that even a small area yields a huge—and heavy—pile of sod. We mounded the sod into the back corners of the property just to get it out of the way for the time being. Eventually, though, the mounds became the inspiration for rock gardens.

Our backyard is small and rectangular and was as flat as a billiard table—except where the last few feet dropped off steeply toward the water retention

Top left: In his dryland rock garden, Charles Mann mixes pink, red, blue, and purple penstemons with orange horned poppies and other xeric plants.

Bottom left: With careful pruning, low-growing rock garden plants, like these mats of pink thyme, stay in scale with a garden railroad. Barbara and Marc Horovitz garden.

Top right: Lavender Crandall's beardtongue *Penstemon crandallii* and yellow daisies of perky Sue *Hymenoxys argentea* in Ellen Wilde's rock garden in front of her home in Santa Fe.

area behind the fence. A row of very large houses was built directly behind us only a few months before we moved in, blocking a mountain view and affording us an unobstructed panorama of kitchens and family rooms. The sod mounds gave us instant height, creating platforms several feet high. Trees and shrubs planted on the mounds would have a head start in creating privacy. The mounds also softened the angular lines of the backyard.

At the time, I was planning to plant trees, shrubs, and perennials—making, as it were, raised mixed borders. I decided to wait a full year before

planting to give the sod time to compost and settle, and to be sure that the grass and weeds were truly dead. That spring I planted vegetables in the mounds (causing the great zucchini glut of 1988 that I'm sure everyone on our block remembers with a shudder). Watering the vegetables regularly helped hasten the composting action. The scads of weeds that germinated in the open soil between the vegetables were easy to dispatch.

In the meantime, we discovered the rock alpine garden at Denver Botanic Gardens. Randy fell in love with the tiny plants. I fell in love with the

Rock gardens in the backyard provide height and relieve the angularity of the rectangular space. Tatroe garden. (Photo by R. Tatroe)

diversity and volume of taxa displayed. At that point we decided to turn our latent mounds into rock gardens. It took us another year to stumble across the local chapter of the North American Rock Garden Society. By then we were already hooked. To our good fortune, the composted sod turned out to be the perfect soil for many rock garden plants. Our underlying soil is mostly heavy, water-retentive, and has a pH of well over 8, not what you would call ideal soil for a group of plants that almost universally demands good aeration and drainage. The composted sod drains quickly, is high in minerals, and contains more humus than the existing soil (which essentially had none).

That first year we had five mounds of varying sizes positioned randomly around the perimeter of the backyard. Initially, we did not purchase rocks but instead recycled sandstone chunks removed from a small dry stacked stone wall in the front yard. More came from the side of the road a few blocks from our home. In the 1980s, the area where we live was fairly rural. When local homeowners renovated their landscapes they would dump the entire previous landscape alongside the roadside. Neighbors rescued eight-foot tall pine trees. We got rock. It was riprap, a chunky granite that is mostly used for erosion control. This is unwieldy rock with no readily apparent facets or strata. I had read Lincoln Foster's book *Rock Gardening* and knew riprap wasn't going to look natural no matter what we did with it. So mostly we just buried it deeply to stabilize the slopes. (Since then, as I could afford to buy more attractive rock, I've dug up and gotten rid of most of the granite.)

As our interest in rock gardening grew over the next decade, so did the rock gardens. Presently they have consumed more than half of our property, front and back. Only the side yard has resisted the invasion of mounds. After the riprap lesson, we started purchasing sandstone boulders, locally called "moss rock" due to the grayish-green lichens that grow on the surface. (Much of the lichen is now gone, killed by the chlorine in our water.)

Although sandstone predominates, we've violated more of Mr. Foster's good advice by

mixing radically different types of rock throughout the garden. We can't help ourselves. When we fall in love with another type of rock, we must have it, referring to the odd boulder here and there as a "glacial erratic." Besides the mounds, we've also created three horizontal rock gardens—a large random-cut red flagstone terrace in front of the house, an area of square red pavers off the paths in the backyard, and a small tumbled beige flagstone garden behind the pond.

Rock gardening, like gardening in general, is a series of experiments. This involves making educated guesses until stumbling upon a plant that is compatible with the environmental conditions, discarding plants that disappoint, and killing an embarrassing number of the ones we would prefer to keep. Unlike many rock gardeners, who are primarily concerned with growing plants well, I also enjoy playing around with the aesthetics of rock gardening, leading to such flights of fancy as polished broken glass mulch, chainsaw-carved wooden gnomes in the "woods," and chiseled stone faces in the dry streambed.

Like all rock gardeners, I've gone through phases, where my goal is to acquire one of every desirable species or cultivar of a particular genus, such as *Stachys* or *Nepeta*. Other phases are chronic, as I've tried to get my hands on every silver-leafed plant known to man. I'm usually indulging in several phases simultaneously, brought about by some article I've read or lecture I've attended. Scraps of paper with lists of coveted plants litter the house and more are written on the back of cash register receipts and greeting cards. Such is the madness of rock gardening. Every catalog that arrives in the mail adds to the flurry of paper lying around the house. As every gardener with a small garden already filled to capacity knows, the problem is fitting all of these new acquisitions into an already overstuffed garden. It comes to a point where grief over losses is short-lived as every dead plant provides space for another on my life list of must-haves.

The plants I grow in my rock gardens are not limited to the low-profile mats, cushions, and buns that are the conventional rock gardener's raison d'être. I prefer the mixed planting of small trees, shrubs, grasses, bulbs, perennials, and annuals typical of arid and semiarid habitats to the tundra paradigm, where every plant in the garden is under a few inches in height. Using a smattering of trees and shrubs also provides shelter for plants that require protection from the baking afternoon sun in midsummer. This imitates a natural model as when, for example, colonies of *Draba oligosperma* grow beneath the boughs of piñon pines in western Colorado.

The Rosette Garden

I have the good fortune to be married to a man, who, although he was president of the local chapter of the North American Rock Garden Society (NARGS) for two terms, has no interest whatsoever in hands-on gardening. What this means in practical terms is that, while Randy shares my interests, he does not ask that I share with him even one square foot of our very limited garden space. It would be ungenerous of me to deny him any plant that catches his fancy.

Plant lovers are generally a fickle lot who fall madly in love with salvias one year and then head over heels for stachys the next. But not Randy. He has been faithful to the silver saxifrage for the past two decades. Every plant sale we ever attended he presented me with a pretty, but doomed, saxifrage for our garden. Occasionally an individual would survive for a time, and then, just as I thought I'd cracked the code, it too, would perish. To his credit, Randy never took this personally. I, on the other hand, was starting to see silver saxifrages as a personal failing.

Silver saxifrages look something like hen and chickens dressed up in formal attire. They are indescribably elegant, forming tight colonies of rosettes decked out in diamonds and platinum. Unfortunately, like their human socialite counterpart, they are difficult to please. I tried everything to achieve the perfect combination of morning light, afternoon shade, and that horticultural oxymoron, "well-drained but moist soil," these aristocrats demand. Nothing worked. The solution

Silver saxifrages and other rosette-shaped treasures are right at home in the specialized microclimates created by a unique set of circumstances in the Rosette Garden. Tatroe garden (Photo by R. Tatroe).

Chunks of blue glass, beads in the shape of scarabs, and a mulch of broken bricks and blue marbles, with blue *Veronica caespitosa,* yellow draba, and white *Schiverekia podolica.* **Tatroe Rosette Garden.** (Photo by R. Tatroe).

came entirely by accident several years ago when we cut down an adolescent blue spruce that was starting to overwhelm its corner of the backyard. The spruce had been hiding a mother lode of silty loam soil beneath its branches. Other parts of our property are cursed—or blessed, depending on how you look at it—with sticky clay fill, probably the residue of every basement excavation on our block. But here we uncovered the stuff that other Front Range gardeners only dream about.

This site is also shaded downhill to the southwest by a pair of Austrian pines, making a snug little glen—the perfect place for a secret garden. I dug in several bags of mushroom compost, along with nitrogen and phosphorus supplements, then laid out a small terrace of white tumbled flagstone from Arizona. Uphill from the terrace is a low rock wall of sandstone that follows the contours of the mound in relaxed curves. The two sites relate to one another, much like the symbol for yin and yang. A third side is open, but shaded slightly by aspens across the path. On a fourth side is a low chain-link fence. We attached a rusting, naturalistic iron bar trellis inside the fence. Planted on the trellis, a native forest grape *Vitis riparia* spreads 15 feet up and down the fenceline and has launched itself into the Austrian pine closest to the fence, further shading the garden.

Plenty of morning sunlight reaches the terrace, but the pines provide shade in the afternoon, keeping this area relatively cool in summer and slowing snowmelt in winter. This is the only place in the backyard where snow piles up and stays for any length of time. With or without snow cover, shade from the pines keeps this spot evenly cold during the winter months, limiting those radical temperature swings that can be so hard on plants. The terrace sits at the top of a fairly steep slope, so fast drainage is also ensured. All of the aforementioned factors contribute to making this terrace a unique microclimate.

As luck would have it, I built the garden the year Randy and I had been to the NARGS annual conference in Tacoma, Washington, where he had picked up *Saxifraga* 'Whitehills' from Siskiyou

Rare Plant Nursery. With little hope, I planted it in the new empty terrace. Lo and behold, this one started spreading like the invasion of Schmoos in the vintage comic strip *Li'l Abner*. Emboldened, I added a few more saxifrages every year. Each in turn, performed equally well—as long as I confine them to the west, more shaded side of the terrace. I don't know exactly how much sun is too much, but there is an obvious line of demarcation beyond which the delicate rosettes sunburn.

Currently, a dozen or so silver saxifrages are tucked between the flagstones and show no signs of stress. They bloom, they multiply, they prosper. When saxifrage expert Rex Murfitt, of Vancouver, B.C., visited our garden, he generously commented that these plants could be difficult in the best of circumstances. He credits the sandstone for our happenstance success. This stone, which is porous, holds water and keeps the soil beneath it cool. Anyone expert in these matters would have suggested trying a trough or a north-facing slope. Flat rock gardens are just not done. But, in my experience, troughs and slopes dry out too quickly. This garden gets by on fifteen minutes of sprinkling twice a week in summer. It is the only place in my entire garden where I can succeed with anything remotely alpine—and pay Randy back for not taking up gardening as a hobby.

Although rock gardening is, first and foremost, about plants, there is no reason we can't have a little fun with our gardens as well. On visits to rock gardens at NARGS annual conferences in the past few years, I've noticed a refreshing trend developing. Art, artifacts, and personal memorabilia are starting to appear in even the most tasteful of gardens. Dick Bartlett, in Lakewood, Colorado, calls his garden "Froggy Bottom." Scores of faux amphibians hide among the plants throughout the garden. In Denver, Gwen Kelaidis sets stone spheres next to her ball cacti to create visual puns.

Nevertheless, what happened next in my terrace was not planned—it just evolved. The mulch in the Rosette Garden was originally pea gravel. The spring after I finished this garden, I noticed that bricks I had used elsewhere as edging had broken up into large, terra-cotta crumbs. These would make handsome mulch—especially in between the light-colored flagstones. There weren't enough to do the entire terrace so Randy and I found a brick salvage yard, purchased more soft-fired bricks, and smashed them with a heavy mallet. The resulting mulch works both in practical terms and as a design element. The effect is much like contrasting grout in tile work.

I am absolutely fascinated with marbles, so it was inevitable that they would eventually find their way into the garden. Popularized as accessories for flower arranging, marbles suddenly became abundant and cheap in the late 1990s. I had acquired a large number of bags of cobalt blue marbles on sale and stored them away, waiting for inspiration to strike. On a visit to Tom and Diane Peace's Denver garden, I noticed that Diane had scattered marbles between the flagstones on their patio. In an act of shameless plagiarism, I distributed the blue marbles I'd been saving on top of the broken brick pieces. Some time later, I scored sky-blue flat "marbles" at a hobby store and these joined the fray. A terra-cotta birdbath sits in one corner of the garden, its color coordinating with the broken bricks. A low stone basin of white lava rock, filled with large glass beads in various shades of blue, marks the intersection between the terrace and a set of stone stairs that leads down the hillside under the pines.

A geometric glass "rose" from a trip to Anchorage inspired me to develop a rosette theme for this little terrace. From then on, I concentrated on other plants that, like the silver saxifrages, grow in rosette form. A couple of carved stone roses from a bead shop reinforce this theme. Fist-sized chunks of blue, white, and green glass from an old glass foundry embellish a low sandstone wall at the edge of the garden. The glass echoes the striations in the rock and the unnatural color introduces an element of surprise to the wall. The interplay of similarities and differences between all these materials contribute to the complex character of this garden.

ROSETTE-SHAPED PLANTS

These rosette-shaped rock garden plants need morning sun and afternoon shade and soil amended with organic matter:

Androsace spp.
Arenaria tetraquetra
Aubrieta deltoidea 'Argenteo-variegata'
Azorella trifurcata 'Nana'
Draba hispanica
Epilobium crassum
Globularia spinosa
Jovibarba spp.
Lewisia spp.
Orostachys spp.
Primula allionii
Rosularia spp.
Saxifraga spp.
Schiverekia podolica
Sedum spp.
Sempervivum spp.
Silene argaea

The Lace Rock Garden

In the summer of 1999, Randy and I (to paraphrase Michael Pollan) seceded from the national lawn and replaced our last remnant of bluegrass lawn with yet another rock garden. Instead of mechanically stripping the sod, this time we killed the lawn with Round-Up and rototilled the dead sod into the underlying soil. This should have been an easy task, and it would have been, had we remembered to soak the area beforehand. As it turned out, the weekend we rented the mechanical tiller, the ground was as impenetrable as a concrete slab. Randy went back to the rental agency three times, trading up to ever-larger machines until he had a monster of a tiller. Only by brute force and determination was he able to till the soil to a dizzying depth of, maybe, 6 inches.

It would have made more sense if we had stopped, watered the area thoroughly to soften the soil to a greater depth, and tried again the following weekend—if it were not for the hills of sand and manure blocking the driveway that had been delivered earlier in the day. If we wanted access to our garage any time soon, things had to proceed as planned. After carting said piles to the backyard, one wheelbarrow load at a time, Randy tilled these in along with a bag of super phosphate.

Colorado State University warns against mixing sand and chopped lawn into clay soil—the resulting mix is the recipe for adobe bricks. But rock gardeners have always ignored this advice. The trick is to add a large enough volume of sand and organic matter, at least one quarter of each by percentage. Because we were able to churn up so little of the soil beneath the lawn, our proportions were probably closer to one-third soil, one-third coarse sand, and one-third well-composted manure. The soil created by this process is almost identical in texture and appearance to the soil we made by piling stripped sod—but this method is a lot faster because it skips the year of composting.

We mounded the soil into the center of the area and used a garden hose to define the perimeter of the garden and the path around it, varying the width of the path and leaving one section wide enough for a couple of chairs to sit in off to one side. Next we divided the mound roughly in two and outlined a smaller path through the center. Using an appliance dolly, we set one 550-pound volcanic rock boulder and two balled and burlapped dwarf conifers on the ground. Then, using shovels and rakes, we contoured soil into naturalistic mounds around all three. This is backward from the way gardens are generally constructed, but I found it easier to position the very heavy elements first and then build the garden around them. Lastly, we placed a few shrubs and the smaller rocks.

The rock we used is a crusty material (sold at area nurseries) locally known as "lace rock." Randy and I were immediately taken with the grotesque shapes, some of which resemble fossils and dinosaur bones. Most rock has striations or fracture lines to guide placement, but lace rock has neither. I laid it on the surface, barely pushed into the soil, with two to three pieces butted up against one other to create pockets for planting. Somewhere during this phase I became curious about this odd rock, so I sent a sample with a friend who works with geologists, to find out what it was. She reported back to me that her coworkers had a good laugh over our rock. It seems we'd purchased hardpan, aka caliche, calcium carbonate deposits that are common in arid regions. When erosion uncovers them, they lie like cradle cap on the surface of the soil. The geologists said this stuff would probably decompose fairly quickly. We were momentarily taken aback until our friend reminded us that geologists think about time in different terms than the rest of us. So far, the caliche is holding up well—only one piece has cracked.

With the exception of the rosette garden, I long ago gave up trying to grow genuine alpines and have instead switched over most of my rock garden to dryland plants. It wasn't so much a conscious decision as a happy accident—dryland plants survived, alpines didn't. Not that I mind greatly. As much as I appreciate the mountains'

The largest shrub in the caliche garden is a prickly pear cactus. Tatroe garden.

majesty, my heart belongs to the desert. My favorite magazine as a kid was *Arizona Highways;* the one place in the United States I wanted to visit more than any other, Arches National Park. Mountain forget-me-nots are undeniably charming, but a purple barrel cactus in the Mojave Desert, a cliff full of agaves blooming in a canyon in Arizona, mats of silvery eriogonums in the White Mountains of California—these are the images that make my heart sing. So I suppose it's only natural that my garden has evolved to reflect this infatuation with the desert.

The southwest side of this garden is devoted exclusively to dryland plants. The caliche lace rock adds to the garden's arid character. When Randy and I visited Death Valley a few years back, the whitened skeletons of dead shrubs were often more hauntingly beautiful than their live counterparts. It seemed only fitting to add a piece of desert "driftwood," an aged, gnarled juniper snag, to the garden. Artwork continues the desert theme in a row of metal kachinas, a lizard tattooed on a rock, a scattering of Apache tears, chunks of petrified wood, and a copper roadrunner.

Because the garden is small, I've chosen small plants that are in scale with the space. Shrubs predominate in desert ecosystems, so I've also included a few of these. When a four-winged saltbush quickly outgrew its space, I replaced it with a similar but smaller saltbush *Atriplex confertifolia,*

Top left: In the caliche garden, nearly black flowers of the dwarf bearded iris 'Jewel Box' harmonize with lavender blossoms of the spring starflower *Ipheion uniflorum* 'Wisley Blue' and lavender-red *Phlox kelseyi* 'Lemhi Purple'. Tatroe garden. (Photo by R. Tatroe)

Bottom left: Lavender-leaf stachys *Stachys lavandulifolia,* with yellow daisies of *Haplopappus acaulis.* (Photo by R. Tatroe)

Top right: White-spined cholla *Cylindropuntia whipplei* and yellow tulips *Tulipa batalinii* 'Bright Gem' in May. Tatroe garden.

a silver-leafed shrub with distinctive seedpods that persist all winter. Another striking silver-leafed shrub, the two-foot tall purple sage *Salvia pachyphylla,* blooms all summer. Its flowers are purplish-blue and the nearly white foliage is strongly aromatic. The largest "shrub" in this garden is a massive, yellow-flowered opuntia, with pads that blush lavender in winter. It's a beast of a thing and requires annual pruning to keep it from overtaking the garden.

The most successful plants, at least when counting the number of survivors, are the buckwheats, with more than a dozen species and subspecies represented. There are several varieties of cushion buckwheat *Eriogonum ovalifolium.* All form dense mats of tiny silvery leaves and flowers of cream, yellow, or pink that mature to rust or red as winter approaches. At the other end of the scale size-wise, *E. niveum* forms 18-inch-tall mounds of white flowers when it blooms in late summer.

For showiness, nothing beats townsendias, some of the earliest flowers to bloom in spring. Preceded only by species crocus, iris, and tulips, *Townsendia nuttalii* and *T. hookeri* are the first flowers to bloom in this garden. In March, their white daisies open, tucked tightly inside the silver cushions. Lavender *T. rothrockii* begins blooming soon thereafter, followed by white-flowered *T. exscapa, T. incana,* and *T. spathulata.* The latecomer of the bunch is a biennial, *T. parryi,* with oversized, two-inch wide lavender daisies that stand several inches above basal rosettes that are dwarfed by the flowers. This plant self-sows in the gravel, covering more real estate each year and blooming on and off all summer.

Species crocus, iris, and tulips are right at home here interplanted or interspersed amongst the Great Basin, Southwest desert, and Great Plains flora, providing riotous color from later winter and throughout the spring season. Cultivars of *Iris reticulata* appear to need some summer moisture to thrive and multiply, but they have persisted, if not prospered, in dry years. Selections of *Crocus*

chrysanthus and *C. sieberi* seem to shrug off the dry conditions. Red-flowered *T. linifolia* and yellow *T. batalinii* 'Bright Gem' have also not missed a beat. My only complaint about these tulips is their foliage, which, although it goes dormant earlier than the larger tulips, still hangs around long enough to shade out and kill a few shade-sensitive plants every spring.

Tucked here and there between the cushions and mats are small hardy cacti. Of these, hedgehog cactus *Echinocereus fendleri* is probably the most flamboyant, sending up huge magenta flowers in mid-spring. There are dozens of other plants in this garden. Standouts include a dwarf mountain mahogany from Utah (a Jerry Morris collection) and several attractive bindweed relatives *Convovulus assyricus, C. boisseri* ssp. *boisseri,* and *C. compactus.* All three form low silver mats with satiny pink or white flowers, varying by species. *Heterotheca jonesii,* a diminutive relative of our local golden aster, is a ground-hugging mat with yellow daisies and blooms all summer.

This arid rock garden does not require much maintenance. I pull a few weeds from time to time but beyond sprinkling a handful of organic fertilizer in spring, that's about it. The drought of 2001–3 did not harm this garden whatsoever. In fact, I suspect that less frequent summer rains are actually better for these plants, most of which originate in much drier places than the Front Range of Colorado.

The irrigated northeastern half of this garden offers a dramatically dissimilar set of conditions. An oddly contorted small tree, *Robinia pseudoacacia* 'Twisty Baby', is open enough to allow ample light through its branches, but has just enough of a canopy to provide sanctuary at the hottest part of the day for lewisias, woody penstemons, tiny aquilegias, gentians, and other temperamental rock garden pearls. Surrounding the lava boulder, the dwarf conifers, and a three-foot tall broom relative, *Cytisophyllum sessilifolium,* are dozens of smallish microclimates that some little-known treasures find to their liking.

Integrating Rock Gardens with Flower Beds

A well-known garden writer once told me that rock gardens and conventional gardens are inherently incompatible. At the time of this conversation, my garden had one foot in the traditional English style (long mixed borders surrounding a small, but central expanse of lawn) and the other in the rock garden realm (mounds of soil and rock rising up here and there out of the borders for no apparent reason). I had done my best to make the rock gardens blend in, arranging them in the overall scheme three-dimensionally, as if they were large shrubs. I varied their sizes, in some cases putting a small mound slightly in front of and off to one side of a large mound, plus took care to make the profiles of the mounds irregular, asymmetrical, and not too cone-shaped.

For all this, there was no denying there was neither an obvious nor a logical geologic explanation for these piles of soil and rock on an otherwise flat plane. I have visited a number of rock gardens and the best, from a traditional design standpoint, anyway, are those built on natural outcroppings of stone, perhaps enlarged and enhanced to expand the garden space. Another effective artifice is converting a steep slope to rock gardens, the stone doubling as a retaining wall and providing an ideal habitat for a collection of rock-loving plants.

When converting a flat lot to rock gardens, two methods stand out. One is a series of freestanding raised beds, arranged within the context of a conventional, more formal garden. The second is grading the entire property into a series of berms and swales so that it imitates a natural landscape. The first abandons any pretext of naturalism, the second eliminates clashes of differing garden styles.

At the time of this mental exercise, my garden was well on its way to being established, with many of the trees and shrubs finally approaching maturity. It didn't make a lot of sense to start over at this point. Grading was out of the question. In any case, the naturalistic arrangement I prefer would stand out in stark contrast against the suburban backdrop of fence lines and rooftops. I'm just not capable of suspending belief at the property line. Neighborhood covenants ban privacy fences on two sides of my property so that was not an option either.

For a time, I tried the cottage garden approach, allowing self-sown seedlings and invasive perennials a free hand throughout the garden. Paths disappeared under swaths of flowers and the distinctions between the rock gardens and the borders did soften noticeably. Things got fairly wild and woolly at this stage. But when the rock gardens began to disappear under California poppies, larkspur, and Queen Anne's lace, it became clear that I could have cottage plants or rock garden plants, but not both, in the same location. (I'll be paying for this indiscretion for the rest of my life—pulling up thousands of seedlings out of the rock gardens as penance).

While still in my cottage garden phase, Randy and I had removed the last of the lawn in the backyard and built the lace rock garden in its place. I was careful to the point of fanaticism to keep self-sowing annuals and biennials out of these areas. The tailored look that resulted led to another epiphany. Instead of attempting to blur the transitions, this time I would outline each area boldly. What the heck, if the various parts of the garden were not going to blend together anyway, I might as well highlight their dissimilarities.

I started with the new rock gardens, the three mounds that replaced the last of the lawn. Originally, I mulched these gardens with the same gray and pink pea gravel as the path surrounding the mounds, because, at the time of construction, I was still in my "blur the edges" phase. To establish a hard outline to the entire area, I ran an edging of used brick along both sides of the path. This resulted in a strong outline, but there still wasn't enough contrast between the areas. So next, I replaced the pea gravel mulch in the gardens with rusty-orange, decomposed granite, collected from a roadside construction site in Park County, Colorado. Now there is no mistaking path from garden.

One garden design recommendation is to first establish hard edges and then "erase" the edges in places. Following this advice, I "erased" the brick edging, literally by removing bricks, wherever two paths intersect so that there was no longer the psychological barrier of stepping over a line to go from one path to another. Where the path goes through the center of the new garden, I pulled some of the stone out from the garden and placed it in the corners where the paths cross to hide the exposed ends of the brick. Then I continued the brick edging another 50 feet into an adjoining section of the garden, stopping it when it ran into a brick terrace on one side and a brick path going into a work area on the other. The effect is now logical to my mind since no part of the edging starts or stops in the middle of nowhere. Admittedly, the whole arrangement is completely artificial, but the various parts no longer fight against one another. The brick provides a measure of continuity, tying several unrelated parts of the garden together.

In other areas, paths became the dividing lines between various parts of the garden. After a couple of years of path building, every previously partly hidden goat trail through the borders and around the rock gardens had been widened and made into a proper path. While most of these are still too narrow for any but the most sure-footed, they do allow better access to the gardens for maintenance. Visiting children and dogs get a kick out of following the network of paths that run throughout the garden, much like a free-form labyrinth.

Whenever I purchased stepping-stone material, I used flat pieces of our locally abundant sandstone, the kind sold for wall construction. These make sturdy steps that go down a slope at the back of the property and up again on the other side as stairs that lead through a small grove of aspen trees. The stairs are laid on top of a French drain, which carries overflow from the pond off the property after a heavy rainfall. Here I was going for the look of a cascade with river rock and boulders of various sizes flanking the stepping-stones. At the top of the stairs, the dry streambed becomes the path that goes past the pond and out onto a brick terrace.

I never toss anything out, so I've always got piles of material stored away until I can figure out where to use it. Much of what I'd been saving was used to make paths throughout the garden. In one corner of the garden, I recycled scrap wall stone into a path that circles behind the largest berm, by putting two or three irregular, but flat and somewhat rectangular, pieces together to form each step. The steps are placed slightly out of kilter to one another for a casual, jaunty effect. In the vegetable garden I made square steps of eight leftover bricks, each laid in a basket-weave pattern. Landscape timbers recycled from a child's play area, cut into 3-foot lengths, and laid in pairs, make a path from the brick terrace to the work area.

The stepping-stones that form the center path in the newest rock garden are off-white tumbled flagstones. This path lined up with two existing paths on either side, one that goes through a flower bed to a faucet, the other leading out to the back gate. Those paths were made with the flat pieces of lichen-encrusted sandstone. In my path-building frenzy, I replaced the sandstone with tumbled flagstone to coordinate with the steps in the rock gardens. It's a

minor change, but rather than changing materials three times along the way, a path of like stones leads from the house wall through several different parts of the garden and exits out the back gate.

When all of these paths were completed, the backyard had been divided into a couple of dozen individual gardens. Each garden is contained within a strong outline and could stand on its own. The borders have been broken up into a series of adjoining flowerbeds, the largest approximately 10 by 10 feet. Instead of appearing chopped up, the garden as a whole resembles a patchwork crazy quilt where each block is random in size and shape and different from all others, but cohesive within the rigid rectangular frame of the property boundaries.

The patchwork quilt arrangement also facilitates plant collecting. English garden writer Gertrude Jekyll's main flower borders at Munstead were a third the size of my entire property and held only eighty different species of plants. Traditional border design requires some repetition along the length of the border for balance. My small garden holds several thousand different plants—there just isn't room for more than one or two of any one species. It's easier to display an assortment of individual species within a small area, treating each block as if it were a large container or flower arrangement, simply because there are fewer elements to coordinate within each.

Each flower bed is planted in a classic florist's asymmetrical triangle with a tall perennial, an ornamental grass clump, or a small shrub in each bed forming a peak off to one side. The plantings in the flower beds echo the shapes of the rock garden berms, lending a measure of uniformity. An unexpected result was the rhythms this arrangement has created. Looking across the peaks and valleys of these individual gardens gives the illusion of a series of waves, of foothills, or of sand dunes. Now, the mounds make perfect sense in relation to the other flower beds.

As a finishing touch, I planted many of the paths with low-growing thymes, veronicas, sempervivums, iceplants, phloxes, bronze fairy fern *Leptinella perpusilla,* brass buttons *L. squal-ida,* and roundleaf germander *Teucrium rotundi-folium,* where they can weave together between the steps. In open gravel paths, I add a few well-behaved annuals like gazanias, miniature Fantasy petunias, and portulacas against the edges for bright spots of color in the summer months when the rock gardens are quiet.

Now, like a labyrinth, my gardens are complex but not chaotic. Within each individual garden, order reigns (no more California poppies mugging tiny eriogonums). But, since the arrangement is ar-tificial anyway, I'm free to experiment with diverse materials and artwork without worrying that I'll ruin a naturalistic effect. Best of all, the rock gardens no longer stand out like frogs on a log.

The Badlands Garden at Raven Ranch

Coloradans Rebecca and Bob Skowron spend their summers scouring the last remaining wild places of the American West. When they are not scrambling into the canyons and potholes of New Mexico, Utah, and Wyoming, they're backpacking into high mountain areas where few tourists ever go. Rebecca's rock gardens, surrounding her home at the northern edge of the ponderosa pine forest known as the Black Forest, honor these vastly dissimilar wilderness environments.

Each separate and distinct garden plays host to a mix of native and exotic plants that represent a spe-cific geographic locale. Natural selection plays a part in determining what garden goes where on her 6.5-acre property. A natural outcrop of stone down-hill from the house is the ideal spot for intrepid plants that require an open exposure and regular ir-rigation, but can otherwise take care of themselves. Nearer to the house are gardens of rarities that merit closer monitoring and attention. When an excava-tion for a greenhouse several years ago left behind a huge pile of soil, naturally Rebecca saw this as an opportunity for a new garden. Off the irrigation

Top: Rebecca Day-Skowron's Badlands Garden at Raven Ranch, with scarlet gilia *Ipomopsis aggregata* in bloom in August.

Bottom: A dryland penstemon *Penstemon caespitosus* ssp. *perbrevis* with a naturalistic mulch of mixed sizes and types of rock.

grid, this hot and sunny site to the southeast and behind the completed greenhouse was the perfect spot for plants from arid places that demand little or no irrigation. The excavated soil was sandy loam so to expand the palette of plants she could grow, Rebecca brought in clay fill to build up the back east-facing side of the mound.

Native plants predominate, but this garden, like all of her gardens, is planted with a blend of natives and exotics from arid regions in other parts of the world. The sandy soil on the west side of the gardens provides the fast drainage that many small cacti, eriogonums, and penstemons require. Plants that naturally occur in heavier soil, which retains more moisture, go on the east side of the mound.

Using rocks carried home from travels across the West, she developed a badlands theme. Distinctive chunks of chalky white stone and ochre and reddish sandstone recreate the striations of color typical of badlands and canyonlands. The rock also helps hold the soil in place and prevent erosion. On one of her trips to the badlands, Rebecca observed that these formations always have caprock, so she recreated this topography by laying blocky stone at the top of the ridge.

The newest extension of this garden is on level ground to the southeast, where Rebecca laid the same white tufaceous rock she used in the adjoining mound to emulate a desert "pavement." The soil here is a mixture of compacted native soil and potting mix left over from her greenhouse operations. Conditions are intermediate to the two sides of the mound, well drained but not as well amended as the loam, compacted but not as heavy as the clay.

Adding to the naturalistic appearance of this garden is mulch of different types of rock, coordinated with the bands of color, and in all different sizes, a departure from the screened gravel more typically used in rock gardens. Rebecca decorates the mulch with crystals and small sandstone spheres, minerals that occur naturally in corresponding rock formations.

This garden is sun-drenched for most of the day but shaded in late afternoon by a ponderosa pine to the west. When planting, Rebecca knocks most of the potting soil off of the plant to expose the roots and works the media into the planting site. Most arid seedlings develop long taproots and these need planting as deeply as possible. She untangles and teases the root down into a deep, narrow hole. After planting, she surrounds the plant with gravel mulch and waters it in thoroughly. The only other time new plants are watered is when they appear to be wilting or if it has not rained for a long spell.

Rebecca's background in ceramic art is apparent in her sensitive composition of materials and plants. Without attempting to make exact copies from nature, her gardens capture the subtle beauty of the cold deserts of the West. Clearly the plants, both natives and exotics, feel right at home.

AlpenRidge Gardens

In suburban neighborhoods, front yard rock gardens are decidedly rare. That didn't stop Sandy and Bill Snyder from replacing their front lawn with a small mountain in the center of their circular driveway. At their home in an older, established neighborhood in Littleton, Colorado, they also transformed the rest of their slightly less than one-acre property into extensive gardens. Some years back, after Sandy retired from the horticultural staff at Denver Botanic Gardens, she vowed to reduce her personal garden's demands on her time. Friends like myself were amused to watch her instead launch into several major projects. One of these was a crevice garden in front of the garage and to one side of her driveway.

The genesis for this new garden was a pile of dirt left behind after a new brick driveway was installed. Inspiration was not immediate. For a couple of years, while Sandy contemplated her windfall, the mound played host to a meadow-style planting of annual flowers. Looking for a new type of garden that would expand the palette of plants she could grow, she engaged Boulder landscape designer Mike Woods, who helped her

build a massive crevice garden of buff sandstone based on a style popularized and widely lectured about by Czech rock gardeners. This type of construction creates hundreds of mini-microclimates for small cushion and mat plants that require a deep root run, dwarf conifers, and other miniature shrubs. The new garden needed to be large to be in scale with the original rock garden 20 feet away and also to block the view of a busy road from the kitchen window.

The first stone slab, 13 by 5 1/2 feet, was so heavy it had to be positioned by a crane. The bottom of the stone was set into a trench 2 feet deep, and the bulk of the top leaned against the mound at a slight slant. To accommodate the smaller slabs, Sandy and Mike dug slots parallel to the first. Conforming to the slope, each successive smaller slab was slotted in, until, at the bottom of the mound, only a few inches of stone protrudes above grade. Half of the slabs go all the way through the mound to ground level. In between these, smaller pieces were set in shallow trenches to give the illusion of more large slabs. A soil mix of equal parts of topsoil, sand, and peat fills the spaces between the stones. After planting, Sandy

Russian arborvitae *Microbiota decussata* is sheltered from the sun by the rock and the shadow of the Snyders' house during the hottest part of the day.

Miniature shrubs growing in Sandy Snyder's Crevice Garden:

Arctostaphylos 'Wood's Compact'

Buxus microphylla 'Kingsville Dwarf'

B. m. 'Tide Hill'

Chamaecyparis obtusa 'Nana'

C. o. 'Reis Dwarf'

Chamaecyparis pisifera 'Tsukumo'

Cotoneaster microphyllus 'Teulon Porter'

Daphne 'Lawrence Crocker'

Ephedra minima

Juniperus chinensis 'Shimpaku'

Microbiota decussata

Picea glauca 'Pixie'

P. pungens 'Blue Pearl'

Pinus mugo 'Jacobsen'

Thuja occidentalis 'Tiny Tim'

miniature elm

topdressed the garden with pieces of broken stone. A microjet irrigation system that waters this garden is on an automated timer. Maintenance consists mainly of pulling the occasional weed and checking for clogged sprinklers.

The garden is on the east side of the house and faces north, an orientation that shelters all but a small section of the garden from direct sunlight

during the hottest part of the day. The stone also helps protect plants from winter damage. Rock gardens generally settle and shrink significantly after construction, but Sandy's stone slabs have not moved at all since the day they were set in place. She credits the heavy clay soil for holding up to the weight of the stone. The surface soil mix has settled some, resulting in deeper crevices. When Sandy plants, she adds soil to maintain the integrity of the design. As she putters in the garden, she takes out plants that are too aggressive, rearranges the mulch to establish boundaries, and creates dams beneath new transplants to slow erosion.

In the backyard is a rock garden Sandy calls her "Terrace Garden." Differing from the rock gardens in the front of the house, both in style and in cultural conditions, this garden was built to accommodate cacti and a passionflower vine, plants with widely disparate needs. Sandy had cacti in other parts of her garden but thought it would be easier, not to mention less painful, if the cacti had their "own place to play." Sandy was also determined to grow a maypops passionflower, a tender vine she was convinced would be hardy in Colorado given the right microclimate. That, and her resolve to be rid of a straight concrete walk that dove steeply down the hillside between the side yard and the back, led to a major excavation on the south side of her home. In the process, she removed a foundation planting of overgrown Pfitzer junipers.

Again, with Mike Woods' assistance, the basement wall was exposed and the soil mounded some 10 feet out and parallel to the house wall. The hillside was graded to tie the side yard into the new mound, creating a garden that is L-shaped and at a right angle to the house. A small terrace against the basement wall, protected on two sides by the garden and on the third by the house, provided just the right environment for the passion vine, which has prospered.

The garden is mostly clay, and paradoxically retains water while at the same time it drains well because of the raised elevation. The east-facing

eties of agaves also get permanent resident status. The side yard section of the garden is home to a mix of xeric shrubs including as *Cowania mexicana*, cercocarpus, genista, and miniature roses. The cercocarpus are sheared as often as needed to keep them compact. Otherwise, this upright shrub has a tendency to split and break apart in snowstorms.

The Terrace Garden is unwatered beyond what nature provides and has turned out to be the one garden that most closely realizes Sandy's vow at retirement to make her gardens less dependent on her. She and husband Bill toured Alaska for five months during the summer of 2004 and when they returned this garden was the least affected by their prolonged absence.

Sandy says her gardens are constantly changing as she "futzes around" until she figures out what she likes. To facilitate such changes, she advises other gardeners not to be too hasty when adding hardscape such as paths and patios, but to instead

Above left: The Terrace Garden in May, with blue scillas and white Atlas daisies. Snyder garden.

Above right: The terrace garden creates just the right microclimate for a maypops vine that has survived Colorado winters for more than a decade. Snyder garden.

side of the garden is reinforced with large boulders of Pueblo river rock. It plays host to several types of dwarf cotoneasters, including a littleleaf cotoneaster *Cotoneaster microphyllus* trimmed into long tendrils that spiral out between the other plants. An arctic raspberry hugs the foot of the mound where extra water collects.

Cacti have priority on the south face, which Sandy says is hotter than heck in summer and warm even in February. She has added drabas, penstemons, small zauschnerias, acantholimons, sempervivums, and orostachys between the cacti. But anything that interferes with the cacti gets the boot. Because they are in character with cacti, several vari-

Plant clumping types of cacti on a level surface so they don't tumble down the slope.

lay out the outlines and live with them for awhile before installing permanent paving materials.

Rock Gardening Sans Rocks

Probably the one thing you expect to find in any rock garden is rock. However, Gwen Kelaidis dispensed with this cliché when she built a pair of large ridges at her home in Colorado. The only rocks in this garden are boulders lining a flagstone staircase that leads through the garden to a front gate. This wasn't the first time Gwen broke with rock gardening conventions. She built her first rockless rock garden in front of a bungalow in east Denver, shortly after she moved here from Wisconsin to join her new husband, Panayoti. (He calls this original effort the beginning of Gwen's orogeny.) As so often happens, practical considerations were what led Gwen to develop her distinctive style. Because of its considerable expense, she left the rock out in this part of the garden and instead looked for inspiration to the rolling hills and dry plains of Wyoming, where many of the plants she planned to grow originate.

When she and her family moved to their new home on an acre in south Denver in 1994, Gwen expanded this concept to cover an eighth of an acre in front of the house. Her garden in east Denver had been built on clay. This time Gwen encountered silty sand with a pH of nearly 8. While she worked on other areas of her property there began a four-year odyssey of soil amendment on the site where her dry rock gardens now reside. Though the silt component helps bind the sand when it's dry, neither sand nor silt does a good job of retaining nutrients nor water. The plan was to add enough organic matter to remedy this situation.

Ever mindful of costs, Gwen offered her yard as a free alternative for dumping clean landscape materials. Landscapers, who pay fees to unload excess soil, sod, and leaves at a landfill, were happy to oblige. That first fall she accepted twenty truckloads (160 cubic yards) of leaves, which were spread 1 to 3 feet deep throughout the site. The following spring, she mounded soil on top of the partially rotted leaves and sowed pumpkins in each hill. Pumpkins were critical to this massive, passive composting operation. Their large leaves shaded the leaf layer, helping to prevent moisture loss and exclude weeds. The regular watering the pumpkins required accelerated the rotting process.

For a time, Gwen's pumpkin patch became a local attraction, as she invited kindergarten classes to learn about gardening and pick their own pumpkins. At the end of four years, this area was covered with 6 to 12 inches of genuine leaf mold, a

material invaluable as a soil amendment that is nearly impossible to find in our region. She hired a contractor with a small bulldozer to push the leaf mold off to one side. He then constructed the berms from the underlying sand, spread the leaf mold back on top, and rototilled the garden to a depth of 12 inches.

The large ridges provide privacy, concealing the main garden from a very public street. Gwen was also concerned that the garden relate to the house, which is catawampus to the compass. When she lays out a rock garden, whether conventional or dry, her goal is to create four different but uniform sets of growing conditions, oriented east–west and

Gwen and Panayoti's dry ridge gardens embrace the front of their home.

Top left; A profusion of sand-loving, dryland wildflowers in Gwen's garden.

Bottom left: At the west ridge in Panayoti's garden, plants flow together.

Top right: White-flowered compact morning glory *Convolvulus boisseri* ssp. *compactus* shimmers alongside purple 'John Proffitt' ice plant.

north–south. The north–south orientation of the garden is on a diagonal to the house itself, an arrangement that is more dynamic than if the house and garden were on parallel axes.

The west ridge is Gwen's, the east is Panayoti's. Neither garden is irrigated, but each reflects slightly different planting philosophies. Panayoti takes a more casual approach, while Gwen carefully considers plant placement. Her goal is to emphasize the steep slope of the hillside. Small trees and shrubs replicate the scattering of trees typical of the hills of Wyoming. She places the tallest specimens at the top of the ridge and then "pours" others down the hillside, tapering them down in size to create an optical illusion of greater height. Gwen plants sparsely, again to represent the western aesthetic where you can "feel the hand of time" and "see the bones of the earth."

When placing plants, she also takes advantage of what she calls the "sponge effect." When a sponge is thoroughly wetted and stood on its end, water rapidly drains from the top to the bottom. Consequently, the bottom of the sponge stays wet much longer than the top. Because a raised mound of soil acts much like a sponge, the trick is to put the most drought-tolerant plants at the top and those that need more water at the base. After planting, Gwen mulches with a sharp, square-edged gravel, one to two stones deep. For convenience and to eliminate the need for a storage area elsewhere in the garden, extra gravel is stored in the paths. When the garden needs more mulch, Gwen simply scoops up a handful and tosses it onto the berm. She recommends getting extra whenever you buy mulch because it can be difficult, if not impossible, to find an exact match at a later date.

Extending the Season in the Rock Garden

It cannot be denied that rock gardens are at their best in early spring. Whether they are alpine or dryland, these mats, cushions, and buns originate where the growing season is short, either due to cold and snow, extremely hot conditions, or a

One of the many buckwheats *Eriogonum umbellatum* ssp. *aureum* 'Kannah Creek' in the Kelaidis's garden.

Above left: Sierra sundrops *Calylophus hartwegii* blooms all summer.

Above right: White buckwheat *Eriogonum wrightii* v. *wrightii* joins long-blooming yellow prairie zinnia *Zinnia grandiflora* in September.

The rock garden is mostly quiet in midsummer, but these rock garden plants bloom in summer:

Allium flavum	Dianthus deltoides	Onosma echioides
Antirrhinum hispanicum 'Roseum'	Dracocephalum renatii	Origanum acutidens
	Eriogonum umbellatum	O. amanum
Calylophus hartwegii	E. flavum	O. libanoticum
Campanula cochleariifolia	E. jamesii	O. rotundifolium
C. poscharskyana	E. ovalifolium	Penstemon richardsonii
C. raineri	Gazania krebsiana	Pterocephalus pinnardii
C. trogerae	G. linearis	Salvia daghestanica
C. zoysii	Gentiana paradoxa	Scutellaria alpina
Centaurea drabifolia	G. septemfida	S. orientalis 'Eastern Star'
Cryptantha virgata	Gypsophila aretioides	Teucrium orientale
Delosperma cooperi	Heuchera pulchella	Thlaspi lilacina
Delphinium grandiflorum	Hymenoxys argentea	Verbascum 'Letitia'
	Linum kingii	

combination of factors. The plants' strategy is to jump into action immediately upon snowmelt, to bloom and to set seed before the return of winter in the case of true alpines, or before the heat and drought of summer arrives in the case of the dryland tundra community.

That's all well and good from an ecological standpoint, but most of us are not content to have flowers in our gardens for only a short period after snowmelt. One solution is to distract visitors' attention from the quiescent mounds with gardens that peak at other seasons elsewhere on the property. Gertrude Jekyll got away with this on a grand scale at Munstead in England with seasonal flower borders, but it probably didn't hurt that she had acreage. For those of us who garden on a small urban or suburban lot, it's more realistic to extend the season by including a percentage of rock garden plants that bloom at times other than at snowmelt.

Only the worst kind of heat discourages the next group of flowers, those that bloom all season. Erodiums, of all types, are the most persistent. I have had erodium flowers in March and October—and every month in between. To ensure there will not be a tattered mix of seedheads and flowers in July, cut the clumps back hard around mid-June. Or deadhead (a tedious business) every few weeks. The sundrops *Calylophus* spp. and the evening primroses *Oenothera* spp. also exhibit lots of stamina. Again, if they get leggy in late spring, cut them back by a third.

Campanula carpatica, and all of its cultivars, blooms practically forever. This willing bellflower does not overrun the garden like some of its close relatives. Summer-persistent yellow forms of corydalis *Corydalis cheilanthifolia, C. ochroleuca* or *C. aurea* are absolutely guaranteed to overrun the garden, so I don't recommend planting them in rock gardens. (But, do find a place for them somewhere else in the garden—they are always in bloom in July.) *Corydalis linstowiana* 'Du Fu Temple' spreads with equal enthusiasm for some gardeners but since this pretty blue variety won't grow in my garden, I can't imagine anyone having too many.

ANNUALS FOR THE ROCK GARDEN

Other good annuals for paths are: tiny marigolds from the Signet series, including Lemon Gem, Tangerine Gem, Gnome, and Lulu

Verbena tenuisecta 'Imagination' (blue and violet) and *V. t.* 'Sterling Star' (silvery blue)

dwarf petunias in the Fantasy series (available in just about every standard petunia color)

little zinnias

creeping zinnias Crystal White, Star Gold, and the Starbright and Profusion series

Zinnia angustifolia 'White Star' and 'Golden Eye'

bright blue flax leaf pimpernel *Anagallis monellii*

apricot *Diascia barberae*

annual vinca *Catharanthus roseus*

Annual zinnias add color to the rosette garden in late summer. Tatroe garden.

Annuals are useful for providing color in the rock garden from summer through autumn. I also plant annual flowers in paths outside my rock garden where they add color without competing with the permanent residents. The ideal annual for rock gardens is one that is small, does not make a pest of itself by flinging seeds all over the garden, and does not require constant deadheading, watering, or fertilizing. It would be convenient if their flowers also stayed open whether sunlight hits them full in the face or not, but I suppose you

Top: California bluebells are a safe companion for xeric rock garden plants. Simply scatter the seeds in early spring where you want them to grow.

Bottom: If watered and fertilized, California poppies can become a pest.

can't have everything. Gazanias and portulacas are two of the best for edging paths even though they do have annoying sunlight requirements. Gazanias open only in full sun, portulacas open whenever they darn well please. Both are so easy and attractive I forgive them their peculiarities.

A few annuals are well behaved enough to plant directly into the rock garden. Among these: magenta rock purslane *Calandrinia umbellata,* golden Dahlberg daisy *Thymophylla tenuiloba,* twinspur *Diascia* spp., golden orange creeping zinnia *Sanvitalia procumbens,* yellow cups *Camissonia cheiranthifolia,* sky-blue southern star *Oxypetalum caeruleum,* and California bluebells *Phacelia campanularia.*

Be forewarned—under no circumstances let loose on your irrigated rock gardens: California poppies, cynoglossum, nigella, and other aggressively self-sowing annuals. I speak from experience. Every spring I weed out thousands of California poppy seedlings. Now confined to my xeric gardens, I will not even allow them to grow in pathways anywhere near a rock garden.

One Final Note on Rock Gardening

Rock garden aficionados will find a way to build rock gardens, regardless of their circumstances. Hence, an article in the Fall 2005 *Rock Garden Quarterly* (the bulletin of the North American Rock Garden Society) lamenting the difficulties of growing rock garden plants atop an apartment building in Manhattan in the midst of a construction boom.

For the non-obsessed, rock gardens still make sense. Far too frequently, hail, wind, or heavy snow batter our gardens, smashing and splintering trees and shrubs, and flattening everything else. Other parts of the country experience events like these every so often, but in the Intermountain West they occur with alarming regularity. After one such storm, my next-door neighbor, newly transplanted from Florida, was stunned by the destruction to his trees. This was as bad as anything he'd seen in four hurricanes. My garden was also badly damaged and the breakage to trees was indiscriminate. The supposedly hard-as-nails bur oak lost as many limbs as "soft" cottonwoods and silver maples.

In sharp contrast, my rock gardens were completely unaffected. The foot and a half of heavy, wet snow that accompanied the first real frost of the season in early October bothered these plants not a whit. In fact, they perked up in response to the 3 inches of water this storm provided. Five hailstorms earlier in the year, same story. I think it's safe to say that if any garden can claim to be weatherproof in our region, the rock garden would be it.

PLANTS FOR DRY ROCK GARDENS

Common Name	Botanic Name	Flower Color	Common Name	Botanic Name	Flower Color
sand verbena	Abronia fragrans	white	hardy living stone	Aloinopsis spathulata	magenta
stemless spikethrift	Acantholimon spp.	pink	balloon pod	Alyssoides graeca	yellow
Greek yarrow	Achillea ageratifolia	white	bladderpod	A. utriculata	yellow
Serbian yarrow	A. serbica	white	mat of gold	Alyssum 'Markgrafii,' A. stribryni	yellow
dwarf yellow yarrow	A. tomentosa	yellow			
false thyme	Acinos alpinus ssp. meridionalis	purple	mountain basket-of-gold	A. montanum	yellow
			Atlas daisy	Anacyclus depressus	white
Persian candytuft	Aethionema armenum 'Warley Rose'	rose/pink	pussytoes	Antennaria spp.	rose/white
			filigree daisy	Anthemis biebersteiniana	yellow
Persian candytuft	A. grandiflorum	pink	silverleaf daisy	A. montana	white
dwarf lady's mantle	Alchemilla erythropoda	yellow	shale columbine	Aquilegia barniebyi	yellow
nodding pink onion	Allium cernuum	pink	wallcress	Arabis ferdinandi-coburgi	white
firecracker onion	A. carinatum ssp. pulchellum	pink	variegated wallcress	A. fernandi-coburgi 'Variegata'	white

Bottom left: Chocolate flower *Berlandiera lyrata* smells sweetly of chocolate late in the day.

Bottom right: Twinspur *Diascia* sp. is the perfect annual for rock gardens.

125

Common Name	Botanic Name	Flower Color
greenleaf wallcress	Arabis x sturii	white
mat manzanita	Arctostaphylos nevadensis	white
kinnikinick	A. uva-ursi	evergreen
sandwort	Arenaria fendleri, A. hookeri, A. montana	white
basket-of-gold	Aurinia saxatilis	yellow
dwarf sage	Artemisia frigida	gray
silver mound	A. schmidtiana	inconspicuous
silver brocade	A. stelleriana	inconspicuous
Colorado aster	Aster coloradoensis	pink
bushy aster	A. dumosus	white
Himalayan aster	A. himalaicus	lavender
red loco weed	Astragalus coccineus	red
ground plum	A. crassicarpus	purple
spoonleaved milkvetch	A. spatulatus	pink
Utah milkvetch	A. utahensis	pink-purple
rock cress	Aubrieta hybrids	purple, pink, white
chocolate flower	Berlandieria lyrata	yellow
spiny throw-wax	Bupleurum spinosum	yellow
purple calandrinia	Calandrinia umbellata	red
poppy mallow	Callirhoe involucrata	magenta
Fendler's sundrops	Calylophus hartwegii ssp. fendleri	yellow
lavenderleaf sundrops	C. lavandulifolius	yellow
halfleaf sundrops	C. serrulatus	yellow
desert primrose	Camissonia tanacetifolia	yellow

Common Name	Botanic Name	Flower Color
cup bellflower	Campanula formanekiana	white
Adriatic bellflower	C. garganica	blue
Adriatic campanula	C. portenschlagiana	blue
bluebell	C. x 'Birch Hybrid'	purple
southwestern paintbrush	Castilleja integra	orange-red
paintbrush	C. sessiliflora	pink, cream, green
dwarf ceanothus	Ceanothus pumilus	purple
draba-leafed centaurea	Centaurea drabifolia	yellow
mouse-ear chickweed	Cerastium candidissimum	white
dwarf snapdragon	Chaenorrhinum glareosum	violet
hardy tiger's jaws	Chasmatophyllum masculinum	yellow
clematis	Clematis fremontii, C. scottii, C. texensis	blue and purple shades
silky morning glory	Convolvulus assyricus	pink compact
morning glory	C. compactus ssp. boisseri	white
double leaf coreopsis	Coreopsis grandiflora 'Baby Sun'	yellow
hardy iceplant	Delosperma spp.	various
maiden pink	Dianthus deltoides	pink
cushion pink	D. freynii	pink
cloud pink	D. nardiformus	pink
fragrant pink	D. petraeus	pink
common draba	Draba aizoides	yellow
cushion draba	D. bruniifolia	yellow
Spanish draba	D. hispanica	yellow
cutleaf dragonhead	Dracocephalum botryoides	purple

Fremont's clematis is native to the dry plains of Kansas and Nebraska.

Common Name	Botanic Name	Flower Color
cushion daisy	*Erigeron caespitosus*	white
compact daisy	*E. compactus*	white to pink
cutleaf fleabane	*E. compositus*	white
New Mexican daisy	*E. scopulinus*	white
mat buckwheat	*Eriogonum* spp.	yellow, white, pink
woolly yellow daisy	*Eriophyllum lanatum*	yellow
yellow cranesbill	*Erodium chrysanthum*	yellow
cranesbill	*E. petraeum* ssp. *glandulosum*	pink
cushion spurge	*Euphorbia epithymoides*	yellow
blue sheep's fescue	*Festuca cinerea*	n/a
fescue grass	*F. glacialis*	n/a
hardy gazania	*Gazania linearis*	yellow
broom	*Genista tinctoria*	yellow
prairie gentian	*Gentiana affinis*	blue
pink geranium	*Geranium cinereum* 'Splendens'	pink
alpine geranium	*G.* x 'Ballerina'	lavender
Dalmatian geranium	*G. dalmaticum*	pink
cranesbill	*G. endressii* 'Wargrave Pink'	pink
Balkan geranium	*G. macrorrhizum*	pink
mat globularia	*Globularia cordifolia*	blue
globularia	*G. neva*	blue
creeping baby's breath	*Gypsophilia repens*	white/pink
spiny goldenweed	*Haplopappus spinulosus*	yellow
Apennine sunrose	*Helianthemum apenninum*	white, yellow
hairy sunrose	*H. canum*	yellow
sunrose	*H.* 'Wisley Pink'	pink
rupturewort	*Herniaria glabra*	green
perky Sue	*Heterotheca argentea*	yellow
Jones' goldenaster	*H. jonesii*	yellow
silver hawkweed	*Hieracium lanatum*	double yellow
St. John's wort	*Hypericum cerastiodes*	yellow
creeping St. John's wort	*H. reptans*	mixed
candytuft	*Iberis saxatilis*	white
evergreen candytuft	*I. sempervirens* 'Little Gem'	white
cutleaf sunflower	*Kalimeris pinnatifida*	yellow
English lavender	*Lavandula angustifolia*	blue/purple
Arizona bladderpod	*Lesquerella arizonica*	yellow
compact statice	*Limonium gougetianum*	lavender
dwarf blue flax	*Linum alpinum*	blue
Balkan flax	*L. capitatum*	yellow
dwarf yellow flax	*L. flavum* 'Compactum'	yellow
dwarf sapphire flax	*L. perenne* 'Dwarf Sapphire'	blue
silver bush lupine	*Lupinus albifrons*	lavender-blue
silky lupine	*L. sericeus*	pale blue
blackfoot daisy	*Melampodium leucanthum*	white

Common Name	Botanic Name	Flower Color
blazing stars	*Mentzelia decapetala*	yellow
coyote mint	*Monardella odoratissima*	lavender
catnip	*Nepeta concolor*	lavender
cushion catnip	*N. phyllochlamys*	pink
lady's eardrop	*Onosma alboroseum*	whitish-pink
yellow lady's eardrop	*O. echioides*	yellow
Turkish oregano	*Origanum acutidens*	lavender
hardy shrimp plant	*O. libanoticum*	pink
roundleaf oregano	*O. rotundifolium*	pink
little pickles	*Othonna capensis*	yellow
locoweed	*Oxytropis sericea*	white
beardtongue	*Penstemon* spp.	blue, white, pink, red
tunic flower	*Petrorhagia saxifraga*	white or pink
Armenian phlomis	*Phlomis armeniaca*	yellow
creeping phlox	*Phlox condensata, P. hoodii, P. bryoides*	white
Bell's bladderpod	*Physaria bellii*	yellow
Newberry twinpod	*P. newberryi*	yellow
cinquefoil	*Potentilla cinerea*	yellow
horse cinquefoil	*P. hippiana*	yellow
cinquefoil	*P. tridentata*	white
mat scabiosa	*Pterocephalus parnassi*	purple
shrub alyssum	*Ptilotrichum spinosum*	purple
frilled flower hardy living stone	*Rabiea albipuncta*	yellow
creeping shrubby iceplant	*Ruschia pulvinaris*	pink
green lavender cotton	*Santolina ericoides*	cream
Mediterranean soapwort	*Saponaria ocymoides*	pink
soapwort	*S. pamphylica* of gardens	pink
grassleaf scabiosa	*Scabiosa graminifolia*	lavender
skullcap	*Scutellaria alpina*	yellow, pink, white, or blue
prairie skullcap	*S. resinosa*	lavender
stonecrop	*Sedum hybridum*	yellow
lanceleaf sedum	*S. lanceolatum*	yellow
Crimean wort	*Sideritis syriaca*	yellow
campion	*Silene hookeri*	red
western campion	*S. petersonii*	pink
goldenrod	*Solidago minutissima, S. spathulata* ssp. *nana*	yellow
cowboy's delight	*Sphaeralcea coccinea*	orange
globe mallow	*S. munroana*	orange
lavenderleaf hedgenettle	*Stachys lavandulifolia*	pink

Drought-tolerant Sunset Crater penstemon *Penstemon clutei* self-sows when it is happy.

Common Name	Botanic Name	Flower Color
orchid hedgenettle	*Stachys monieri*	pink
Caucasian stachys	*S. nivea*	white
night-blooming ice plant	*Stomatium mustilinum*	yellow
tansy partridge feather	*Tanacetum densum ssp. amani*	yellow
wall germander	*Teucrium chamaedrys*	purple, white
Asian germander	*T. orientale*	lavender
Mediterranean germander	*T. polium*	purple
low germander	*T. syspirense*	pink
thyme	*Thymus spp.*	lavender, pink, white
concrete leaf living stone	*Titanopsis calcarea*	yellow
Easter daisy	*Townsendia spp.*	purple, pink, white
shrubby mullein	*Verbascum dumulosum*	yellow
speedwell	*Veronica spp.*	blue
hummingbird mint	*Zauschneria californica*	red
blue mint	*Ziziphora clinopodioides*	pink

Above: Pale yellow lady's eardrop is a tough plant for unirrigated rock gardens only.

Right: Blue speedwell with yellow hardy ice plant *Delosperma nubigenum.*

Gardening in Shade

Overleaf: Gardening in the shade in a grove of Gambel oak. Jerry and Harlyn Mlynck's garden in Colorado Springs.

Above: Woodland wildflowers are often understated—pearlwort *Sagina subulata* 'Aurea' in full bloom with purple-leafed ajuga. (Photo by R. Tatroe)

Shade is a rare commodity in the relatively new suburb where I live and garden. Copious shade is nearly always the result of trees casting shadows—and trees are scarce in the Intermountain West except in creek beds, flood plains, and at higher elevations where extra moisture is available naturally. The one place there is often an overabundance of shade is in older, urban neighborhoods where trees planted decades ago now shade entire city blocks. When Randy and I moved into our seven-year-old development in 1987, there were no mature trees in the entire neighborhood. Shade provides welcome relief from Colorado's searing summer heat, so one of my first priorities was to plant trees. In case an arboretum comes to mind, more than half of these bit the dust before they were big enough to cast a shadow of any size.

HAIL KILLED SEVERAL—both directly from accumulated weight that snapped off overburdened limbs and indirectly from disease organisms that gained access through hail inflicted wounds. I've lost other trees to early and late snowstorms, those unseasonable blizzards that drop a foot or two of snow and literally knock trees down. (The March blizzard of 2003 that snapped a 25-foot-tall pine in half in my garden and damaged one-fourth of the trees in the Denver metro area is all too typical.) Four different species of maples developed chlorosis (yellowed leaves caused by iron deficiency due to our highly alkaline soil) and eventually had to be removed. The bacterial disease, fire blight, felled a crabapple and an eating apple. Borers got a pear and a peach.

After a decade and a half of tree torture, shade still mostly eludes me. Meanwhile, in one of those perverse turns of human nature, I've become fascinated by the wealth of plants that tolerate, or actually require, shade. I'm determined to grow as many of these as I can fit into the few shady spots in the garden. A ponderosa pine in the front of the house and an Austrian pine in the back play host to dozens of shade plants, resembling brooding hens trying to cover as many eggs as possible at one sitting. Still, I have some experience with the frustration shade can generate.

A silver maple, which survived and in fifteen years reached 30 feet in height, gave me a taste of the kind of shade that stymies other, more generously tree-endowed gardens. The soil beneath this maple was strangled with a network of fibrous roots, making it impossible to dig without a strong will and a mattock. These same roots deprived plants growing beneath the maple of both water and nutrients. Even so, I was able to find a few plants that were up to the silver maple's challenge. So why does shade continue to baffle and defeat so many gardeners?

Dappled light beneath a honey locust is ideal for a wide range of perennials, including yellow foxglove *Digitalis grandiflora*. **Arbogast garden, Centennial, Colorado.**

I suspect it might be because most of us have a greater familiarity with sun-loving plants. Children are drawn to showy flowers. Among my first memories are of black-eyed Susans growing along the roadsides in Maryland where I lived as a child and of my grandmother's towering hollyhocks in her Wisconsin garden. New gardeners are often attracted to these old favorites and other ubiquitous garden perennials, such as tall bearded iris, Shasta daisy, and chrysanthemum—sun-lovers all. Woodland wildflowers with their understated, and sometimes, frankly bizarre flowers may be an acquired taste, unless you were lucky enough to grow up near an undisturbed woodland.

Might the fact that so few gardeners in our region are native born and raised add to the conundrum? Most of us came here from places where we learned a different horticultural language, so to speak. Rhododendrons, azaleas, mountain laurels, and lacecap hydrangeas, solid choices for shade in other parts of the country, are not well suited for life in the Intermountain West for a variety of reasons. Many of these are plants adapted to the acidic soils of the deciduous forests of the Pacific Northwest or the Northeast and are utterly intolerant of the prevailing alkalinity in our region. Furthermore, they may struggle with our low atmospheric humidity. Other familiar shade plants are not hardy enough to withstand winters here. Hardy broadleaf evergreens may be fried by our intense winter sunshine—or they may be desiccated by relentless, fierce winds. Planting such maladapted old friends nearly always results in their failure and reinforces the impression that gardening in the shade is, if anything, even more of a challenge here.

Garden writers perpetuate the myth that gardening in shade is impossibly difficult. Just about every book on shade gardening apologizes for the "limited selection" of plants for shade. One explanation for this might be because garden writers tend to be plant collectors whose gardens represent a modern day Noah's Ark, with one of every species known to man. Most gardeners are satisfied with fewer choices and will find the hundreds of flowers and shrubs that do thrive in shade in our region more than adequate.

Shade and Its Endless Variables

Before deciding which plants are adapted to your garden, it is important to understand the endless variables of shade. Most garden books and nursery catalogs generally divide shade into three categories: light, medium, and dense. But shade is much more complex. There as many microclimates in shade as there are in full sun. Many factors affect the level and quality of shade, including: number of hours of direct and indirect sunlight, time of day and time of year that shade patterns occur, and environmental conditions. For example, house walls have a different effect on plants than do trees.

Light shade (shade that lasts for only a few hours each day) and dappled shade (the type of shade in a lath house or under an open branched deciduous tree, such as a honey locust) hardly count as shade at all in our sun-drenched climate. I've had tomatoes set fruit in light shade. The only plants that might not do well in light shade are those with desert origins and those few that, like most of the penstemons, require direct sunlight for the entire day and object to even the slight shading that comes from being too crowded in a flower bed.

Open shade (shade on the east and north sides of structures or tree and shrub masses) is another situation that will hardly affect plant selection at all. These spots tend to be very sunny in the early hours of the morning and shaded in the hottest part of the day. Most plants get sufficient light, at least in spring and early summer, before longer shadows are cast.

In fact, dappled shade and the open shade provided by eastern and northern exposures are often the best locations to grow traditional garden plants, many of which are absolute sun-lovers in other regions. Roses, lilies, and a host of perennials benefit from five to six hours of unobstructed morning sunlight followed by the protection shade provides during brutally hot summer afternoons. This is the perfect place for the "oasis" garden—a garden of plants that is not strictly adapted to this region but that the gardener can't bear to live without. If you absolutely must have rhododendrons, the east or north side of the house is where they will most likely survive. Here they are protected from the drying winter sun and summer heat. Another benefit is that the same plant grown on the east side of the house will need less water than its counterpart in full sun.

The most difficult open shade microclimate is the west side of the house. Here shade occurs in the morning hours. Then the sun hits full force in the afternoon—at the same time of day when the highest temperatures are recorded. Except on those days when thunderstorms threaten, which can be most afternoons in the late spring and summer. This combines the worst of both worlds. It's too shady for true sun-worshippers like the aforementioned penstemons. Plus, on days without cloud cover, the heat from the afternoon sun is further intensified by heat reflected from the structure itself, making conditions far too toasty for woodland flowers. On alternating days plants may either fry or receive no sunlight whatsoever.

"Part shade," "medium shade," and "moderate shade" all describe conditions similar to those found in open woodlands. This is not the near-total darkness found on the floor of a mature conifer forest but the soft light that gets through where the trees thin out at the forest edge. A grove of aspens creates this effect as sunlight filters through the foliage. In such places, the undergrowth is tangled and varied. A comparable environment exists in the garden whenever two to three hours of sunlight hits the area directly or when there is a half day of indirect or reflected light. The majority of shade plants are compatible with medium shade.

A few situations go beyond what any plant can reasonably be expected to endure. In truly dense shade, where little or no sunlight reaches, almost nothing will grow. Dense shade might be found beneath a deck or a mature spruce, under wide eaves on the north or east side of the house, or between towering walls in urban areas. So, why fight it? This is bound to be the coolest, most comfortable spot in the garden in summer. If the area is large enough, why not build a patio or a deck? Or, simply spread cedar mulch and set out a few pots of

Even true sun-lovers like yellow-flowered sulfur buckwheat get enough light to bloom in the open shade beneath a Scots pine *Pinus sylvestris* in the Kelaidis' garden.

Crabapples and pines create the medium shade conditions found in open woodlands. Shady Lane at DBG.

houseplants, indulging them in a summer vacation out of doors.

The amount of light any area receives can change dramatically from season to season. North- and east-facing microclimates that get ten hours of morning sunlight in June may be totally eclipsed by the house later in the season. The northeast-facing front of my house basks in nearly full sun early in the growing season, but by the end of summer not one ray of sunlight reaches this area. Every winter a "glacier" of unmelted snow forms here after the first heavy snowfall and sticks around until spring, protected from melting by the shadow of the house.

The quantity and quality of light also changes over time. As young trees mature, the shadows they cast become increasingly dense and the area they shade grows larger with each passing season. Sun-loving peonies and iris cease blooming and once healthy junipers develop diseases, their resistance lowered as the light dims. Successful gardens change with the circumstances.

All plants need light to conduct photosynthesis, but they do differ in their light requirements and shade-tolerance depending on their geographic origins. Woodland plants are genetically adapted to low light levels. Most have characteristically large leaves to capture any available light efficiently. Many bloom early in the year to catch the sun's rays and the attention of pollinators before the trees leaf out. With oversized leaves, the pulmonaria is prototypical of shade plants. Its flowers bloom as soon as the snow melts, long before deciduous shrubs and trees break their winter dormancy. It, like most plants with woodland origins, can be damaged if subjected to too much sunlight.

Guessing which shade plants will thrive in your own given set of conditions is always a bit of a gamble. It helps to recognize the symptoms a plant exhibits when it is getting too much or too little sunlight. Shade-loving plants subjected to too much direct sunlight appear scorched, which tells the whole story. They are, in fact, sunburned. Badly burned plants may die from their injuries.

Signs that a plant is getting too little sunlight are usually subtler. Often the only indication that something is wrong is when a perfectly healthy-looking plant fails to bloom. More serious light deprivation may cause the plant to lean toward the light and grow taller, skinnier and paler, and eventually to expire. Don't be alarmed though, when an otherwise healthy plant leans toward the light but does not exhibit any other signs of distress. In this case the plant is simply being opportunistic, trying to grab a few more rays of sunlight.

Figuring out the light needs of a plant before you try it can be frustrating. Nursery catalogs and garden books attempt to give some sort of a shade/sun designation in their descriptions. But the experiences of gardeners from other parts of the country can be misleading for gardeners in our region. Many perennials, for example, need afternoon shade to grow at all in the Deep South. The same plants might prefer full sun in our climate, where the nights are cool and the air less humid.

In recent years, many new plant introductions have come from the Pacific Northwest, where sunny days can be rare events. A plant that insists on full sun in Seattle might be perfectly content with, and indeed might demand, three to four hours of sunshine in Denver. The best thing to do is to make an educated guess—and be prepared to move any plant that is not thriving.

Gardening Under Trees

Urban forests create their own special shade conditions. Gardening successfully under large trees depends a lot on the type of tree. Those with heavy dense canopies, like my silver maple, can effectively prevent any sunlight from reaching the ground. Open branched trees such as honey locusts are better choices. Faced with an over-abundance of tree-cast shade, consider hiring an arborist to prune out a few large limbs or limb up mature trees to allow in more light from the sides. Many older neighborhoods are choked with bird-planted saplings of weedy trees such as Siberian elms. Consider removing these and

With leaves large enough to capture every ray of sunlight that penetrates the gloom, pulmonarias are prototypical of plants that evolved in shade.

Take care when gardening under trees—cutting roots or raising the soil level can kill a valuable tree. PlantAsia at DBG.

thinning out groves of green ash, maples, and cottonwoods.

Tree roots present additional problems. Shallow-rooted trees are difficult to garden under. Maples and spruces are among the worst offenders, forming an impenetrable mat of roots on the soil surface, but clay soil encourages surface rooting of many otherwise deep-rooted trees. Digging a few test holes will reveal whether you have a challenge on your hands. If you can dig at all, you can plant in that area.

You might be tempted to raise the soil level by piling soil over compacted tree roots or digging out a section of roots, but doing either can kill the tree. So, first consider how much you value this tree. I wouldn't recommend taking the risk with a mature oak or a linden but my silver maple was fair game. Since I didn't care whether it lived or died and wouldn't have been heartbroken if I had hastened its demise, I tore up roots and added soil with reckless abandon. (Naturally, it didn't die— that required a professional crew and a chainsaw).

Besides filling up every square inch of available soil, tree roots are also greedy and gluttonous, grabbing up all of the water and nutrients, effectively out-consuming more genteel companions at their feet. When gardening beneath trees, it is helpful to dig in plenty of compost or well-rotted manure to replicate the humusy conditions found on the floor of a deciduous tree forest. This is one instance when sphagnum peat moss is worth its hefty cost. Because it holds up to twenty times its weight in water, this product helps the soil retain moisture. A thick mulch of shredded leaves or pine needles also helps conserve soil moisture.

Plants growing under trees require more frequent irrigation than those in shade cast by a structure. So before planting thirsty hostas and ferns consider whether providing the extra water is practical or whether this is a good use of such a scarce resource. Where space allows, putting the hostas on the east or north side of the house and choosing a drought-tolerant ground cover for under the tree might be a better option.

Or not. This brings up another consideration unique to our region. Gardeners with expansive clay soils should not place irrigated gardens next to their foundation walls. Doing so risks expensive-to-repair damage to the foundation or the basement. Most house warranties prohibit any planting within a specified distance from the house walls. After the warrantee expires, it is generally safe to plant drought-tolerant shrubs next to the foundation and water these by hand until they are established. Of course, the safest alternative is to leave areas next to the foundation unplanted.

The Silver Maple's Demise

The silver maple was here when we purchased our home. Since it was one of the only trees on the property, we decided to leave it be for the time being, planning to take it out at a later date when other, more appropriate, trees became established. Looking back, I realize what a huge error in judgment this was. Every year as this tree provided a larger umbrella of shade for our house, it became more indispensable. At the same time, the larger the tree grew, the more of a challenge it was to garden beneath it. Young silver maples are not difficult to garden under, but mature silver maples are another matter entirely.

Every winter I contemplated evicting this beast. But then came summer and interior comfort won out. In the meantime, I discovered a palette of perennials that would grow in shade beneath the maple where there was essentially no soil. These included bear's breech *Acanthus balcanicus*, larkspur, sea holly *Eryngium planum*, and rose campion *Lychnis coronaria*, a silver-leafed biennial with magenta or pale pink flowers. This situation called for tough, even invasive plants, so I also allowed comfrey to establish a small colony here where little else would grow. In March of 2001, I had finally had enough. Anticipating carnage, I hired a tree company to cut the maple cut down at a time of year when there wasn't much up for the work crew to damage. To protect the garden beneath the tree, we covered the area with sheets of plywood set on bricks. This

was so effective that crocuses in full bloom were undamaged in the process.

Gardening Under Pines

A ponderosa pine in front of my house and a pair of Austrian pines in the back provide more straightforward medium shade environments. Put in the first year we moved into our home, these trees have quickly grown to respectable size. As they've grown taller, each year I've pruned off two or three lower limbs to make room to maneuver beneath their branches. Pines subjected to this treatment are not harmed, nor do they look unnatural if no more than about one-third of the trunk is exposed at any one time.

Bear's breech is one of a handful of perennials tough enough to survive underneath a silver maple. (Photo by R. Tatroe)

Top: Shade-loving perennials crowd together beneath a ponderosa pine.

Bottom: Magenta wild geraniums, golden columbine, white goat's beard, 'Pewter Moon' coral bells, and the brown spikes of roundleaf alumroot *Heuchera cylindrica*. (Photo by R. Tatroe)

Pines are very effective at blocking rainfall from reaching the soil at their base, instead directing runoff along the branches and out to the "drip line" where their roots are actually growing. As a result, gardening under pines nearly always requires irrigation to compensate for the extremely dry soil beneath their branches. Pines don't seem to mind the extra water as long as the soil they are growing in is well drained. I water these areas once a week without apparent damage to the trees.

Sheltered beneath the ponderosa pine in the front yard are two beds, the south side bordering the walk to the front door and the north side between the driveway and the flagstone terrace. Light strikes the outer edges of these areas when the sun is low in the sky early and late in the day. Direct sunlight never reaches the flowers planted under the pines. In these beds I can play around with traditional shade plants like hellebores, hostas, and pulmonarias.

Designing a garden in shade is really no different than designing any other flower bed—with a couple of minor exceptions. Colors look different in shade than in sun. Dark colors in cool tones—blues, reds, and purples—have a tendency to recede in any situation. In the dark they may disappear entirely. Light colors have the opposite effect. White, silver, and the complete pastel range stand out in incandescent contrast against a dark backdrop and so brighten up shaded areas considerably. Colors that show up well at dusk are the best choices for heavy shade. Similarly, variegated foliage is valuable for bringing in the illusion of light, creating a dappled effect where sunlight never actually reaches.

On the north side of the pine, I've used several types of variegated foliage, along with white and pale flowers. Conventional wisdom counsels against combining different types of variegation, but I find in some instances, they are not only compatible, but highly so. The leaves of the edible strawberry *Fragaria ananassa* 'Variegata' are boldly splashed with white. Their runners reach out and entwine tufts of silver-edged sedge *Carex*

conica 'Hime Kansugi', a grasslike plant that shimmers in the soft light. In the same vicinity *Pulmonaria* 'Spilled Milk' is so heavily washed with silver it shines with the ethereal quality of dragonfly wings. Next to the trunk of the pine where no direct light ever reaches, a mass of unremarkable greenery of the goat's beard *Aruncus dioicus* erupts into a delicate foam of white plumes in early summer, its flowers echoing the white of the variegated foliage in this bed.

A couple of alum roots join this grouping. One is a peculiar, little-known western native with brown flowers *Heuchera cylindrica*—definitely a "designer plant" in the same category as bronze-hued *Carex buchananii* and brown-flowered primroses. But its coppery flowers make perfect sense when placed next to *Heuchera* 'Pewter Moon' which has similar coloration. The exquisite large leaves of this heuchera are marked with silver patches heavily divided by dark bronze veins, reminiscent of a stained-glass window.

Close to the path is a clump of variegated sylvan woodrush *Luzula nivea*, another handsome grass imposter, with wide blades finely edged in silver. Other low perennials line the walk where more sunlight penetrates the gloom. The hardy geranium *Geranium cinereum* 'Splendens' lives up to its name with splendid magenta flowers. Siberian bellflower *Campanula poscharskyana* molds itself around the flagstones and sends up hundreds of lavender-blue bells in late spring. Pale yellow fumewort *Corydalis ochroleuca* has self-sown throughout this area (requiring at least one session each spring on hand and knees pulling out hundreds of seedlings—this little weed is too pretty to ban and too small to deadhead easily).

Further back from the walk, purple blossoms of the native wild geranium *Geranium viscosissimum* and golden yellow celandine poppy *Stylophorum diphyllum* brighten the shade in early summer. This duet features impressively large and handsome foliage and carries their flowers high aloft on tall stems.

On the driveway side of the bed, several invasive spreaders grow up, over, and around one another,

Top left: Lady's mantle has tiny chartreuse flowers and elegant, downy foliage.

Top right: Goat's beard *Aruncus dioicus* sends up white plumes in late spring.

Bottom: Golden columbine *Aquilegia chrysantha* self-sows in shady places.

making a tapestry of foliage and flowers. I continually battled yellow archangel *Lamiastrum galeobdolon* in my garden in England (and lost), so it was with some trepidation that I finally decided to see what it would do in my Colorado garden. It still spreads with great glee, but is not so difficult to control in this drier, less fertile situation. Other well-known pests, lady's mantle *Alchemilla mollis,* the mourning widow *Geranium phaeum,* and the snowdrop anemone *Anemone sylvestris* make good companions—they are all up to one another's grab for more territory. While I wasn't looking, this gang of three consumed the better-behaved yellow-leafed spotted dead nettle *Lamium maculatum* 'Beedham's White'. Other spotted nettles could have stood their ground against these hooligan neighbors, but the chartreuse varieties are meek and mild-mannered and cannot compete.

In the southwest corner of the backyard, for the first ten years, ground-cover junipers grew beneath two Austrian pines. When I removed the junipers to make room for flowers, I discovered that this was the best soil on my entire property, a silty loam. Amending this area with mushroom compost created the perfect soil for woodland wildflowers. The garden is still relatively new, but so far a mix of unusual bulbs and wildflowers thrive in the shelter of the pines. The uncommonly good soil greatly expands the numbers of plant choices. The season starts with a succession of unusual bulbs, including the delicate greenish-yellow bells of *Fritillaria pontica* in April. About the same time blooms the checkered lily *Fritillaria meleagris,* also known as Guinea hen flower or snake's head fritillaria. With a herringbone pattern of purple and white, this flower never fails to catch the notice of visitors who exclaim over their unique coloration. Crowds of English bluebells *Hyacinthoides non-scripta* mingle with the western native *Camassia quamash* 'Blue Melody', with distinctive variegated foliage and star-shaped pale blue flowers.

Orange seems an unlikely color for a shade-loving flower, but in summer, three lilies of woodland origin, bloom resplendent in orange hues. The first to bloom, a western native, leopard lily *Lilium pardalinum,* has nodding burnt orange,

A small grove of aspens and Austrian pines creates a shady glen in a very hot backyard. Tatroe garden.

Cream and sage-gray comfrey *Symphytum grandiflorum* **'Goldsmith' with maroon and cream auricula primroses. (Photo by R. Tatroe)**

maroon-spotted flowers. Also native, more commonly to the eastern United States but occasionally found in the Rocky Mountains, is the wood lily *Lilium philadelphicum* with upright-facing orange flowers. *Lilium henryi* from China, is the beanpole of the three, with stems that reach 5 to 6 feet and lean on the lower branches of the pine.

After the lilies finish in late August, colchicums take over. These shade-loving bulbs resemble pink crocuses and flower without accompanying foliage. The foliage comes up in spring, then disappears and stays dormant while the flowers are up. Where the sunlight never penetrates grow red-flowered *Trillium sessile*, yellow merry-bells *Uvularia grandiflora*, wood aster *Aster divaricatus*, bugbane *Cimicifuga mairei*, with fragrant white flowers, and several species of hellebore. At the outer edge of the pine boughs, where light hits directly for a few hours each day, ivory-flowered monkshood *Aconitum septentrionale* 'Ivorine', Rocky Mountain columbine *Aquilegia caerulea*, and the purple woodland penstemon *Penstemon whippleanus* recreate a stylized mountain scene.

Learning by Trial and Error

Although my experience with shade is not vast and the percentage of shade in my own garden is relatively small, the northeast side of my house provided me with a hard lesson. We moved here in September and at that time this side of the house was completely shaded. I decided this was the ideal place for ferns and hostas. (It was the *only* place for ferns and hostas—there was not another square foot of shade on our entire property.) We took out some overgrown pfitzer junipers along the foundation that were threatening to obscure the living room window and amended the soil with 4 to 6 inches of organic matter. Then I planted a selection of bare root ferns and hostas, along with Meserveae hollies, bleeding hearts, and a few other plants recommended for shade.

Several things transpired over the next couple of years. First, it became apparent that early in the year this part of the garden is anything but shaded. Sunlight hits this area in spring through early summer directly from sunrise until well after noon, a total of seven hours each day. By anyone's definition this is "full sun." Moreover, I had not anticipated how potent the spring sunshine is in Colorado. With no haze or cloud cover to act as filters, shade lovers sunburned badly. Later that summer the light shifted, things recovered and I was lulled into a false sense of complacency. The following year there was a bad hailstorm, and with no trees to block the hail, this area looked like it had been gone over with a salad shooter. Other parts of the garden outgrew the damage but my shade garden, which was right next to the front door where there was no way to avoid looking at it, was in tatters for the rest of the season.

The last straw was when we discovered water leaking into the crawl space. Our house was seven years old when we bought it and even though the previous owner had given us a package of instructions from the builder, I had neglected to read them thoroughly. When I did after the fact, I discovered that our house is built on bentonite clay soil and was highly susceptible to water damage. At that point I dug up thirsty ferns and hostas and gave them away. Then began a search for plants that could handle full sun for half the growing season and full shade for the rest of the year. They also had to get by on very little irrigation. Of course, no such list existed—even though nearly every new house on the high plains presents exactly the same situation.

The bleeding hearts were a clue. They like strong sunlight in spring but go dormant by the time this area is plunged into deep shade later in the season. Virginia bluebells are equally happy here as are false Solomon seal and camassia. None of these are drought-tolerant plants by any definition, but they get plenty of water from the melting accumulation of snow to get through their spring growth spurt. These plants are spring ephemerals, a group of flowers adapted to deciduous forests. They come up in spring to take advantage of light, moisture, and nutrients before the trees come out of dormancy. After blooming, they go dormant, their foliage dying back

Pink bleeding hearts and blue camassia—spring ephemerals like these take advantage of spring moisture and then disappear during the heat of summer. (Photo by R. Tatroe)

Left: Traditional perennial flowers appreciate morning sunlight and protection from the sun during the hottest hours in the afternoon. Tatroe garden.

Above: Plants with chartreuse foliage like *Centaurea* 'Gold Bullion' brighten a blue, yellow, and white color scheme.

to the ground; spring ephemerals don't need much water during their dormancy, making them ideally suited to the conditions here.

Deciduous shrubs hide the holes left when these flowers melt away. What I needed were shrubs rated for sun or shade that were also xeric. Admittedly, there aren't many, but there are more than you might imagine. Daphnes don't mind these conditions, nor do many of our native shrubs, such as the little leaf mock orange and sumacs, which put up with a similar environment in the canyonlands of the Southwest. Shrub roses are another option, preferably the varieties that bloom only once in spring. These don't need sunlight later in the season to stimulate a second flush of flowers.

Over the years I've tried and tossed out a half dozen shrubs for various reasons. A variegated 'Carol Mackie' daphne was glorious for a time—until its wide-spreading branches were crushed by a succession of heavy snows. A more upright green-leafed 'Somerset' daphne continues to thrive, cloaking itself in deliciously fragrant flowers in spring and again in late summer. No one would ever accuse white forsythia *Abeliophyllum distichum* of actually thriving, but I keep this nondescript little shrub because it flowers very early with the daffodils and grape hyacinths. Pressed up against the house wall, Korean spice viburnum *Viburnum carlesii*, blooms only a bit later, its pink buds opening to white flowers that are exceedingly fragrant.

Of the shrubs, roses predominate. Because they do so well in this protected spot, I replace every shrub failure with a rose. 'Lady of the Dawn', a semidouble confection of ivory blushed pink and gold, normally gets four feet tall. Placed near the corner of the front porch, I anticipated the scent of "fresh-cut apples" every time I passed by. The label's promise of heavenly fragrance has not met my expectations, but by the third year this rose was so happy with this location that it sent out canes seven feet long that literally obstructed the front entrance. (To prevent bloodied visitors, I prune it back hard after the first flush of flowers in early summer.)

A few flowers other than spring ephemerals either tolerate or appreciate this exposure. Golden

EPHEMERAL PERENNIAL FLOWERS THAT GO DORMANT AFTER BLOOMING

Common Name	Botanic Name	Height	Color	Hardy To:	Water Needs
monkshood	*Aconitum* spp.	5'	varies	-40°	moderate/moist
wood anemone	*Anemone nemerosa*	12"	white, blue or pink	-40°	moderate
rue anemone	*Anemonella thalictroides*	4"	pink	-40°	moist
jack-in-a-pulpit	*Arisaema* spp.	varies	varies	-40°	moist
bulbous oat grass	*Arrhenatherum elatius* ssp. *bulbosum* 'Variegatum'	18"	n/a	-30°	moist
Italian arum	*Arum italicum*	12"	green	-40°	moist
Dutchman's breeches	*Dicentra cucullaria*	8"	white	-20°	moderate
bleeding heart	*D. spectabilis*	2–3'	pink or white	-40°	moderate
shooting star	*Dodecatheon meadia*	18"	pink	-40°	moist
leopard's bane	*Doronicum cordatum*	15"	pink	-30°	moist
liverleaf	*Hepatica americana*	6"	various	-30°	moist
June grass	*Koeleria macrantha*	12"	n/a	-30°	dry
spring vetchling	*Lathyrus vernus*	12"	pink, white, or purple	-20°	adaptable
Virginia bluebells	*Mertensia virginica*	18"	blue	-40°	moist
fernleaf peony	*Paeonia tenuifolia*	2'	magenta	-30°	moderate
Oriental poppy	*Papaver orientale*	3'	various	-50°	adaptable
Solomon's seal	*Polygonatum* spp.	24"	spring white	-40°	moist
pasqueflower	*Pulsatilla* spp.	6"	blue, white, or red	-50°	adaptable
bloodroot	*Sanguinaria canadensis*	6"	white	-40°	moist
golden banner	*Thermopsis* spp.	24–30"	yellow	-30°	moderate
wake robin	*Trillium* spp.	18"	varies	-40°	moist

Variegated bulbous oat grass is an attractive foil to roses and other perennial flowers.

Virginia bluebells.

'Golden Wings' rose appreciates the cooler afternoon temperatures of an open east-facing exposure. (Photo by R. Tatroe)

columbine *Aquilegia chrysantha* from the canyons of New Mexico is a prolific self-sower, but none of its seedlings venture out into the full sun only a few feet away. Straw foxglove *Digitalis lutea*, feverfew, moneyplant *Lunaria annua*, and muskmallow *Malva moschsata* also put up with these extremes. All four have self-sown abundantly throughout this flower bed.

A Lightly Shaded Transition Zone

Several feet farther out from the house wall is a transition zone where I can water more freely without fear of damaging the house foundation and where sunlight hits for more hours of the day for a greater part of the season. Here I can grow many things that wouldn't withstand the onslaught of the full sun in other parts of the garden. Roses do very well in this site even though they are watered only once a week, about half as often as they demand in the backyard where the orientation is toward the southwest. Even quite a distance from the house wall the soil dries out much more slowly because it is shaded for a few hours during the hottest part of the day.

A Y-shaped stone path dissects the flower bed to the east of the front door. The long leg of the 'Y' leads from the front walk to the flagstone terrace. The short side provides access to a faucet. To one side is an exuberant 'Golden Wings' rose, its large floppy yellow blossoms accented with burnished gold crowns of conspicuous stamens. Another rose, 'Dainty Bess', delicate both in constitution and demeanor, sits protected like a cherished younger sister chaperoned by two older siblings at a dance by 'Golden Wings' to the west and 'Mary Rose' to the east. Bess is a thing of exquisite beauty, with huge flowers composed of five massive pale pink petals surrounding a cluster of maroon stamens. 'Mary Rose', a vigorous David Austin old-fashioned double rose, is medium pink.

This is the place I try out oddball perennials, ones whose hardiness is uncertain, as well as several varieties of tall garden phlox, sun-lovers that seem to appreciate some respite from the heat of the day.

This is the only spot where I've had any luck with Jacob's ladder *Polemonium caeruleum,* a dainty perennial with fernlike foliage and spikes of lavender blue flowers in May. Drumstick primrose *Primula denticulata,* in several shades of pink, appreciates the very heavy moisture-retentive soil and the early morning sunshine. The perennial forget-me-not *Brunnera macrophylla* 'Langtrees' comes up and blooms the minute the snow melts, its clusters of tiny true blue flowers in contrast to large rough leaves splattered with white spots—as if a slightly careless housepainter has been at work.

The Sunset Garden

The narrow side yard on the west side was initially the most problematic spot in the garden. Adjacent to a five-acre open space, there were no structures or trees to block the full force of the afternoon sun. When we moved into our home in September 1987, nothing was here but a 14 by 50-foot strip of lawn bordered by a utilitarian fence of chain link and two-by-fours. A section of 6-foot-tall privacy fence and a gate spanned the opening between the perimeter fence and the house. Entered from the front yard off the driveway, this was the only access to the backyard.

Behind the orphaned fence panel lurked one of those giant tractor tires that parents bring home for their kids to play in (and then wish they hadn't when they discover that the tire turns anything that touches it black). The tire was home to a half dozen mature black widow spiders. Two purple sand cherries, one on each corner of the house, were the only other living things occupying the space. This was the hottest spot on our entire property. And it had all of the charm of a dog run. Because it was a relatively small space and looked so embarrassingly bad, remedying this situation was our number one priority that first fall.

We got rid of the tire and, with the help of our two teen-aged sons, stripped the sod by hand. Next we dug in a truckload of compost. By now it was quite late in the year, but we forged ahead anyway and planted shrubs and trees gleaned from

A 'Canada Red' chokecherry shades the west side of the Tatroe house.

Top: Red and orange shades of daylilies bring sunset tones into the garden.

Bottom: Sultry purple hellebores with white-splotched *Arum italicum* 'Pictum'. (Photo by R. Tatroe)

end-of-season clearance sales. (This was fortuitous, as it turned out. Shrubs and trees that have survived an entire summer in pots in a nursery are a good bet in the Darwinian scheme of things—every one of them survives to this day.) Lastly, we laid out a meandering path to de-emphasize the tunnel effect of the long, narrow space.

The following spring, a 'Canada Red' chokecherry, an upright juniper, and two reddish-purple 'Rosy Glow' barberries were thriving, giving us a false sense of how difficult this site would turn out to be. Naively, I planted flowers, which did very well until summer arrived—and then the heat did them in. This was when I discovered that the side of the house was too hot to touch with a bare hand in the heat of the day. Heat continued to radiate from the wall well into the evening hours.

I tried many different types of flowers, and only a few were truly successful. In the meantime, the shrubs and trees were doing just fine. Over the years, I added 'Gold Flame' and 'Magic Carpet' spireas, beautybush *Kolkwitzia amabilis*, false indigo *Amorpha fruticosa*, rose of Sharon, shadblow serviceberry *Amelanchier canadensis*, variegated dogwood, wayfaring tree *Viburnum lantana*; and a selection of shrub roses (a single-flowered gallica; 'Alika'; 'Pink Meideland'; 'Scarlet Meideland'; 'Henry Kelsey'; the David Austin rose 'Sweet Juliet', and a few unnamed miniatures. All of these have been successful regardless of weather, water availability, or changing light circumstances.

Also flourishing at the sunny southwest end of the walk is a massive 10-foot-tall red-leafed rose *Rosa glauca* that started life as a 6-inch-tall seedling. Birds planted Virginia creeper at its feet. These have grown into a network of vines that shroud the rose and travel yards in each direction along the fenceline. A less vigorous rose would have been smothered long ago. The rose and the Virginia creeper are particularly attractive together in autumn when their foliage becomes orange and scarlet, respectively. Bright scarlet rose hips on wine-colored canes and the vine's blue fruit add even more color.

Over the next ten years, conditions in this garden changed quite radically. The chokecherry developed into a magnificent specimen, as tall as our two-story house wall, shading a good third of the area during the growing season. Other shrubs have also matured and afford protection beneath their branches. On a hot afternoon, this is now one of the most pleasant places in the garden. It should have been a simple matter to expand the palette of perennials that would grow here by choosing from the dozens adapted to shade. But about the same time the garden matured, water shortages became a fact of life.

A wide range of woodland plants would be right at home amongst the shrubs and trees—if only I could spare the water for them. Hostas and primroses that were successful for a time suffered badly, but pulmonarias and a few intrepid ferns persisted. Also outlasting the drought were bergenia, brunnera, many varieties of clematis, toad lily *Tricyrtis formosana,* wood dittany *Cunila origanoides,* orange-flowered *Geum* x *borisii,* Christmas rose *Helleborus niger* 'Maximus', bottlebrush grass, and the hardy fountain grass cultivars 'Hameln' and 'Cassian'. All of these subsisted on one-half inch of water per week during the extremely hot summers of 2002 and 2003.

This garden is built upon a sultry color palette of orange, red, purple, and apricot flowers intermingled with burgundy and silver foliage. My inspiration was a photo in a magazine of a harvest arrangement of eggplant, purple string beans, red onions, lavender mums, and magenta dahlias. The color scheme echoes the blazing sunsets that frequently set the horizon alight just beyond the fenceline. I've concentrated on perennials with both flower and foliage color that reinforce the sunset theme. Daylilies cover every nuance of this color range and so a number of these provide the underpinnings for this garden in midsummer. They need some light to bloom well, so I've placed daylilies in spots where a modicum of sunlight gets through. Of these, dark colored varieties, in reds, scarlets, and purples, are prone to fading in full sun. They hold their color much better in this partly shaded situation.

Some flowers in the sunset theme are more shade-tolerant and can be positioned where less light penetrates. Because there is a plethora of heucheras with red flowers or reddish-purple foliage, I've used a large selection of these tough plants, adding more as new introductions become available ('Amber Waves', 'Cascade Dawn', 'Cherries Jubilee', 'Chocolate Ruffles', 'Dale's Strain', ' Plum Pudding', 'Silver Scrolls', 'Swirling Fantasy', 'Obsidian', and *Heuchera villosa purpurea*). Other purple-leafed plants that do well here include: *Persicaria* 'Red Dragon', purple-leafed wood spurge *Euphorbia amygdaloides* 'Purpurea', *Eupatorium* 'Chocolate', Japanese parsley *Cryptotaenia japonica* 'Atropurpurea', and New Zealand hairy sedge *Carex comans* 'Bronze '.

To mimic the effect of dappled sunlight, I've also added a number of white and cream variegated plants, including pulmonarias ('Excalibur', 'Majesty', Milky Way', 'Opal', 'Raspberry Splash', and *Pulmonaria longifolia* ssp. *cevennensis*), and *Heuchera* 'Snow Angel'. Adding an airy touch are several fairly drought-tolerant ferns: *Dryopteris dilitata* 'Lepodata Cristata', *D. filix-mas* 'Undulata Robusta', *Polystichum acrostichoides,* and the Japanese painted fern *Athyrium niponicum* 'Pictum', with foliage washed in both silver and purple.

The Raised Planter

When we built a grape arbor over the patio, we incorporated into it a raised planter 12 feet long, 3 feet wide, and 2 feet deep. Crosshatched slat panels covered with clematis screen the planter on two sides and abut the house wall on the third. A Niagara grape grows on the trellis overhead and further shades this area. No direct sunlight reaches the planter, but it's fairly bright just the same because of its southwest orientation. Of all of my shade gardens, this is the one I can most easily manipulate.

The soil is a mixture of approximately half clay and half organic matter. Because it is a planter, I can water daily if necessary in the summer months without violating watering restrictions. Even

Blue and white hardy geraniums beneath a golden hops vine in Mary Ellen Tonsing's garden in Littleton, Colorado.

though I generally water no more than once or twice a week, having the option gives me a place where I can grow a few desirable perennials that wouldn't get enough water elsewhere in the garden. Here I can grow *Ligularia* 'The Rocket', its handsome, heart-shaped, purple-tinged leaves, toothed at the edges. Nearby is *Lobelia* 'Queen Victoria', with purple leaves and bright red flowers. Finely cut, silvery foliage of *Dicentra* 'Luxuriant' brightens the gloom, with rose-red flowers all summer. The white trumpets of 'Honey Bells' hosta perfume the adjoining patio for several weeks in late summer. This is also where houseplants can safely spend the summer out-of-doors, left in their containers and dropped in between the permanent residents.

Shade Gardening in Established Gardens

In an older neighborhood in Littleton, Colorado, Mary Ellen Tonsing's experience with shade is typical of urban areas across our region. Unlike those of us in newer suburbs, creating shade was not a consideration—she already had more than enough. Her home, an original farmhouse built in 1915, sits off to one side of the one-acre property, surrounded by trees. Remnants of an earlier garden remained when she moved into the home thirty years ago. A few unusual trees and shrubs such as hemlocks and uncommon varieties of honeysuckles were planted among the trees. A large greenhouse the same vintage as the farmhouse sat at the back of the property.

The largest garden "room," across the driveway from the house, is screened by a row of towering blue spruces. Three other sides of this large rectangle are lined with mature shade trees that were planted to provide privacy from a busy street and from neighboring properties. Beds surrounding a Victorian gazebo in the center of the garden get enough sunlight for traditional perennials and roses. The rest of the garden around the perimeter of this area is shaded beneath the large trees.

Today these mixed borders of shrubs, wildflowers, ferns, perennials, and dwarf evergreens are as

Though other ferns may do well in this region, depending on microclimates, Mary Ellen recommends these as the best adapted:

Common Name	Botanic Name	Height	Hardiness Zone
dwarf maidenhair	*Adiantum aleuticum* 'Subpumilum'	3–4"	5
Himalayan maidenhair	*A. venustum*	8–12"	5
European lady fern (many cultivars)	*Athyrium felix-femina*	1–2'	4
Japanese painted fern	*A. niponicum* 'Pictum'	15"	4
holly fern	*Cyrtomium fortunei*	12–30"	5
bulblet bladder fern	*Cystopteris bulbifera*	18–36"	3
golden-scaled male fern	*Dryopteris affinis*	2–3'	4
Champion's wood fern	*D. championii*	1–3'	5
autumn fern	*D. erythrosora*	18–24"	5
male fern (and cultivars)	*D. filix-mas*	2–4'	4
Goldie's wood fern	*D. goldiana*	3–3'	3
Mexican wand fern	*D. pseudo-filix-mas*	30–48"	5
Siebold's wood fern	*D. sieboldii*	1–2'	6
oak fern	*Gymnocarpium dryopteris*	9–12"	2
limestone oak fern	*G. robertianum*	9–18"	2
Christmas fern	*Polystichum acrostichoides*	1–2'	3
soft shield fern	*P. setiferum* 'Divisilobum Plumosum'	18"	5

Japanese painted fern and black mondo grass.

lush and colorful as any gardener could hope. But Mary Ellen remembers when she was concerned that nothing would grow in such heavy shade. In the mid-1980s, she started volunteering at the Rock Alpine Garden at Denver Botanic Gardens. When Panayoti Kelaidis, curator at that time, learned of her frustrations, he gave her lists of plants that would grow in shade. Every time Panayoti introduced her to a new family of plants, Mary Ellen built a new border to accommodate them.

As luck would have it, the soil in this garden was more friable, better drained and more organic than most found in the Front Range. Mary Ellen suspects the topsoil was never removed and that this area had once been a field where crops were grown. Even so, the pH is still too high for many of the acid-loving plants that are the standard fare in shaded gardens in other parts of the country. Still, through trial and error, Mary Ellen has developed a unique blend of hundreds of flowering shrubs and perennials well suited to her site.

Several tall shrubs planted beneath the trees provide extra screening from the neighboring properties and the street. One of these, beautybush *Kolkwitzia amabile* is a big, rangy shrub with yellow-throated coral-pink flowers in spring followed by bristly brown seed capsules that persist into summer. Probably the most striking characteristic of this shrub is bark that exfoliates much like a paper birch. Also a good understory shrub for blocking out street noise and unsightly views is 10-foot-tall Ural false spirea *Sobaria sorbifolia*. With handsome dark green foliage, this shrub suckers freely into an ever-expanding thicket. In early summer, false spirea produces fluffy white plumes up to 10 inches long. Mary Ellen is also extremely fond of *Viburnum* x *bodnantense*, one of the first shrubs to flower in the new year, often as early as February. Though damaged by weather some years, the soft pink and sweetly fragrant flowers are a reminder that spring is just around the corner.

Other shrubs in her borders include weeping hemlock *Tsuga canadensis* 'Bennett', Japanese rose *Kerria japonica* 'Picta', *Viburnum carlesii*, *Cotoneaster salicifolius repens*, *Rhododendron* 'Faisa', and Japanese maple *Acer palmatum* 'Seiryu'. 'Bennett' is a slow-growing dwarf form of

Canada hemlock, with dark green needles toward the center of the shrub highlighted by pale green new growth at the tips. The bright yellow flowers of the kerria glow in the dark in spring, and the creamy white variegation of the leaves lighten and brighten the shade the rest of the season. Small-leafed 'Faisa' rhododendron has lavender flowers. Finely dissected leaves of *Acer palmatum* 'Seiryu' emerge bright green tinged red in spring, turning yellow and crimson in autumn.

The most powerfully and sweetly scented of the viburnum clan, the Korean spice viburnum *Viburnum carlesii,* bears coral-blushed white flowers in spring. Furry leaves become wine red in the fall. Weaving through a large area of the long border is the unusual low and spreading form of willowy cotoneaster *Cotoneaster salicifolius* 'Repens', which travels along the ground throwing out sprays of lustrous dark green foliage decorated with red fruits. In the largest border, 100 feet long and 25 feet deep, hundreds of species of shade-loving perennials co-exist. Masses of arisaemas, trilliums, heucheras, tiarellas, asarums, black liriope, hellebores, geum, pulmonarias, cyclamens, brunnera, astilbe, and polemoniums create a rich tapestry of spring flowers and elegant foliage on the "forest floor."

Arum italicum stands out in spring and fall, producing bright green, arrow-shaped leaves, some marked in white. If these are winter-killed they reappear in spring. After the hooded white jack-in-the-pulpit-style flowers open, the foliage melts away. In late summer, the plant sends up stalks with bright orange berries, startlingly naked without their foliage. As these fade, the handsome foliage returns. Another arum, *A. maculatum,* also does well for Mary Ellen. Called lords-and-ladies, it is similar to *Arum italicum* but flowers slightly earlier in spring. The berries of both of these are toxic, so use care when planting it in a garden where small children play.

Of the hellebores, a particularly nice subspecies of Lenten rose *Helleborus orientalis,* is from the Caucasus in Russia; *H. o. abchasicus* is Mary Ellen's all-time favorite. Its greenish flowers are spotted, striped and washed with reddish-purple.

In early spring, the star of the show is the double bloodroot *Sanguinaria canadensis* 'Flore Pleno', an Eastern woodland wildflower with bright white star-shaped flowers. Surprisingly easy to grow, it once commanded a king's ransom, until the connoisseur's demand for this extraordinary plant was somewhat sated. From Japan and Korea comes another graceful woodland wildflower, yellow waxbells *Kirengeshoma palmata*, which produces pale yellow nodding flowers in late summer and fall.

Nothing will grow under the grand old spruces next to the driveway except cyclamen. But these magnificent flowers have multiplied in the dry shade to form carpets of exotically marbled and patterned foliage in spring. The leaves disappear during the summer months and then, in late summer, multitudes of tiny violet-like flowers bloom in every shade of pink imaginable. A few are pure white.

Before planting anything new, Mary Ellen digs in plenty of peat moss to make the soil more water retentive. She recommends moistening peat moss with hot water before mixing it in—otherwise it will pull all of the water out of the soil. She mulches the beds thickly with pine needles collected in the fall from two of her children's mountain properties. The pine needles lay in piles over the winter to allow grass seeds to drop out, then are spread in early spring. Regardless of how hot it gets in summer, the shade borders are watered only once or twice a week. The thick blanket of pine needles helps prevent soil moisture loss. Recent transplants get extra water from a watering can until they are established and growing strongly. As Mary Ellen says "The plants adapt."

A Garden in the Woods

Forty miles south of Denver, Rebecca Day-Skowron, owner of Rocky Mountain Rare Plants seed company, gardens in shade beneath natural groves of deciduous Gambel oaks and ponderosa pines on parts of her property. Located on the northern edge of the Black Forest at 6,500 feet in elevation, the conditions here are radically differ-

'Nova Zembla' rhododendron thrives in Rebecca Day-Skowron's shade garden.

ent from those in my own garden and from those in much of the Front Range. Winters are colder, but the trade-off is enviable soil—well-drained sandy loam with a pH that is nearly neutral.

Better known as an authority on rock alpine gardening, Rebecca's first love is eastern woodland wildflowers. A childhood in Ohio imprinted her with fond memories of playing and traipsing through the woods hunting wild morel mushrooms and wildflowers. Wood anemones, Jack-in-the-pulpit, bloodroot, and trilliums were abundant in the deciduous forests of gum, sassafras, maple, and beech. Her high-altitude shade gardens play host to many of the same flowers she treasured as a child, including trilliums and wood anemones transplanted from her grandfather's Ohio woods.

Most of Rebecca's shade collections are sheltered under one large pine with a thicket of scrub oak on either side. While only a small amount of direct sunlight reaches the ground in early morning, a great deal of filtered light makes its way through the pines' open crowns. More light passes

Japanese creeping primrose *Primula kisoana* in pine duff. (Photo by R. Tatroe)

through the bare branches of the oaks before they leaf out in the spring. A robust *Clematis alpina* ssp. *rubra* clambers over the oaks and up into the pines smothering itself in dark red bells each spring and then finishing up the year by opening up a few more flowers in late summer. When she started the garden ten years ago, Rebecca left this area unamended except for adding iron sulfate to acidify the soil. She has used Miracid as a foliar fertilizer once or twice a year since and allows pine needles to accumulate where they fall as a mulch. The garden is irrigated twice a week to keep the soil slightly and consistently moist.

The first thing gardeners from other parts of the metro area notice in her garden are the Himalayan blue poppies *Meconopsis betonicifolia*. This aristocrat of the poppy family is just about impossible to grow where soils are alkaline and days are hot, so its appearance stops most visitors in their tracks. The true blue, crinkled flowers bloom alongside red rhododendrons in mid-June, saturating the quiet glen with color. Because they are such a rarity in the Front Range of Colorado, Rebecca has a party every year to celebrate the blue poppies' bloom. Rhododendrons, too, thrive under the pines, including evergreen 'Manitou' (pale pink flowers), 'Ramapo' (purplish), and 'Nova Zembla' (red). Oddly enough, 'PJM', the rhododendron most often recommended for this region, has never been a success for Rebecca. Labrador tea *Ledum groenlandicum*, another ericaceous shrub from cool, moist environs of North America also does well here.

Another surprise for area gardeners is seeing a healthy flowering dogwood *Cornus florida* 'Rainbow' with the low ground cover bunchberry *Cornus canadensis* romping underneath. This pretty little tree with yellow variegated foliage has never broken stride, blooming every year. Its leaves turn brilliant red in autumn. Rebecca found her specimen at a now defunct home improvement store one year and has never seen it offered for sale again anywhere else.

All of the usual suspects for shade are here, including large patches of epimediums, bergenia, asarums, bleeding hearts, coralbells, hostas and ferns. *Astilbe chinensis* 'Pumila' has formed a large colony that blooms pink in late summer. A few rarities make themselves at home here as well. Rebecca points with pride to a large patch of *Primula kisoana,* a Himalayan plant that is reportedly difficult to grow. Here it spreads with unrestrained glee. Nearby is *Epigaea repens,* commonly called trailing arbutus, a pink-flowered evergreen mat of a shrub that dislikes alkaline soil—not a good choice for most of the Intermountain West. The connoisseur of aroids will also enjoy seeing little *Arisaema flavum,* a species from the Himalayas with heavily divided leaves and a yellow and purple spadix, and *Arisarum proboscideum,* the mouse-tail plant, so-called because its spathes end in long, curled "tails."

Scattered throughout the plantings are *Corydalis solida,* an early-blooming bulb with upright racemes of rose-purple tubular flowers over ferny foliage. The whole colony quietly melts away when hot weather arrives in force. A close relative with staying power and similar foliage is *Corydalis linstowiana* 'Dufu Temple' that takes over when the *Corydalis solida* exits, sending up blue flowers continually until frost.

The only problems that Rebecca has encountered in this garden are slugs—she snips these in half with sharp scissors—and a few invasive plants. The most persistent is the spreading native bluebell *Mertensia lanceolata,* which was well ensconced under the oaks and pines before the garden was built (and will probably still be there long after the garden is gone). Rebecca digs these out as they emerge. Only one plant, *Geranium pratense,* routinely developed mildew, so it got the boot. A bench in the shade is Rebecca's favorite spot in the garden to sit and rest—usually with a cat on her lap—while she contemplates unfinished tasks in other, needier parts of her garden.

Dealing with Drought in the Shade Garden

Those with sunny gardens may have an easier time dealing with water restrictions and drought. For gardeners with sun, it's a simple matter of switching to better adapted plants—and our options are vast. It's hard to feel too sorry for ourselves when we replace beloved but water-guzzling lobelias with glorious desert penstemons. Meanwhile, gardeners overendowed with shade can have a rough time finding plants that tolerate both drought and shade.

Arid lands are open places where shrubs and trees are widely spaced. Other than the few shade-tolerant plants that grow in the shadow of north- or east-facing cliffs, there aren't many plants in the desert or the high plains that evolved in shade. Forests of piñon and pine that occur at drier and lower elevations of the West are also relatively open places. Companion plants tend to grow between rather than beneath the trees. Most woodland and shade plants in the nursery trade are imports from wetter climates where the annual

Shady places too dry for plants are ideal places to sit and escape summer's heat. Horovitz garden.

precipitation may be two to three times greater than ours, even in an average year.

The gardener coping with shade and drought needn't give up, but drastic measures might be necessary. In an era when "save the urban forest" is a rallying cry in our region, it seems heretical to suggest it, but every tree is not a good tree. Trees use extraordinary amounts of water. One strategy to conserve water while gaining more light is to cut down weedy or sickly trees. An arborist can help you decide which trees are extraneous and which are worth keeping. Valuable old shade trees—ash, catalpa, cottonwood, hackberry, honey locust, horse chestnut, Japanese pagoda tree, Kentucky coffeetree, lindens, red maples, and oaks—should never be removed unless there is a very good reason. But even these can be limbed up or pruned to let in more light.

There's not much you can do about it when the shade results from the neighbor's "pop-up." No plant can survive without some light and water, but even a small amount of sunlight and irrigation can greatly expand the plant palette. To improve the water-holding capacity of the soil, before planting dig in plenty of peat moss and compost. After planting, apply an organic mulch to help reduce evaporation.

The following lists contain hundreds of plants that are both cold hardy and adapted to at least some level of shade. Most of these require either moderate or consistent levels of moisture. Gardeners with generous amounts of shade would be wise to treat shade gardens as "oasis" zones, limiting themselves to small beds of such thirsty plants. A large proportion of the shade areas can be chosen from the admittedly much more limited selection of flowers, shrubs, and trees designated in the lists as "adaptable."

ANNUALS FOR SHADE

Flowering annuals produce more flowers in light or medium shade. For heavy shade, choose annuals with attractive foliage. All of the following can be grown either in containers or in the ground.

Common Name	Botanic Name	Water Needs
flowering maple	Abutilon hybrids	moderate
floss flower	Ageratum houstonianum	moist
joyweed	Alternathera spp.	moderate
asparagus fern	Asparagus densiflorus	moderate
annual woodruff	Asperula orientalis	adaptable
red orach	Atriplex hortensis ssp. rubra	moist
wax, fibrous, tuberous	Begonia hybrids	moist
amethyst flower	Browallia speciosa	moist
Canterbury bells	Campanula medium	moderate
spider plant	Chlorophytum comosum	moist
farewell-to-spring	Clarkia unguiculata	moderate
larkspur	Consolida ambigua	adaptable
Chinese forget-me-not	Cynoglossum amabile	moist
foxglove	Digitalis purpurea	moist
snow-on-the-mountain	Euphorbia marginata	adaptable
fuchsia	Fuchsia hybrids	moist
Coppertone mallow	Hibiscus acetosella 'Coppertone'	moist
polka-dot plant	Hypoestes phyllostachya	moist
busy lizzie	Impatiens walleriana	moist

Common Name	Botanic Name	Water Needs
sweet potato vine	Ipomoea batatas	adaptable
bloodleaf	Iresine lindenii	moist
edging lobelia	Lobelia erinus	moist
sweet alyssum	Lobularia maritima	moderate
moneyplant	Lunaria annua	adaptable
monkey flower	Mimulus x hybrids	moist
forget-me-not	Myosotis sylvatica	moist
baby blue eyes	Nemophila menziesii	moist
flowering tobacco	Nicotiana alata	moderate
flowering tobacco	N. sylvestris	moderate
cupflower	Nierembergia hippomanica	moist
petunia	Petunia x hybrida	adaptable
California bluebells	Phacelia campanularia	dry
Darcy sage	Salvia darcyi	moderate
butterfly flower	Schizanthus pinnatus	moist
coleus hybrids	Solenostemon scutellarioides	moist
black-eyed Susan vine	Thunbergia alata	moist
wishbone flower	Torenia fournieri	moist
pansy viola	Viola x wittrockiana	moist

Hardy cyclamen.

Most bulbs perform best in seasonal shade cast by deciduous trees and shrubs, rather than in the year-round dense shade beneath evergreens. Tropical bulbs will not survive winter in our region. Use them as annuals or dig them up and store them in a cool place over the winter.

Common Name	Botanic Name	Size	Bloom Time	Color	Hardy To:	Water Needs
lily leek	*Allium moly*	12"	early summer	yellow	-20°	adaptable
Grecian windflower	*Anemone blanda*	3"	spring	various	-20°	adaptable
tuberous begonia	*Begonia* spp.*	12"	summer	various	tropical	moderate
spring meadow saffron	*Bulbocodium vernum*	6"	spring	pink	-30°	moderate
fancy-leafed caladium	*Caladium* spp.*	20–24"	various	n/a	tropical	moist
camass	*Camassia* spp.	varies	late spring	blue or white	-30°	moderate
glory-of-the-snow	*Chionodoxa* spp.	8"	early spring	blue, pink or white	-40°	adaptable
meadow saffron	*Colchicum* spp.	3–8"	fall	pink or white	varies	moderate
autumn crocus	*Crocus speciosus*	6"	fall	lavender or white	-30°	moderate/dry
snow crocus	*C. tommasinianus*	3"	early spring	various	-30°	dry
alpine violet	*Cyclamen* spp.	6"	various	pink or white	-20°	adaptable

Common Name	Botanic Name	Size	Color	Bloom Time	Hardy To:	Water Needs
winter aconite	*Eranthis cilicica*	3"	yellow	early spring	-30°	moderate
winter aconite	*E. hyemalis*	3"	yellow	early spring	-40°	moderate
foxtail lily	*Eremurus himalaicus*	6'	white	early summer	-40°	moderate
dog's tooth violet	*Erythronium 'Pagoda'*	6–12"	yellow	spring	-30°	moderate
pineapple lily	*Eucomis spp.**	12–24"	greenish-white	summer	tropical	moist
checkered lily	*Fritillaria meleagris*	10"	purple and white	spring	-40°	moderate
Black Sea fritillary	*F. pontica*	12"	greenish-white	spring	-30°	moderate
little yellow bell	*F. pudica*	3"	yellow	spring	-30°	dry
snowdrop	*Galanthus spp.*	4–10"	white	spring	-50°	moderate
Spanish bluebell	*Hyacinthoides hispanica*	12"	blue, pink or white	spring	-40°	moderate
English bluebell	*H. non-scripta*	12"	blue	spring	-20°	moderate
spring starflower	*Ipheion uniflorum*	6"	blue or white	spring	-20°	moderate
summer snowflake	*Leucojum aestivum*	12–20"	white	summer	-30°	moderate
spring snowflake	*L. vernum*	6–12"	white	spring	-30°	moderate
Henry's lily	*Lillium henryi*	3'	orange	summer	-30°	moderate
leopard lily	*L. pardalinum*	5'	orange	summer	-30°	moderate
wood lily	*L. philadelphicum*	18"	orange-red	summer	-30°	moderate
turk's cap lily	*L. martagon*	3-4'	various	summer	-30°	moderate
magic lily	*Lycoris squamigera*	18"	pink	fall	-30°	moist
grape hyacinth	*Muscari spp.*	4–12"	blue, white or violet	spring	-40°	adaptable
orchid narcissus	*Narcissus 'Thalia'*	16"	white	spring	-40°	adaptable
Star of Bethlehem	*Ornithogalum umbellatum*	6"	white	spring	-30°	adaptable
striped squill	*Puschkinia scilloides*	5"	blue and white	spring	-40°	adaptable
Siberian squill	*Scilla siberica*	6"	blue or white	spring	-50°	adaptable

* tropical bulbs

A ground cover of sweet woodruff. Shady Lane at DBG.

A few of the following can be aggressive spreaders, either by seeds or rhizomes. Save those marked with an asterisk for a meadow-style planting.

Common Name	Botanic Name	Height	Form	Hardy To:	Water Needs
big bluestem	Andropogon gerardii	4-6'	upright, arching	-40°	adaptable
Korean feather reed grass	Calamagrostis brachytricha	3'	upright	-30°	adaptable
New Zealand hairy sedge	Carex comans 'Bronze'	18"	upright tufts	-20°	moderate
miniature variegated broad-leafed sedge	C. conica 'Marginata'	18"	tufts	-20°	moist
morning star sedge	C. grayi 'Morning Star'	18"	upright	-20°	adaptable
creeping variegated broad-leafed sedge	C. siderosticha 'Variegata'	10-16"	tufts	-20°	moist
northern sea oats	Chasmanthium latifolium	3'	upright	-30°	adaptable
tufted hairgrass	Deschampsia caespitosa	2-3'	tufts	-30°	moist
amethyst blue fescue	Festuca amethystina	1'	tufts	-30°	adaptable
manna grass	Glyceria maxima 'Variegata'*	2'	tufts	-20°	moist
golden grass	Hakonechloa macra 'Areola'	18"	arching	-20°	moist
velvet grass	Holcus lanatus*	5"	tufts	-20°	moderate
bottlebrush grass	Hystrix patula*	3'	upright	-20°	adaptable
gold-margined woodrush	Luzula sylvatica 'Marginata'	2'	tufts	-20°	adaptable
hairy melic	Melica ciliata*	18"	upright	-20°	adaptable
variegated moor grass	Molinia caerulea 'Variegata'	2'	clump	-20°	moist
switch grass	Panicum virgatum	3'	clump	-30°	adaptable
black flowering pennisetum	Pennisetum alopecuroides 'Moudry'	2-3'	clump	-20°	adaptable
ribbon grass	Phalaris arundinacea 'Feesey's Form'*	3'	upright	-30°	moist
autumn moor grass	Sesleria autumnalis	18"	upright tufts	-20°	moderate
green moor grass	S. heufleriana	2'	mound	-20°	moderate
frost grass	Spodiopogon sibiricus	3'	upright	-20°	moderate

* can be invasive

Northern sea oats.

Pigsqueak *Bergenia cordifolia.*

Common Name	Botanic Name	Size (height)	Bloom Season	Color	Hardy To:	Water Needs
bear's breech	*Acanthus balcanicus*	5'	summer	purple	-20°	adaptable
lady bells	*Adenophora* spp.	30"	midsummer	blue	-40°	moderate
bishop's weed	*Aegopodium podagraria 'Variegatum'* *	12"	late spring	white	-40°	moderate
bugleweed	*Ajuga* spp. *	6–12"	early summer	pink, blue	-40°	adaptable
lady's mantle	*Alchemilla* spp.	6–18"	early summer	chartreuse	-40°	adaptable
Peruvian lily	*Alstroemeria 'Ligtu Hybrids'*	varies by cultivar	summer	varies	-20°	adaptable
bluestar	*Amsonia* spp.	3'	early summer	blue	-50°	moderate
pearly everlasting	*Anaphalis margaritacea*	24"	late summer	white	-30°	adaptable
snowdrop anemone	*Anemone sylvestris*	18"	spring	white	-40°	moderate
columbine	*Aquilegia* spp.	6–24"	early summer	varies	-40°	adaptable
goat's beard	*Aruncus* spp.	1–3"	early summer	varies	-40°	moderate
ornamental ginger	*Asarum* spp.	varies by species	varies	varies	varies	moderate
blue wood aster	*Aster cordifolius*	4'	late summer/fall	lavender or blue	-50°	moderate
white wood aster	*A. divaricatus*	2'	fall	white	-20°	moderate
bushy aster	*A. dumosus*	16"	fall	lavender, violet, or white	-50°	moderate
masterwort	*Astrantia* spp.	2'	summer	white, pink, or red	-30°	moderate
Balkan lace	*Athamanta turbith ssp. haynaldii*	2'	early summer	white	-20°	moderate
pigsqueak	*Bergenia* spp.	18"	spring	white, pink, or red	-20°	moderate
heartleaf brunnera	*Brunnera macrophylla*	18"	spring	blue	-40°	adaptable
bellflower	*Campanula* spp.	varies by species/ cultivar	varies	varies	varies	varies
blue cohosh	*Caulophyllum thalictrioides*	30"	summer	white	-30°	adaptable
plumbago	*Ceratostigma plumbaginoides**	6"	fall	blue	-20°	adaptable
turtlehead	*Chelone* spp.	3"	fall	pink, violet	-30°	moderate
bonnet bellflower	*Codonopsis* spp.	1–2"	summer	blue	-30°	moderate
lily-of-the-valley	*Convallaria majalis**	6"	spring	white or pink	-20°	adaptable
cordydalis	*Corydalis* spp.	varies by species	varies	varies	varies	varies
American dittany	*Cunila origanoides*	8–16"	summer	white	-20°	moderate
bleeding heart	*Dicentra eximia, D. formosa*	12	spring	pink or white	-30°	moderate
gasplant	*Dictamnus albus*	30"	summer	pink or white	-40°	adaptable
foxglove	*Digitalis* spp.	varies by species	varies	varies	varies	adaptable
fairy bells	*Disporum sessile*	6"	spring	white	-20°	moderate
barren wort	*Epimedium* spp.	varies by species/ cultivar	spring	varies	varies	adaptable
wood spurge	*Euphorbia amygdaloides*	24–30"	spring	chartreuse	-20°	moderate
cushion spurge	*Euphorbia epithymoides*	18"	spring	yellow	-30°	moderate
Japanese fleece flower	*Fallopia japonica**	3–5'	spring	white	-30°	adaptable
meadow sweet	*Filipendula* spp.	varies by species/ cultivar	varies	varies	varies	adaptable
sweet woodruff	*Galium odoratum**	1'	spring	white	-30°	adaptable
gentian	*Gentiana* spp.	varies by species/ cultivar	varies	blue	varies	moderate
hardy geranium	*Geranium* spp.	varies by species/ cultivar	varies	various	varies	adaptable
variegated ground ivy	*Glechoma hederacea 'Variegata'**	4" and spreading	spring	white	-30°	adaptable
hellebore	*Helleborus* spp.	varies by species/ cultivar	varies	varies	varies	adaptable

Common Name	Botanic Name	Size (height)	Bloom Season	Color	Hardy To:	Water Needs
coral bells, alum root	Heuchera spp.	6–18"	spring	white, pink or red	-30°	moderate
foamy bells	x Heucherella cultivars	18"	summer	pink	-30°	moderate
hosta	Hosta spp.	varies by species/ cultivar	varies	varies	-40°	moderate
forest poppy	Hylomecon japonica	12"	spring	yellow	-20°	moderate
candy tuft	Iberis sempervirens*	9–12"	spring	white	-50°	adaptable
false rue anemone	Isopyrum biternatum	6"	spring	white	-50°	moderate
archangel	Lamiastrum galeobdolon 'Variegatum'*	12"	spring	yellow	-30°	adaptable
yellow archangel	L. g. 'Herman's Pride'*	12"	spring	yellow	-30°	moderate
spotted dead nettle	Lamium maculatum*	6"	summer	pink, white	-40°	adaptable
lily turf	Liriope spicata*	12"	summer	violet	-20°	adaptable
rose campion	Lychnis coronaria	24"	summer	pink or magenta	-30°	adaptable
loosestrife	Lysimachia spp.	varies by species/ cultivar	varies	varies	varies	moderate
black mondo grass	Ophiopogon planiscapus 'Niger'	6"	early summer	white to pale pink	-20°	moderate
strawberry wood sorrel	Oxalis crassipes 'Rosea'	4"	all summer	pink	-20°	moderate
woodland peony	Paeonia obovata	18"	spring	rosy pink	-30°	moderate
Claude Barr penstemon	Penstemon 'Claude Barr'	2"	late spring	purplish-blue	-40°	moderate
woodland phlox	Phlox divaricata	6–18"	spring	blue, pink or white	-30°	moderate
prairie phlox	Phlox pilosa	6–18"	spring	blue, pink or white	-30°	moderate
creeping phlox	Phlox stolonifera*	6–18"	late summer	blue, pink or white	-40°	moderate
obedient plant	Physostegia virginiana	3"	summer-fall	pink or white	-30°	moderate
green dragon	Pinellia pedatisecta	6"	summer	green	-20°	adaptable
primrose	Primula spp.	varies	varies	varies	varies	moderate
self-heal	Prunella vulgaris*	12"	summer	blue, purple or white	-20°	moderate
lungwort	Pulmonaria spp.	12"	spring	varies	-20°	moderate
rue	Ruta graveolens	30"	summer	yellow	-30°	adaptable
iris moss	Sagina subulata	2'	summer	white	-30°	adaptable
Turkish sage	Salvia recognita	24"	summer	pink	-30°	dry

Top: Alexander loosestrife *Lysimachia punctata* 'Alexander'

Bottom left: Blue flowered pulmonaria in a shaded bed. Shady Lane at DBG.

Bottom right: Barrenwort *Epimedium alpinum* ssp. *rubrum.*

PERENNIALS FOR SHADE, *continued*

Common Name	Botanic Name	Size (height)	Bloom Season	Color	Hardy To:	Water Needs
burnet	*Sanguisorba* spp.	3–5'	summer	reddish-purple	-30°	moderate
London pride	*Saxifraga* x *urbium*	6"	spring	white	-10°	moderate
two-row stonecrop	*Sedum spurium**	30"	summer	red	-30°	adaptable
lamb's ears	*Stachys byzantina**	24"	summer	pink	-30°	adaptable
celandine poppy	*Stylophorum diphyllum**	24"	summer	yellow	-40°	moderate
comfrey	*Symphytum grandiflorum**	18"	spring	varies	-30°	adaptable
kittentails	*Synthyris missurica**	7"	summer	violet	-60°	moderate
partridge feather	*Tanacetum densum* ssp. *amani**	6"	summer	yellow	-40°	dry
feverfew	*T. parthenium*	24"	late spring	white	-40°	adaptable
meadow rue	*Thalictrum* spp.	varies by species/cultivar	spring	varies	-20°	moderate
spiderwort	*Tradescantia* spp.	18"	summer	varies	-40°	moderate
toad lily	*Tricyrtis* spp.	36"	autumn	purple	-40°	moderate
clover	*Trifolium* spp.	varies by species/cultivar	varies	varies	varies	moderate
periwinkle	*Vinca minor**	6"	spring	varies	-30°	adaptable
violet, pansy	*Viola* spp.	varies by species/cultivar	spring/autumn	varies	-50°	adaptable

Orchid Frost deadnettle
Lamium maculatum 'Orchid Frost'.

* can be used as ground covers

ROSES FOR SHADE

All roses do best with a good soaking once or twice a week. Really dense shade will inhibit flowering, so site these where they receive at least a little sunlight, particularly during their bloom season.

Rose	Color	Classification	Rose	Color	Classification
Ballerina	medium pink	polyantha	Nevada	bluish-pink	shrub
Blanc Double de Coubert	white	rugosa	New Dawn	pale pink	climber
Carmencita	pink	hybrid shrub	Nymphenburg	salmon pink	modern shrub
Cecile Brunner	pale pink	climber	Paulii	white	rugosa
Complicata	pink	shrub	Pink Grootendorst	medium pink	rugosa
Cornelia	coppery apricot	shrub	Prairie Dawn	salmon pink	modern hybrid
Dr. Van Fleet	bluish-pink	rambler	Queen Margrethe	pastel pink	shrub
F. J. Grootendorst	medium pink	rugosa	*Rosa canina*	pink	species
Felicia	pink	polyantha	*Rosa eglanteria*	pink	species
Félicité Parmentier	pink	alba	*Rosa glauca*	pink	species
Fruhlingsgold	yellow	hybrid spinosissima	*Rosa mundi*	pink striped	gallica
Golden Showers	yellow	climber	*Rosa rugosa* 'Alba'	white	rugosa
Harrison's Yellow	yellow	shrub	*Rosa rugosa* 'Rubra'	blue red	rugosa
Iceberg	white	floribunda	*Rosa setigera*	deep pink	species
Jens Munk	pink	rugosa	*Rosa x alba* 'Semiplena'	white	alba
Knockout	red	shrub	Sally Holmes	cream	shrub
La Belle Sultane	crimson	gallica	Stanwell Perpetual	pale pink	hybrid spinosissima
Lavender Lassie	lavender pink	hybrid musk	Sweet Briar	light pink	species
Maiden's Blush	bluish-pink	alba	The Fairy	pale pink	polyantha
			Zephirine Drouhin	medium pink	climber

Most of the following require protection from winter sun and wind.

Common Name	Botanic Name	Attributes/Comments	Size	Hardy To:	Water Needs
white forsythia	Abeliophyllum distichum	white flowers/early spring	4' x 4'	-30°	moderate
chokeberry	Aronia spp.	white flowers/black or red berries/red fall color	6' x 6'	-30°	adaptable
New Jersey tea	Ceanothus americanus	white flowers	4' x 5'	-30°	moderate
mountain mahogany	Cercocarpus montanus	yellow flowers/seedheads	6' x 6'	-20°	dry
redtwig dogwood	Cornus spp.	white berries/red fall color	varies by species/cultivar	varies	moderate
rock spray	Cotoneaster horizontalis	red berries/red fall color	2 x 6'	-30°	adaptable
burkwood daphne	Daphne x burkwoodii 'Carol Mackie'	pink flowers	5' x 5'	-20°	adaptable
daphne	D. x transatlantica 'Jim's Pride'	white flowers	2' x 2'	-20°	adaptable
wintercreeper	Euonymus fortunei	good foliage plant	varies by cultivar	-30°	adaptable
spreading euonymus	E. kiautschovicus 'Manhattan'	semievergreen	4' x 6'	-20°	moderate
dwarf euonymus	E. nanus ssp. turkestanicus	purple flowers/coral seed capsules	3' x 6'	-50°	adaptable
rose of Sharon	Hibiscus syriacus	attractive flower/color varies by cultivar	12' x 6'	-30°	adaptable
panicle hydrangea	H. paniculata 'Grandiflora'	white flowers	8' x 8'	-40°	moderate
waxflower	Jamesia americana	white flowers	3' x 3'	-20°	moderate
common juniper	Juniperus communis	evergreen	1-3' x 3-6'	-50°	adaptable
Japanese kerria	Kerria japonica	yellow flowers	5' x 5'	-30°	adaptable
twinberry	Lonicera involucrata	pink flowers/black berries	6' x 6'	-20°	moderate
Oregon grape holly	Mahonia aquifolium	yellow flowers/evergreen/ blue berries	6' x 6'	-40°	adaptable
creeping mahonia	M. repens	yellow flowers/blue berries/ red fall color	18" x 3'	-30°	adaptable
Russian carpet cypress	Microbiota decussata	evergreen	18" x 6'	-50°	moderate
mountain lover	Paxistima canbyi	evergreen/purple in winter	10" x 10"	-30°	moderate
littleleaf mock orange	Philadelphus microphyllus	white flowers	4' x 4'	-20°	adaptable
firethorn	Pyracantha coccinea	white flowers/evergreen/ red berries	6' x 6'	-20°	moderate (choose hardy varieties)
three-leaf sumac	Rhus trilobata	yellow flowers/red fall color/ red fruit	6' x 6'	-30°	adaptable
clove currant	Ribes aureum	yellow flowers/black fruit/ red fall color	6' x 6'	-30°	adaptable
thimbleberry	Rubus parviflorus	white flowers/fruits	6' x 6'	-20°	moderate
boulder raspberry	R. deliciosus	white flowers	6' x 6'	-50°	adaptable
Ural false spirea	Sorbaria sorbifolia	white flowers/yellow fall color	6' x 8'	-30°	moderate
coralberry/snowberry	Symphoricarpos spp.	varies by species	varies by species/cultivar	-20°	moderate
yew	Taxus spp.	evergreen	varies by species/cultivar	varies	moderate
Burkwood"s virburnum	Viburnum x burkwoodii	white flowers/purple fall color	10' x 10'	-30°	moderate
fragrant virbunum	V. x carlcephalum	white flowers	8' x 8'	-20°	moderate
Judd's viburnum	V. x juddii	white flowers	6' x 6'	-30°	moderate
Allegheny viburnum	V. x rhytidophylloides 'Alleghany'	white flowers/black fruit/ orange fall color	10' x 10'	-20°	adaptable

Common Name	Botanic Name	Attributes/Comments	Size	Hardy To:	Water Needs
hardy kiwi vine	Actinida kolomikta 'Arctic Beauty'	leaves marked pink and white	15-20'	-30°	adaptable
silver vine	A. polygama	leaves marked silver	12-15'	-30°	adaptable
mountain fringe	Adlumia fungosa	pink flowers/biennial	6-10'	-20°	adaptable
five-leaf akebia	Akebia quintana	reddish purple	30'	-30°	adaptable
monk's hood vine	Ampelopsis aconitifolia	berries/yellow fall color	25'	-30°	moderate
variegated porcelain vine	A. brevipedunculata 'Elegans'	white flowers/blue berries	10'	-30°	moderate
Dutchman's pipe	Aristolochia durior	yellow-green flowers	30'	-30°	moist
trumpet vine	Campsis radicans	red, salmon, or yellow flowers	30'	-30°	adaptable
American bittersweet	Celastrus scandens	orange fruit	20'	-40°	adaptable
alpine clematis	Clematis alpina cultivars	color varies by cultivar	10'	-30°	adaptable
Praecox clematis	C. x jouiniana 'Praecox'	pale blue flowers	5'	-20°	moderate
large-petaled clematis	C. macropetala cultivars	color varies by cultivar	12'	-30°	moderate
sweet autumn clematis	C. terniflora	white flowers	20'	-20°	moderate
Athens yellow bleeding heart	Dicentra scandens	yellow flowers	8'	-10°	moderate
wintercreeper	Euonymus fortunei	attractive foliage	12'	-20°	adaptable
English Ivy	Hedera helix	evergreen	12'	-30°	adaptable
hop vine	Humulus lupulus	attractive fruits	25'	-30°	adaptable
climbing hydrangea	Hydrangea anomala ssp. petiolaris	white flowers	20'	-20°	moist
winter jasmine	Jasminium nudiflorum	yellow	12'	-20°	moderate
trumpet honeysuckle	Lonicera sempervirens	color varies by cultivar	20'	-30°	adaptable
Boston ivy, Virginia creeper	Parthenocissus spp.	attractive foliage	varies	-30°	adaptable
Japanese hydrangea vine	Schizophragma hydrangeoides	white flowers	20'	-20°	moist
tenturier grape	Vitis vinifera 'Purpurea'	purple leaves	20'	-20°	adaptable

Trumpet honeysuckle.

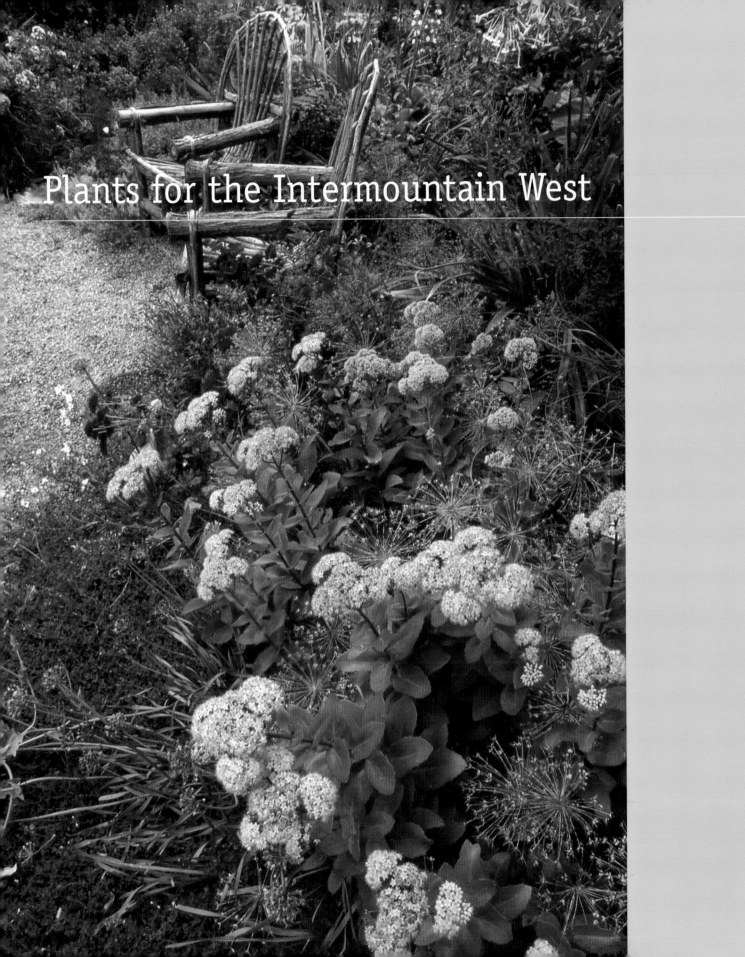

Plants for the Intermountain West

Overleaf: A wider variety of perennials grows in the Intermountain West than in "perennial paradises" like Eugene, Oregon. *Sedum* 'Matrona' in the Tatroe garden.

Above: Non-native tall bearded iris is as vigorous as the yuccas in Dan Johnson's garden.

*I*n the summer of 1998, Randy and I attended the annual meeting of the North American Rock Garden Society in Eugene, Oregon. The cool, misty climate there is not ideal for traditional rock garden plants. But, oh, the perennials. If there is a paradise for perennials, Willamette Valley is the place. The gardens we visited were resplendent with rare and lovely wand flowers *Dierama* spp., as large as major household appliances. Delphiniums and foxgloves were as tall and stately as those that grew in our village in England. After we returned home, I told Randy that I intended to move to Oregon. He spent the rest of that summer pointing out Colorado's attributes. Nothing he said dissuaded me—that is, until he brought up dryland plants. Would I be able to grow acantholimons, eriogonums, and townsendias in a maritime climate? Certainly not as well as in sunny, dry Colorado.

Goldenrod, firetails *Persicaria amplexicaulis* 'Speciosa', and variegated maidengrass. Ornamental Grass Garden at DBG.

OUR REGION'S HORTICULTURAL vernacular is distinctive and that's part of its charm. With the exception of the few that prefer constant moisture, soft light, and mild winters, flowers do very well here. Second to grasses, flowers are the prevailing vegetation in much of our region. Trees and shrubs have no place to hide when the weather turns nasty, but perennial flowers go dormant in winter (a few indulge in summer dormancy as well) to escape the vagaries of our climate. If badly damaged, perennials generally grow new tops. Dry air, cool nights, and cold winters thwart many insect and disease problems. Combined with plentiful sunshine and strong UV light, these are ideal conditions for growing healthy and vigorous perennials. Despite Oregon's bounty, I can actually grow a wider variety of perennials in my Colorado garden. They may not get as large or grow as vigorously, but this is not always a disadvantage. Hellebores in the Pacific Northwest can get as large as an easy chair and take up more space than I care to give them. In Colorado, where they achieve only a fraction of their potential size, I can fit several cultivars of hellebores in the space a single plant would require in Eugene.

Flora from the cold deserts of the world are right at home in the Intermountain West, with very little change to existing conditions. Plants from damper climates also do well as long as the soil is amended (when necessary to suit their needs) and irrigation is available. Tropical flowers relish our hot summers and can be grown as annuals, to be tossed out at the end of the season. Or, they can spend the winter indoors as houseplants. The roots of many popular tropicals like cannas, dahlias, and gladiolas can alternatively be stored in a cool place during their winter dormancy. Then, if all goes well, you can enjoy these plants again year after year.

In the Intermountain West, we really do have the best of all worlds—as long as supplemental irrigation is available. When that is not an option, we can turn to a plethora of plants from the cold deserts and steppes of North and South America, central Europe and Asia, the Middle East, and parts of Africa. Collectors bring us new and exciting choices every year, plants suitable for our region that can be a real challenge to grow in climates long considered more hospitable than our own. The more of these we include in our gardens, the more our gardens develop a regional character—and the more the rest of the horticultural community will come to admire our prowess. Gardeners from other places are often astounded at our success with reputedly temperamental plants. In other climates, daphnes have a bad habit of dying with no apparent explanation. In our region, daphnes can be as vigorous as junipers (and, like junipers, we remove them when they get too large for their allotted space).

Right Plant, Right Place

Books abound on the topic of choosing the best plant for a particular site. The premise is to make a perfect fit between plant and site. Good intentions aside, most plant purchases are, like puppies, impulse buys rather than thoughtful decisions. Nothing else accounts for planting a pair of blue spruces on either side of a front sidewalk that eventually will be 10 to 20 feet wide. Or, even more commonplace, pfitzer junipers (10 by 10 by 20 feet at maturity) planted as foundation plantings under a window. Obviously, the homeowner did not do the math. Besides mature size, several critical factors must be considered when choosing the best plant for a particular site. The most obvious of these are heat and cold tolerance, and drainage, sunlight, water, and soil requirements. Not so obvious is how much crowding a plant can handle.

In this regard, there are three general categories of plants. The first, botanists call these *ruderals*, are plants that repopulate bare ground after a natural or manmade disturbance has destroyed all or most of the existing vegetation—in other words, the "Band-Aids" of the plant world. Fireweed, the first colonizer to appear after fire or landslide in the mountains, is probably the best-known example in our region. Its magenta spikes are a neon sign announcing that healing has begun. Once the forest grows back, fireweed dies out. Plants like these have limited value in gardens because their job is to cover as much disturbed ground as quickly as possible.

In the second group are the *competitors*, what one ecologist calls "urban dwellers." These plants grow together in the tightly knit proximity of meadows and prairies. This community demands the good life, where soil is fertile and moisture relatively abundant. The bulk of our traditional perennials and ornamental grasses come from this category. These plants are perfectly happy growing cheek to jowl with their neighbors and relatives.

The third group contains the loners of the plant world, the *noncompetitors*. They dwell where conditions are too severe for anything else to grow. These solitary plants scratch out a living where things are tough—where soil is either infertile or absent entirely, where moisture is severely limited, or where wind, cold and heat, or toxic soil push the limits of what plant life can endure. Rock garden plants primarily fall into this last category.

The practical application of learning the social requirements of each plant becomes apparent when you try to make compatible groupings in the garden. We understand that weeds overrun more polite companions. But many meadow and prairie plants also menace noncompetitors, most of which cannot grow if even slightly crowded. Plant labels provide at least some cultural information regarding sunlight, water, and drainage requirements. Discovering a plant's crowding tolerance can be more of a challenge. Penstemons as a whole cannot abide close quarters, nor can most true alpines or plants with desert origins. Naturally, there are exceptions. Some desert wildflowers in the Southwest take advantage of the shade and extra organic matter trapped beneath shrubs, packing themselves in as tightly as commuters in a Tokyo subway car.

On more than one occasion, I've badly misjudged a plant's needs. No wonder the western bleeding heart *Dicentra formosa*, a wildflower that grows on open rocky slopes in its native Oregon, was not happy planted beneath pine trees in my garden, where little direct sunlight reaches. Most of the time, all we have to go on is educated guesses, and we end up having to make adaptations in any case. The coastal mountains of Oregon, where this dicentra originates, are significantly cooler in summer and wetter in winter than where I live. After seeing where it flourished in the wild, I decided to try this plant again, this time on the south side of a pine where it can bask in full sunshine in the morning and where snow accumulates in winter. It's possible this spot may be more to its liking, but it's never a sure thing. Just as you might kiss a lot of frogs to find a prince, you sometimes go through a lot of trial and error to match up plant and place.

Signature Plants of the Intermountain West

Some years ago, when a friend converted a section of her garden to xeriscape, her husband objected. To him, the plants looked "weedy." My friend's husband's reaction is not atypical. For many, xeriscape is an acquired taste. When I developed a plant list for a local park system in the early 1990s, I was cautioned not to use the term "xeriscape," lest the neighbors find out what we were up to and complain. Even those of us who wholeheartedly endorse xeriscaping appear conflicted. Every article ever written on the topic includes the phrase "xeriscape is more than cactus

Penstemons don't like crowding.

Xeric gardens have a distinctive vernacular. Spikes of Grecian foxglove *Digitalis lanata* in Tom and Diane Peace's Denver garden.

and yucca." This attitude is puzzling—these are exactly the type of plants that best represent our arid and semiarid lands. If we were to overcome our collective cultural bias against them, cacti, yucca, and other xeric fare could become signatures for our region, plants that we could point to with real pride of place.

Many, but not all, of these potential signature plants are regional natives. Wherever they originate, drought-tolerant plants (aka, xerophytes) share a commonality in physical appearance. In other words, desert plants look like desert plants.

Xeric plants employ a variety of defensive strategies to deal with heat and aridity. These contribute to their unique character—and to the widely held perception that, because they are so different from the more familiar temperate flora, desert plants are too uncouth for polite company. The leaves of xerophytes are generally small or finely cut with less surface area to dry out. Additionally, a large percentage of desert natives have silver or shiny foliage that reflects the intense solar radiation of their native habitat. Many of their leaves and stems are covered in fine hairs to shade the surface.

Top left: The small, finely cut foliage of cliffrose *Cowania mexicana* is typical of xeric shrubs.

Top right: A felted surface helps prevent moisture loss. Biennial giant silver mullein *Verbascum bombyciferum*.

Bottom: Giant-flowered purple sage *Salvia pachyphylla* has leathery leaves that resist drying out in its high desert native habitat.

Mountain mahogany *Cercocarpus ledifolius* sheds its leaves during periods of extended drought.

Others store water in succulent foliage and stems. Leaves that are leathery or waxy to the touch also help mitigate moisture loss. The leaves of a few specialized shrubs, like the curlleaf mountain mahogany *Cercocarpus montanus,* curl up during dry spells to further reduce surface area, and shed their leaves during extended periods of drought. Thorns and strongly aromatic foliage repel grazing animals in a land where plants can't afford to be passive.

Not all adaptations are so readily apparent. Desert shrubs often develop extensive root systems that harvest water over a wide area or delve deeply to tap into underground water sources. Others, like yuccas and desert four o'clocks, have unimaginably huge taproots that store water underground to help the plants get through dry times. Long-lived xeric plants usually adopt more than one method for coping with drought. Compared to more familiar Japanese maples and yews, desert plants may look wild and unkempt, but, to attract scarce pollinators, their flowers are often spectacular. In good years, deserts put on stunning floral shows that bring admiring tourists from far and wide. Few sights are as arresting as scarlet globe mallow glowing against black lava rock or hillsides of California poppies stretching for as far as the eye can see.

Local nursery people have a saying: "More plants are killed by over- than by under-watering." This is especially true of xerophytes, which must be allowed to dry out between waterings. It's the interval that is tricky—too short and the transplants drown, too long and they die of drought. Check new transplants frequently until they are established (putting out new growth) and water as soon as the rootball becomes bone dry. Depending on time of year, weather conditions, and the water-holding capacity of the soil, perennial flowers generally become established within the first few weeks. Shrubs and trees may take several years. Once established, most of the following can survive on natural precipitation, but watering once or twice a month results in better flowering and a fuller, lusher garden.

There are so many variables that it's impossible to come up with hard and fast guidelines for how much and how often to water. This explains why most garden writers and catalogs default to some variation of *low, medium,* and *high.* But plants don't care about averages. Their water needs change markedly from season-to-season and year-to-year, depending on weather conditions.

Learning to water is an art. Even genuine desert plants need irrigation from time-to-time. Let your garden be your guide—and be aware that even the best of us get it wrong more often than we care to admit. Don't feel too bad, though. We live in a region

Top left: Many xeric plants, like the banana yucca *Yucca baccata,* have deep taproots that store water.

Top right: Bush morning glory *Ipomoea leptophylla* emerges from an oversized tuber that helps it survive dry years.

Bottom: Fiery orange flowers of desert mallow *Sphaeralcea ambigua* attract pollinators from far and wide.

where even Mother Nature kills a lot of plants. The following are the best watering guidelines I've come across. From the *Agua Fria Nursery Catalog:* "Once established, **xeric** plants should be watered every 3–4 weeks during dry periods. **Moderately xeric** plants should be watered every 2–3 weeks. Plants needing **moderate watering** should be watered every 1½–2 weeks. Plants needing **regular watering** should be watered every week." (Agua Fria Nursery, 1409 Agua Fria Street, Santa Fe, New Mexico 87501)

By no means are the following lists comprehensive. I've included just a sampling of some of the more widely available natives and adapted imports that are appropriate choices for unirrigated or lightly irrigated zones. All of the plants recommended for dry rock gardens (p. 125) are also good choices for xeriscapes. The division is purely arbitrary, based mostly on size and fashion. Keep in mind that watering recommendations are always subjective—each plant's water requirements can vary widely throughout our region, depending on rainfall, soil type, and relative humidity, to name just a few of the factors that are part of this complex equation.

SIGNATURE PLANTS: ADAPTED PERENNIALS

Common Name	Botanic Name	Flower Color	Water
moonshine yarrow	Achillea x 'Moonshine'	yellow	dry/moderate
lily-of-the-Nile	Agapanthus Headbourne Hybrids	blues and white	dry/moderate
hummingbird mint	Agastache spp. and cultivars	various	moderate
creeping basket-of-gold	Alyssum montanum	yellow	moderate
desert blue stars	Amsonia jonesii	blue	dry/moderate
golden columbine	Aquilegia chrysantha	yellow	moderate
prickly poppy	Argemone polyanthemos	white	dry
butterfly weed	Asclepias tuberosa	orange	moderate
king's spear	Asphodeline lutea	yellow	dry/moderate
white aster	Aster ericoides	white	dry
Dream of Beauty aster	A. kumleinii of gardens	pink	dry
Greek horehound	Ballota pseudodictamnus	pink	dry/moderate
calamint	Calamintha grandiflora	pink	dry/moderate
lesser calamint	C. nepeta	lilac	dry/moderate
winecups	Callirhoe involucrata	magenta	dry/moderate
harebells	Campanula rotundifolia	blue	moderate
Jupiter's beard	Centranthus ruber	coral red	dry/moderate
sugar bowls	Clematis hirsutissima	purple	moderate
sea kale	Crambe maritima	white	dry/moderate
miner's candle	Cryptantha virgata	white	dry
purple prairie clover	Dalea purpurea	magenta	dry/moderate
Jimson weed	Datura spp.	white	dry
twinspur	Diascia integerrima 'Coral Canyon'	coral pink	moderate
Grecian foxglove	Digitalis lanata	bronze	dry/moderate
narrow-leafed foxglove	D. obscura	orange	moderate

Common Name	Botanic Name	Flower Color	Water
canary clover	Dorycnium hirsutum	pink	dry
prairie purple coneflower	Echinacea angustifolia	pink	dry/moderate
globe thistle	Echinops ritro	blue	dry/moderate
buckwheat	Eriogonum spp. and cultivars	yellow	dry/moderate
woolly sunflower	Eriophyllum lanatum	yellow	dry/moderate
sea holly	Eryngium spp.	blue	dry/moderate
wallflower	Erysimum asperum	yellow-orange	moderate
flowering spurge	Euphorbia corollata	white	moderate
blanketflower	Gaillardia aristata	red and yellow	dry/moderate
whirling butterflies	Gaura lindheimeri	white	moderate
wild geranium	Geranium caespitosum	rose-purple	dry/moderate
prairie smoke	Geum triflorum	salmon	moderate
horned poppy	Glaucium spp.	yellow or orange	dry/moderate
white statice	Goniolimon tataricum	white	dry/moderate
Maximilian's sunflower	Helianthus maximiliani	yellow	moderate
hairy golden aster	Heterotheca villosa	yellow	dry/moderate
hyssop	Hyssopus officinalis	blue	moderate
bush morning glory	Ipomoea leptophylla	pink	dry
sky rocket	Ipomopsis aggregata	red	dry/moderate
blue flag	Iris missouriensis	blue	moderate
red hot poker	Kniphofia spp.	orange/yellow	moderate
English lavender	Lavandula angustifolia	lavender	moderate
tree mallow	Lavatera thuringiaca	pink	dry/moderate
gayfeather	Liatris punctata	pink	dry/moderate
Siberian sea lavender	Limonium gmelinii	blue	dry/moderate
sea lavender	L. latifolium	white	dry/moderate
blue flax	Linum perenne	blue	dry/moderate
fringed puccoon	Lithospermum incisum	yellow	dry

Common Name	Botanic Name	Flower Color	Water
silver lupine	*Lupinus argenteus*	lavender	dry/moderate
silver horehound	*Marrubium rotundifolium*	inconspicuous	moderate
desert four o'clock	*Mirabilis multiflora*	magenta	dry
wild bergamot	*Monarda fistulosa*	lavender	dry/moderate
catmint	*Nepeta x faassenii*	lavender	dry/moderate
white evening primrose	*Oenothera caespitosa*	white	dry/moderate
Missouri primrose	*O. macrocarpa*	yellow	moderate
Lambert's locoweed	*Oxytropis lambertii*	lavender	dry
poppy	*Papaver* spp.	various	dry/moderate/moist
beardtongue	*Penstemon* spp. and cultivars	various	dry/moderate
Russian sage	*Perovskia atriplicifolia*	lavender	moderate
scorpionweed	*Phacelia hastata*	white	dry/moderate
hardy Jerusalem sage	*Phlomis russeliana*	yellow	dry/moderate
Santa Fe phlox	*Phlox nana*	pink	moderate
purple groundcherry	*Physalis lobata*	purple	dry
woolly cinquefoil	*Potentilla hippiana*	yellow	dry/moderate
paper flower	*Psilostrophe tagetina*	yellow	dry/moderate
prairie coneflower	*Ratibida columnifera*	red or yellow	dry/moderate
rosemary	*Rosmarinus officinialis* 'Arp'	lavender	dry/moderate
wild petunia	*Ruellia humilis*	lavender	dry/moderate
sage	*Salvia* spp. and cultivars	various	dry/moderate
gray santolina	*Santolina chamaecyparissus*	yellow	dry/moderate
yellow pincushion flower	*Scabiosa ochroleuca*	yellow	dry/moderate
silver groundsel	*Senecio longilobus*	yellow	dry
Mexican catchfly	*Silene laciniata*	orange	moderate
meadow goldenrod	*Solidago canadensis*	yellow	moderate
globe mallow	*Sphaeralcea* spp.	various	dry
lamb's ears	*Stachys lanata*	pink	moderate
prince's plume	*Stanleya pinnata*	yellow	dry
flameflower	*Talinum calycinum*	magenta	moderate
snow daisy	*Tanacetum niveum*	white	dry/moderate
golden banner	*Thermopsis montana*	yellow	moderate
western spiderwort	*Tradescantia occidentalis*	purple	moderate
mullein	*Verbascum* spp.	various	dry/moderate
Great Plains verbena	*Verbena bipinnatifida*	purple	moderate
plains verbena	*V. wrightii*	purple	moderate
showy goldeneye	*Viguiera multiflora*	yellow	dry
hummingbird trumpet	*Zauschneria* (syn. *Epilobium*) spp. and cultivars	scarlet	moderate
prairie zinnia	*Zinnia grandiflora*	yellow	dry

Not all xeric plants have small flowers. Those of Missouri primrose are the size of teacups.

Common Name	Botanic Name	Water
white fir	Abies concolor	moderate
bigtooth maple	Acer grandidentatum	moderate
Utah serviceberry	Amelanchier utahensis	dry
leadplant	Amorpha canescens	dry
false indigo	A. fruticosa	moderate
pinemat manzanita	Arctostaphylos nevadensis	dry/moderate
greenleaf manzanita	A. patula	dry/moderate
bigleaf sage	Artemisia tridentata	dry
four-wing saltbush	Atriplex canescens	dry
shadscale	A. confertifolia	dry
western river birch	Betula occidentalis	moderate
silver butterfly bush	Buddleia alternifolia spp. argentea	dry/moderate
yellow bird of paradise	Caesalpinia gilliesii	dry/moderate
littleleaf pea shrub	Caragana microphylla 'Tidy'	dry/moderate
bluemist spirea	Caryopteris x clandonensis	moderate
deerbrush	Ceanothus fendleri	moderate
mountain mahogany	Cercocarpus brevifolius	dry
dwarf mountain mahogany	C. intricatus	dry
curl-leaf mountain mahogany	C. ledifolius	dry
mountain mahogany	C. montanus	dry
fernbush	Chamaebatiaria millefolium	dry
desert willow	Chilopsis linearis	dry/moderate
chitalpa	x Chitalpa tashkentensis	dry
rabbitbrush	Chrysothamnus nauseosus	dry
smokebush	Cotinus coggygria	dry/moderate
cliffrose	Cowania mexicana	dry
Arizona cypress	Cupressus arizonica	dry
Spanish gold broom	Cytisus purgans	moderate
green joint fir	Ephedra viridis	dry
Apache plume	Fallugia paradoxa	dry
cliff fendlerbush	Fendlera rupicola	dry
desert olive	Forestiera neomexicana	moderate
single leaf ash	Fraxinus anomala	dry/moderate
velvet ash	F. velutina	dry
hop sage	Grayia spinosa	dry
pea buckthorn	Hippophae rhamnoides	dry/moderate
rock spirea	Holodiscus dumosus	moderate
wax flower	Jamesia americana	moderate
juniper	Juniperus communis	dry
alligator juniper	J. deppeana	dry
one-seed juniper	J. monosperma	dry

Common Name	Botanic Name	Water
Utah juniper	J. osteosperma	dry/moderate
Rocky Mountain juniper	J. scopulorum	dry
winterfat	Krascheninnikovia lanata (syn. Ceratoides, Eurotia)	dry
bush honeysuckle	Lonicera involucrata	moderate
blue-leaf honeysuckle	L. korolkowii	dry/moderate
wolfberry	Lycium pallidum	dry
desert holly	Mahonia fremontii	dry
redberry desert holly	M. haematocarpa	dry
squaw apple	Peraphyllum ramosissimum	dry
Lewis mock orange	Philadelphus lewisii	dry/moderate
littleleaf mock orange	P. microphyllus	moderate
pine	Pinus aristata	dry
piñon pine	P. edulis	dry/moderate
limber pine	P. flexilis	dry
Ponderosa pine	P. ponderosa	dry
Scots pine	P. sylvestris	moderate
plains cottonwood	Populus deltoides	moderate
quaking aspen	P. tremuloides	moderate
wild plum	Prunus americana	dry/moderate
desert peach	P. andersonii	dry/moderate
western sand cherry	P. besseyi	dry/moderate
chokecherry	P. virginiana	dry/moderate
Douglas fir	Pseudotsuga menziesii	moderate
hop tree	Ptelea trifoliata	dry
antelope bitterbrush	Purshia tridentata	dry/moderate
Gambel oak	Quercus gambellii	dry/moderate
Colorado foothills oak	Q. x mazeii	moderate
desert live oak	Q. turbinella	dry
wavy leaf oak	Q. undulata	dry
sumac	Rhus glabra	dry/moderate
three-leaf sumac	R. trilobata	dry
staghorn sumac	R. typhina	dry/moderate
golden currant	Ribes aureum	moderate
Smith's buckthorn	Rhamnus smithii	dry/moderate
New Mexico locust	Robinia neomexicana	dry
boulder raspberry	Rubus deliciosus	moderate
desert sage	Salvia dorii	dry
giant flowered purple sage	S. pachyphylla	dry
silver buffaloberry	Shepherdia argentea	moderate
Rocky Mountain ash	Sorbus scopulina	moderate
snowberry	Symphoricarpos albus	dry/moderate
coralberry	S. orbiculatus	dry/moderate

Cacti, Agaves, and Yuccas

As a fancier of both rocks and cacti (and yucca, too), I've long wondered how cactus got to be the bane of xeriscapes. I suspect it's those stereotypical Sun City gravel landscapes in Arizona and Southern California that give rock and cacti such a bad name. But it's not the materials that make these landscapes so unappealing—it's the bad design. No one gets nearly as indignant over the comparable, and much more commonplace, water-guzzling alternative of wall-to-wall turfgrass.

Ironically, some of the most celebrated and sophisticated landscapes in the Southwest are composed of little more than rocks and cacti. In these minimalist landscapes, cacti are used as living sculpture. In fact, one of the biggest environmental challenges facing Arizona is stopping its citizens from loving their cacti to extinction. Natural areas are being stripped bare of wild-collected cacti, and these plants go for astronomical prices on the black market. In sharp contrast, a friend of mine caught Colorado neighbors digging up every clump of cacti on their acreage—not to sell, but to put out with the garbage.

This attitude is inexplicable, especially since few plants are better equipped to deal with our fickle climate. Plus, it's a missed opportunity. When cacti bloom, they are the life of the party. No flower exhibits more razzamatazz than the 3- to 4-inch-long magenta trumpets of hedgehog cactus *Echinocereus fendleri*. Claret cup *Echinocereus triglochidiatus* is no shrinking violet either, its flowers fire-engine red. Cactus flowers come in a wide range of colors. Whether shockingly bright or pastel shades, one thing they all have in common is a crystalline quality that makes them glow as if lighted from within.

Flowers are only a small part of the cactus's allure. The perfect symmetry of the many ball- and barrel-shaped varieties gives them a genuine personality, if only because these forms are so rare in nature. Though many of these cacti grow in grasslands in the wild, one of the best ways to display small cacti is tucked up against rocks, playing up the

Fire engine–red flowers on claret cup cactus *Echinocereus triglochidiatus*.

A dish garden of nonhardy succulents with pink-flowered *Sedum* 'Bertram Anderson' and variegated thyme. Tatroe garden.

dissimilarities between the two. Larger prickly pear cactus, cholla, hardy agaves, and yuccas are among the few truly architectural plants that we can grow in our cold winter climate. They bring drama to the garden when silhouetted against a bare wall where they can engage in shadow play. Or they make a theatrical statement when isolated or underplanted with low-growing dryland flowers.

Growing up in California with a mother who had similar inclinations may have something to do with why cacti and succulents are among my favorite plants. Her tastes ran to agaves, jade plants, and echeveria. Plant nurseries tend to lump these together with cacti. As a kid who tagged along on shopping trips, I was fascinated with pottery

dishes that contained a mixture of cacti and succulents, often decorated with a ceramic donkey to emphasize their Mexican flavor.

Though my garden in Colorado includes every hardy succulent, cactus, yucca, and agave I can get my hands on, I'm still most smitten with cacti that are small enough to fit in a dish. My parents' 50-foot-long hedges of opuntia and aloe vera in California terrified me. I was also creeped out by a neighbor's front yard planted exclusively with monster cacti and agaves, crammed together, and towering over my head. It wasn't until I visited the venerable cactus and succulent gardens at the Huntington Botanical Garden that I realized that what my parent's neighbor's front yard lacked

CACTI, AGAVES, AND YUCCAS

Hardy cacti, agaves, yuccas, and their relatives: for greater likelihood of success, plant these in fast-draining soil next to a large rock.

Common Name	Botanic Name	Common Name	Botanic Name
agaves	*Agave havardiana*	**prickly pear cactus**	*Opuntia aurea*
	A. kaibabensis		*O. basilaris*
	A. lechuguilla		*O. cymochila*
	A. neomexicana		*O. erectoclada*
	A. parryi		*O. glomerata*
	A. toumeyana ssp.bella		*O. macrocentra*
	A. utahensis ssp. nevadensis		*O. phaeacantha*
	A. virginica		*O. polyacantha*
chollas	*Cylindropuntia grusonia*		*O. pottsii*
	ssp.clavata		*O. violacea*
	C. davisii	**yuccas**	*Yucca angustissima*
	C. echinocarpa		*Y. baccata*
	C. imbricata		*Y. baileyi*
	C whipplei		*Y. brevifolia*
sotol	*Dasylirion wheeleri*		*Y. elata*
red yucca	*Hesperaloe parviflora*		*Y. filimentosa*
beargrass	*Nolina microcarpa*		*Y. glauca*
	N. texana		*Y. harrimaniae*
			Y. neomexicana
			Y. pallida
			Y. rostrata
			Y. rupicola
			Y. schottii
			Y. sterilis

(Small hardy cacti are listed on p. 118)

Top: **Prickly pear cactus can stand in for shrubs in the xeric border. WaterSmart Garden, DBG.**

Bottom left: **Hardy beargrass *Nolina microcarpa*.**

Bottom right: **Few plants are more architectural than the hardy agaves. Kelly Grummons' garden, Denver.**

were the basic design elements of varying size and scale (everything was supersized), negative space (there were no open areas), and contrast (a few desert annuals and flowering shrubs would have broken the monotony). It took me years to get over my prejudices and start using opuntias as shrubs. Their sculptural quality and incredibly beautiful flowers finally won me over. (Not to mention that in Colorado, opuntias don't grow into 10-foot-tall hedges.) All cacti that are cold hardy enough to grow outside here are restrained compared to their southwestern relatives.

I still indulge my childhood fascination by growing non-hardy cacti and succulents in dish gardens that live indoors for the winter and outdoors from May through October. A few specimens go solo in their own pot, but most are mixed. I do embellish my dishes (impressions made early in life die hard). Minerals from rock shops, as well as marbles and spheres, complement the plants. Small sculptures of toads, lizards, horned toads, and other desert creatures fashioned out of stone, ceramic, or bronze replace the hackneyed donkey. In one dish, I've worked in a small blue bottle found in road construction along I-25 in Denver. Others are embellished with assayer's crucibles from Leadville, Colorado, or with pieces of desert driftwood.

Grasses

No group of plants is more appropriate to Intermountain West gardens. Before the days of livestock grazing and fire suppression, grasses predominated in even the driest parts of our region. This is our good fortune because, at the moment, it would be hard to find another group of plants that is more universally coveted. From California, to the Deep South, and to the horticultural trendsetters in the Pacific Northwest, gardeners everywhere have embraced these versatile plants that German plantsman Karl Foerster, in the early part of the twentieth century, called "the hair of Mother Earth." In fact, gardens where grasses outnumber flowers are becoming increasingly commonplace. With origins as diverse as desert and pond, there is an ornamental grass for every conceivable cultural condition, from hot, dry xeriscape to damp shade.

As their popularity increases, the selection of grasses and grasslike plants gets larger every year. From miniature mondo grass *Ophiopogon japonicus* 'Pygmaeus', which, at 2 inches, is a good candidate for planting between paving stones, to 14-foot-tall hardy pampas grass *Saccharum ravennae*, there's an option for every garden and landscape design situation as well. Large grasses make great accents or screens even in small gardens. Medium-sized grasses are good fillers and provide texture. Short varieties are handy as edgers and for enscribing patterns in low ground covers.

Generally, grasses don't make much of an impact on the garden until late summer and early autumn. Because they emerge from winter battered and broken, most gardeners cut grasses back to the ground at some point in early spring. For several months thereafter, the clumps make a gradual comeback and are barely noticeable while floral displays grab all the attention. Then suddenly, in late August, grasses take center stage. Some stand tall and regal, others are arching and graceful. No longer simply a neutral foil for flowers, the grasses become stars in their own right, adding drama and excitement to gardens as the season starts to wind down. If that weren't enough, many ripen to yellow, gold, orange, red, or burgundy as summer slips into autumn.

Most gardeners are familiar with no more than a half dozen varieties of ornamental grasses, despite their enormous appeal. The standards—blue oat grass *Helictotrichon sempervirens*, blue sheep's fescue *Festuca cinerea*, maiden grass *Miscanthus sinensis*, and feather reed grass *Calamagrostis* spp.—do represent some of the best qualities we've come to expect from ornamental grasses, including ease of care, good looks for a long season, and a tolerance of a wide range of garden conditions. But why stop there?

Any good grass encyclopedia reveals dozens of other grasses that are suitable for our region. First, there are the offbeat cultivars of the most widely

Top: Silky threadgrass enlivens a planting of salmon twinspur and sandpaper verbena *Verbena rigida*. Hudson Gardens, Littleton, Colorado.

Bottom: Nothing beats grasses for adding texture and movement to the garden. Plains Garden, DBG.

Annual and frost-tender perennial grasses that can be grown as annuals:

Common Name	Botanic Name
quaking grass	Briza maxima
squirrel tail grass	Hordeum jubatum
hare's tail	Lagurus ovatus
ruby grass	Melinus neriglume
purple majesty millet	Pennisetum glaucum
purple fountain grass	Pennisetum setaceum 'Rubrum'
feathertop	P. villosum
broom corn	Sorghum vulgare
black tipwheat	Triticum durum
variegated corn	Zea mays 'Quadracolor'

Grasses for xeriscapes:

Common Name	Botanic Name
silver beard grass	Andropogon saccharoides
purple three-awn	Aristida purpurea
mountain mist grass	Blepharneuron tricholepis
side oats grama	Bouteloua curtipendula
blue grama	B. gracilis
feather reed grass	Calamagrostis x acutiflora 'Karl Foerster'
tall wheatgrass	Elytrigia elongata
weeping love grass	Eragrostis curvula
sand love grass	E. trichoides
blue avena grass	Helictotrichon sempervirens
June grass	Koeleria spp.
silky threadgrass	Nassella tenuissima
Indian rice grass	Oryzopsis hymenoides
little bluestem	Schizachyrium scoparium
Indian grass	Sorghastrum nutans
prairie dropseed	Sporobolus heterolepis
giant sacaton	S. wrightii
needle-and-thread grass	Stipa comata

Grasses for sun with regular irrigation:

Common Name	Botanic Name
quaking grass	Briza media
northern sea oats	Chasmanthium latifolium
blue sheep's fescue	Festuca cinerea
Japanese blood grass	Imperata cylindrica 'Red Baron'
maiden grass	Miscanthus sinensis
purple moor grass	Molinia caerulea
switchgrass	Panicum virgatum
fountain grass	Pennisetum alopecuroides
reed canary grass	Phalaris arundinacea
hardy pampas grass	Saccharum ravennae
autumn moor grass	Sesleria autumnalis
blue-green moor grass	S. heufleriana

used varieties, such as the variegated version of feather reed grass *Calamagrostis* x *acutiflora* 'Overdam'. This is an upright, stately grass, 3 to 4 feet tall, with shimmering golden-edged leaves. The purplish flower spikes appear in June and age to buff within a few weeks, then persist all summer and into winter. Fall-blooming feather reed grass *Calamagrostis brachytricha* lays claim to some of the most attractive flowers of any of the grasses, with delicate reddish purple sprays that hold up well to winter's depredations. This grass' shade tolerance makes it especially useful in a family of plants that generally prefers abundant sunlight.

Blue sheep's fescue, a stiff silvery-blue clumping grass, is available in a dozen improved selections—most with more intense coloration than the species. 'Elijah Blue' and 'Sea Urchin' are two that are most widely available. Less well known is large blue fescue *Festuca amethystina,* an extremely finely textured grass that is slightly taller and more arching than its close relative. The miscanthus clan is also a large and varied group. If you're acquainted only with the popular 6-foot-tall 'Gracillimus', you might give some of the other cultivars a try. Several, like 'Yaku Jima', 'Adagio', and 'Nippon' are shorter and more compact, often a better fit for small gardens. 'Morning Light' has fine-bladed white variegated leaves that develop a pink cast in fall, as do most of the variegated varieties.

While grasses generally bloom in summer and fall, blue-green moor grass *Sesleria heufleriana*, produces ephemeral flowers in April that open black and then become flecked in creamy yellow. This is a tussock-former with blades that are green on one side, blue on the obverse. The seedheads of summer-blooming rattlesnake grass *Briza media* really do resemble this snake's distinctive rattle. Shaped like golden lockets and suspended from two-foot tall slender stems, they make a soft rustle in the slightest breeze.

Best in light shade is silky spike melic *Melica ciliata*. In my garden, this grass thrives under aspens. The June flowers of silky spike melic look a lot like the foam boppers you can buy at sporting events. Silky spike melic throws progeny around prolifically. To prevent a small meadow from forming, cut the flowers off after they start to fade (to create a meadow, plant two and just stand back). Tufted hairgrass *Deschampsia caespitosa* can also tolerate quite a bit of shade. Most cultivars were developed in Germany and bear names that indicate the jewel-like beauty of their flowers, among them 'Goldgehange' (gold pendant), 'Goldschleier' (gold veil), 'Goldtau' (gold dew), and 'Tautraeger' (dew-bearer). Bulbous oat grass *Arrhenatherum elatius* ssp. *bulbosum* 'Variegatum', is a sweet little grass burdened with an overly long botanic name. Its green and white blades appear breathtakingly silver from a distance. If allowed to get too hot or dry at midsummer, the clump will go dormant, coming to life again later in the summer when the weather cools off. (For more grasses for shady sites, see page 159.)

Backlighting showcases grasses. To take advantage of this effect, site grasses where either the morning sun or the last rays of the afternoon illuminates them. No grass plays with light more effectively than silky threadgrass *Nassella tenuissima* (syn. *Stipa tenuissima*), a very fine-bladed grass that is not always reliably hardy. This is never a problem for us because there are always enough seedlings to replace clumps that die, but not so many to make this grass a pest. Also reportedly frost tender, weeping love grass *Eragrostis curvula* has survived -14°F in my garden without damage. Green in summer, golden in winter, this grass is very drought tolerant.

Conventional wisdom mandates spring planting of perennial types of ornamental grasses, but Mikl Brawner of Harlequin's Garden in Boulder, Colorado, advocates fall planting as well. As long as the grasses go into the ground several weeks before the ground freezes and the transplants are watered whenever they dry out over the winter, fall planting is equally successful.

Portable Microclimates: Container Gardening

Not too many years ago, I would have said the phrase that best describes the Intermountain West is "anything goes." Unlike gardeners in wet climates, who struggle to grow maladapted dryland plants in soggy conditions, we can grow equally maladapted moisture-loving plants just by adding water. Although I have never tried to alter my extremely alkaline soil enough to grow acid-loving rhododendrons and blueberries, I know plenty of gardeners who have done just that and gotten away with it. Anything is possible as long as water is cheap and plentiful. And wherever supplemental irrigation is readily available, the argument that nearly "anything goes" is still valid. But looming water shortages dictate that we need to limit the amount of garden we devote to moisture-loving plants. Anyone trying to grow a quarter acre of such plants is, sooner or later, going to get socked with huge penalties on their water bills.

Container gardening allows us to have it all without violating either watering restrictions or common sense. This is the one microclimate we can absolutely control. We choose the soil. As sun or shade patterns change through the seasons, we can manipulate the light simply by moving the container. Bringing the container indoors, or just the plants in it, overrides the limitations of lack of winter hardiness. Temporarily covering the container with a sheet easily thwarts freak weather during the growing season. Containers add color to otherwise sterile hardscapes. Place pots on porches and patios, or use window boxes or hanging baskets anywhere they can be suspended, including from tree branches. Drop pots into beds and borders, either as decorative elements in their own right, or to fill temporary holes left by all manner of minor disasters.

One real advantage to growing annuals in containers is the ease of protecting them from our capricious weather. One late freeze in June and

Orostachys spinosa. Kelaidis garden.

all of the tropicals in your garden turn black—September snows do in most annuals, regardless of their origins. While I was covering dozens of individual portulacas with one-gallon plastic nursery pots in anticipation of an arctic front one September, it occurred to me how much easier it would be to protect these plants if they were all huddled together in one place. Since then, I've planted frost-tender annuals exclusively in containers and use only frost-resistant species, like gazanias and petunias, out in the garden. When frost threatens, I cover the containers and leave the gazanias and petunias to fend for themselves.

All cacti and succulents benefit from being planted in a custom growing mix with a large percentage of porous scoria that prevents excess moisture from accumulating at all seasons. Again, growing these plants in containers allows you complete control over their exacting cultural requirements. I place the few cacti and succulents that need to be kept dry during summer rains beneath the eaves on the front porch and the back patio. A collection of nonhardy cacti and succulents, many in brightly decorated, but also non–frost-proof Mexican Talavera pottery, add color, flair, and texture throughout my garden. They sit on the "steps" of the dry waterfall, on benches, and on stones—anyplace that needs a boost of color—then come inside for the winter. Hardy succulents can remain outside year round as long as their container is also weather-resistant.

In late summer, I distribute containers of annual flowers throughout the garden. Before changing

Left: A mixed planting of tender succulents. Designed by Karen Haataja.

Top right: A collection of hardy cacti in blue pots. Kelaidis garden.

Bottom: Drop in an attractive container wherever the garden needs a pick-me-up. Don Johnson garden.

light conditions necessitate a move, they reside on the front porch and back patio. The northeast-facing front porch gets plenty of sunlight early in the season, but not enough for sun-lovers later in the year. On the back patio, once it is fully leafed out, a massive concord grape on the arbor blocks sunlight for anything but true shade plants, such as coleus and impatiens, from about mid-July onward. This really isn't such a bad arrangement. Shade cloth on the arbor protects new transplants in containers in spring while they are vulnerable to weather fluctuations. By late summer, the garden is looking tired and can use some help. Dropping in pots brimming with annual flowers is an instant pick-me-up.

Perennial Flowers: The Redheaded Stepchildren of the Mountain West

More than once I've been asked to talk about "new and underused" perennials. There are plenty of these, but *all* perennials are underused in our region. Beyond the occasional daylily or tall-bearded iris, perennials are not all that common in home landscapes. If flowers are included at all, they are generally limited to annuals in a pot, a planter, or a bed. The only perennials that are commonplace in residential landscapes are those used as ground covers. Municipal and commercial plantings are little better. Landscapers have discovered ornamental grasses in a big way—but very few perennial flowers interrupt the "amber waves of grain" look that many of these represent.

What a missed opportunity. Grasses and flowers are a perfect match. Nature almost never paints a scene where one stands without the other. Percentages change, but plains, steppes, and meadows all recreate this natural model. There is no better place than the Intermountain West to grow all types of perennials. Our only limitations are winter hardiness (it's our good fortune that so many varieties of perennials are cold hardy) and soil pH (in general, perennials are not terribly particular about soil type). Xeriscaping has popularized many dryland perennials, but most traditional perennials, such as Shasta daisies, daylilies, lupines, and peonies, appreciate exactly the same cultural conditions and irrigation as bluegrass lawn. There is no reason why everyone who has a lawn can't carve out at least one bed to grow such perennials.

While we can choose from among literally thousands of perennials, every year a few more, previously obscure or unknown, make their way into our gardening lexicon. Some of these become instantly indispensable. Red horned poppy is one such plant. Until the turn of the millennium, we had yellow horned poppies and pale sherbety-orange horned poppies, but no red ones. Then in the spring of 2003, as if by some cosmic synchronicity, red horned poppies were in every garden I visited.

Plant breeders and plant explorers bring us a never-ending parade of new perennials. A few, like hardy ice plants, are truly new to cultivation here. Others are natives with newly recognized garden potential. The whole tribe of agastaches, wildflowers from the American Southwest, falls into this category. Some are new and improved forms of familiar flowers, either hybrids, intentionally bred or naturally occurring, or mutations that caught someone's eye. The changeling might have flowers or foliage markedly different from the norm, or it might be taller or shorter. A handful of plant breeders deliberately select for superior plants—more profuse flowering, and with better disease-, insect-, and weather-resistance.

New from South Africa is *Berkheya purpurea*, a striking purple, lavender, and white daisy that promised to join the ranks of the tender African daisies we use as annuals—until it survived several winters at Denver Botanic Gardens. There's also the moon carrot *Sesile gummiferum* of Plant Select® fame, and *Lallemantia canescens*, a gorgeous short-lived perennial from the Middle East, with purplish-blue spikes. Not all plants are strictly newcomers. *Stachys inflata*, one of my favorites, was a gift from Panayoti Kelaidis in 1991, but it was never commercially available until High Country Gardens of Santa Fe listed it in their catalog in 2006. My policy is to

As in nature, grasses and perennials make perfect partners in the garden. Scarlet hummingbird trumpet *Zauschneria californica*.

Brilliant orange and red horned poppies suddenly showed up in gardens all across the Intermountain West.

Recent additions to the ranks of indispensable perennials for Intermountain West gardens:

Common Name	Botanic Name
Balkan lace	*Athamanta turbith* ssp. *haynaldii*
Cisco woody aster	*Aster venustus*, (syn. *Xylorhiza venusta*)
silver spike	*Berkheya purpurea*
stork's bill	*Erodium trifolium*
red horned poppy	*Glaucium* spp.
mountain hollyhock	*Iliamna rivularis*
lavender false sage	*Lallemantia canescens*
scorpionweed	*Phacelia hastata*
Darcy's sage	*Salvia darcyi*
Mohave sage	*Salvia pachyphylla*
moon carrot	*Seseli gummiferum*
	Sideritis phlomoides
shrubby lamb's ears	*Stachys inflata*
pyrethrum daisy	*Tanacetum cinerariifolium*

Top: Silver spike *Berkheya purpurea* from **South Africa is hardier than first thought.**

Bottom left: Lavender false sage *Lallemantia canescens* from the **Middle East.**

Bottom right: Scorpionweed *Phacelia hastata* is native to the **Front Range of Colorado.**

try every new introduction at least once. You never know. Each one has the potential to turn out to be your new favorite plant.

Annual Flowers

Once, while shopping for flowers, I overheard a couple discussing the relative merits of annuals and perennials. He insisted that perennial flowers were the better value because they come back every year. "You only have to plant them once." I can't deny his logic but the annual/perennial debate isn't an either/or proposition. The best gardens contain some of each. I can't imagine a garden without annuals. Perennials do enjoy longer lives than annuals, but the tradeoff is volume. This gentleman will likely be disappointed when he discovers that most perennials bloom for only a week or two.

Keeping a garden of perennials in color the whole summer is an exercise in choreography that involves a great deal of thought. When one flower goes over, another must be poised to take its place. A garden where perennial flowers mix it up with annuals requires less coordination. Perennials come and go, but annuals carry on, providing color throughout the season. Annuals have other uses, too. Many types grow incredibly fast, making them ideal for temporary screening or infill, while newly planted shrubs and trees grow to mature size. I once took out a large bridal veil spirea to make room for a tree that will eventually reach 15 feet and screen the west side of my property. In the meantime, I fill the void every year with annual red-leafed 'Carmencita' castor beans and burgundy sunflowers—both guaranteed to reach 5 or 6 feet within weeks of transplanting.

For a time, gardening with annual flowers was considered déclassé. Perennials and mixed borders were the height of fashion, annuals the stock-in-trade of municipal park plantings and old tires recycled into planters. It wasn't until the recent surge in the popularity of container gardening that

the fortunes of annual flowers reversed. The number of new annuals introduced each year has increased exponentially, with variations on old favorites and quite a number of plants previously unknown to horticulture.

Ten years ago, who had ever heard of calibrachoa, angelonia, scaveola, or plectranthus? Partly, it's spillover from the current tropical craze. Factors such as an increase in plant exploration, a concerted attempt to improve existing flowers, and "branding" of new introductions all contribute to the current wealth of possibilities. We all benefit from the greater selection and better disease- and weather-resistant plants. One good example is

sun-tolerant coleus, until recently a confirmed shade lover. New cultivars tolerate sun or shade with equal aplomb, making them the perfect choice for patios like mine that are sunny in spring but shaded later in the season.

Many of the most promising new annuals are actually frost-tender perennials that won't survive our cold winters, but that bloom the same season when started from cuttings or seed. We grow these as annuals, planting them outside only after all reasonable risk of frost is past. At the end of the season, we can either bring them inside or toss them into the compost bin. Another current trend is using hardy perennials with particularly attrac-

Annual lavender verbena stays in bloom when red coral bells wimp out from summer's heat.

Pink zinnias and chartreuse sun-tolerant coleus.

tive foliage, like heucheras, artemisias, lamiums, and vincas, in containers. At the end of the season they can be planted in the garden to overwinter, and dug up again and replanted into a container the following spring. If the container is frost-proof, and you can remember to water them occasionally, hardy perennials can be left in their containers in a protected area all winter.

Cool-season annuals are those that fare better where summer temperatures don't get so uncomfortably hot. If you want to see for yourself, drive up to a mountain community in July and compare their lobelias, snapdragons, brachycome, clarkias, China pinks, and agrostemma with yours. Plains dwellers generally succeed with cool-season annuals only in

the rare cool summer. These flowers prefer temperatures that are too brisk for tomatoes—good tomato years are bad cool-season annual years.

If you want to give them a try anyway, plant cool-season annuals in a sheltered location that receives morning sun and afternoon shade. Or, adopt the traditional bedding-out philosophy of creating seasonal displays and plant cool-season annuals for spring color. Then plan to rip them out when they start to look ratty, usually around the middle of June. (It's easier to lose your flowers if it seems like it was your idea in the first place.) A few of these annuals—snapdragons, sweet alyssum, and calendulas, for example—bloom for a couple of months in spring and early summer, but will rebloom later in the year if their stems are cut down to basal foliage after they finish their first round of blooms. You may want to leave these in place over the summer if they don't look too awful.

Summer is the season when flower beds can develop a serious case of what more than one garden writer has called "the gaps." Tulip foliage that has been hanging on seemingly forever finally succumbs to the heat. You gleefully pull out those unsightly brown leaves only to discover you have just ripped bare a large section of the flower bed. Whatever originally cavorted with the tulips has long since departed. Or, you cut down a patch of perennials that only a few short weeks ago were the glory of the garden and find that now there is nothing left but stubs and expanses of exposed soil—with all the appeal of a clear-cut logging site. To further add to your troubles, scores of cool-weather annuals have fainted dead away from weeks of relentless heat. And, then there are Oriental poppies, bleeding hearts, and other spring ephemerals. After they have finished blooming, these massive flowers collapse like an undercooked soufflé.

In a perfect world, garden centers would sell annuals all summer. But this is not economically feasible where the growing season is as short as ours. Sales of annual flowers fall off sharply after the spring buying frenzy and by midsummer, they are nearly impossible to find. The shrewd gardener prepares for garden calamities by purchasing a few extra containers of annuals in spring. Skip the pansies and look for the real heat-lovers like coreopsis, salvias, gazanias, and portulacas. Deciding which are which is not difficult. The sun-worshipers are sturdy and perky even when their pots dry out. Anything obviously suffering from heat stroke is not a good choice. Store your reserves in a cool, partly shaded place and water them regularly until you need them. If you missed the last of the annual flowers, early July is not too late to poke in a few seeds of morning glories, scarlet runner beans, nasturtiums, sunflowers, cosmos, and zinnias. Just be sure to keep the soil damp until they germinate.

Red corn poppies in Charles Mann's meadow garden.

Scarlet flax doesn't come in six-packs. Sow the seed directly into the garden.

Flowering perennials and shrubs generally take a breather in July and August. Most of the color in the midsummer garden comes from heat-loving summer annuals. Due to our extreme fluctuations in spring temperatures, summer annuals can get off to a slow start. They may refuse to budge the entire month of June (or, heaven forbid, shrink in size). Then July's heat triggers them to grow and by August the plants are hearty and full of flowers. Warm-season annuals, as their name implies, excel in summer heat. It's no use planting any of these heat-lovers much before June 1. As a general rule, this group is utterly frost intolerant and temperatures below 50°F can stunt their growth. One great thing about summer annuals is that you can plant them in July and August, the hottest part of the summer. As long as you don't let them dry out (or get too wet), heat won't set them back whatsoever.

There are dozens of annual flowers that are not well known, oddly enough, because they are too easy to grow. In an era where most flowers begin their lives in plastic cell-packs, those that don't adjust well to greenhouse culture tend to be overlooked. These free-and-easy annuals and biennials prefer a more casual genesis. Scatter their seed in the garden and they are good to go. As an added bonus, flowers that germinate in situ are more drought-tolerant than those transplanted out as seedlings.

Some gardeners can't abide serendipity in their gardens. They want their plants to stay put and have no use for the anarchy of self-sowing annuals, biennials, and perennials. I, on the other hand, rely on these spunky flowers to fill in all of the bare spots and knit my flower beds together. To be sure, my taste runs to bursting at the seams, my garden as chockablock as an antique market stall. For me, larkspur, love-in-a-mist, California poppy, bread poppy, columbines, rose campion, red orach, echium, silky thread grass, feverfew, blue flax, Armenian poppy, money plant, violets, verbascum, hollyhocks, corydalis, and mountain basket-of-gold are reliable old friends. These flowers come back in various parts of the garden, year after year, from seeds sown or plants purchased well over a decade ago.

Self-sowing annuals and biennials best grown from seed (sown where they are to grow):

Common Name	Botanic Name
corncockle	Agrostemma githago*
hollyhock	Alcea ficifolia, A. rosea ‡
amaranth	Amaranthus spp. (all types)
false bishop's flower	Ammi majus
common dill	Anethum graveolens
prickly poppy	Argemone mexicana ‡
red orach	Atriplex hortensis ‡
tickseed	Bidens ferulifolia, B. humilis
borage	Borago officinalis ‡
pot marigold	Calendula officinalis* ‡
bachelor's buttons	Centaurea cyanus* ‡
honeywort	Cerinthe major 'Purpurascens'*
larkspur	Consolida ambigua* ‡
plains coreopsis	Coreopsis tinctoria ‡
golden smoke	Corydalis aurea ‡
cosmos	Cosmos spp. ‡
Chinese forget-me-not	Cynoglossum amabile* ‡
dragonhead	Dracocephalum nutans ‡
viper's bugloss	Echium vulgare ‡
California poppy	Eschscholzia californica ‡
western wallflower	Erysimum asperum ‡
blanketflower	Gaillardia pulchella
bird's eyes	Gilia tricolor
sunflower	Helianthus annuus
flower-of-an-hour	Hibiscus trionum ‡
Mexican tulip poppy	Hunnemannia fumariifolia
candytuft	Iberis umbellata*
standing cypress	Ipomopsis rubra* ‡
tidy-tips	Layia platyglossa
mountain phlox	Linanthus grandiflorus*
scarlet flax	Linum grandiflorum
honesty	Lunaria annua ‡
Texas bluebonnet	Lupinus texensis*
rose campion	Lychnis coronaria* ‡
Tahoka daisy	Machaeranthera tanacetifolia ‡
mallow	Malva spp.*
blazing star	Mentzelia spp. ‡
four o'clocks	Mirabilis jalapa
baby blue eyes	Nemophila menziesii*
love-in-a-mist	Nigella damascena* ‡
corn poppy	Papaver rhoeas* ‡
California bluebells	Phacelia campanularia*

*cool-season annuals, the remainder are warm season
‡ Cold-hardy seed that can be sown in fall

Annuals and biennials for dry zones:

Common Name	Botanic Name
desert marigold	Baileya multiradiata
rock purslane	Calandrinia umbellata
Madagascar periwinkle	Catharanthus roseus
Rocky Mountain beeplant	Cleome serrulata
spiderflower	C. 'Sparkler Blush'
livingstone daisy	Dorotheanthus bellidiformis
Mexican daisy	Erigeron karvinskianus
snow-on-the-mountain	Euphorbia marginata
treasure flower	Gazania rigens
sweet potato vine	Ipomoea batatas
lantana	Lantana spp.
statice	Limonium perezii
statice	L. sinuatum
blazing star	Mentzelia spp.
Bigelow's monkey flower	Mimulus bigelovii
lemon mint	Monarda citriodora
horsemint	M. pectinata
flowering tobacco	Nicotiana sylvestris
petunias	Petunia spp., Explorer, Tidal Wave, and Wave series
sage	Salvia coccinea
autumn sage	S. greggii
creeping zinnia	Sanvitalia procumbens
plains Navajo tea	Thelesperma filifolium
Dahlberg daisy	Thymophylla (syn. Dyssodia) tenuiloba
Imagination verbena	Verbena tenuisecta

A few things, like bachelor's buttons, have disappeared over time, as conditions in my garden have changed. They were once abundant, but obviously needed more elbow room. Many of these flowers, like California bluebells, are desert ephemerals. These opportunistic wildflowers germinate quickly after rain falls, many flowering and completing their entire life cycle in a few short weeks. Our relatively wet summers (compared to their Mojave Desert origins) occasionally coax California poppies, and a few otherwise short-lived annuals, into staying around throughout the summer months to rebloom every cool spell and again in the fall.

Seed packets provide specific cultural information, advising the best time and method for planting for each particular species. A good general one-size-fits-most approach is to rough up the soil with a rake, broadcast the seed, then smooth the soil with the back of the rake. Sow the seed in late fall or spring just before rain or snow is forecast. If the storm passes your garden by, water using a very gentle spray to prevent washing the seeds out of the soil. In rock or gravel mulched areas, simply scatter the seeds over the mulch where they will settle into the nooks and crannies.

When things really heat up, it's time to plant annual vines. Most have tropical or subtropical origins and absolutely insist on hot days and warm nights to do more than sit and sulk. Garden centers sell container-grown seedlings as well as seeds. Seedlings provide a couple weeks' head start over seeds, but the selection is limited compared with the dozens of different kinds of seed available. Every garden center sells seeds of common vines such as nasturtiums, sweet peas, morning glories, and scarlet runner beans. More unusual types may take some searching.

All annual vines appreciate well-amended humusy soil and regular watering. Those requirements met, most annual vines are positively foolproof. Add soil, water, and sunshine—and stand back. Many of these vines are vigorous enough to cover an entire shed within a few weeks. Use annual vines to hide eyesores like chain-link fencing or to provide instant shade on an arbor over the patio. Send them up perennial vines—when the clematis is out of bloom, it might as well act as a trellis to another season of color. If you're lucky, the bloom times of both will coincide for a sumptuous, layered effect. Annual vines can also be allowed to tumble down the sides of containers and hanging baskets. Simply poke a few seeds into the soil around the edge of the pot. Or stick a small trellis or wire pyramid into a large container and train the vine both up and out.

Bulbs for Low-Maintenance Color

In a culture where instant gratification is the prevailing marketing objective, flowering bulbs are an imperfect fit. When you plant bulbs, the various brown lumps offer only the promise of flowers to come two to eight months hence. With the exception of the few types sold in containers, when they're at their peak you can't actually buy them. This disjunction between availability and culmination may explain the underuse of a class of plants so perfectly suited to our region. Tulips get good press, as do daffodils and lilies, but only the popular florist types with big flowers and long stems. Hundreds of their smaller or quirkier relatives hardly ever make an appearance.

With few exceptions, bulbs are exquisitely adapted to our climate and conditions. Tropicals such as canna, pineapple lily, and gladiola aren't winter hardy but they do withstand heat better than many annuals, blooming after even stalwarts like petunias wimp out in midsummer. Most spring-blooming bulbs actually prefer dry summers. In fact, the very existence of a bulb suggests a plant that originates in a habitat where at least part of the year it is too hot, too cold, or too dry for optimal growth. Developing a bulb allows the plant to bide its time underground until conditions improve, measurably increasing its chance of survival. Everything the plant needs is packed into this ingenious storage unit—roots, stems, leaves, and flowers—all ready to leap into action at the appropriate time.

Contrary to what many of us have been led to believe, America's favorite bulb, the tulip, is better suited to life in the Intermountain West than in Holland. Hailing from the steppes of Central Asia—places such as Afghanistan, Iran, Iraq, Syria, and Turkey—tulips are perfectly adapted to cold winters and hot, dry summers. For centuries, the Dutch have been breeding hybrids that are more tolerant of summer damp, but tulips betray their arid origins by rotting if kept too wet during their summer dormancy. Species tulips are, as a rule, not only drought tolerant, but drought demanding.

Simply by choosing a selection of early-, mid-, and late-season varieties, it is possible to have tulips blooming for a full three months. The earliest tulips start in March, including the Kaufmanniana hybrids, and cultivars of *Tulipa humilis*, *T. biflora*, *T. polychroma*, and *T. turkestanica*. Kaufmanniana hybrids bear huge, nearly stemless flowers in the shape of six-pointed stars when fully open. Often the interior of the flower is radically different from the outer petals. These tulips come in an array of brilliant colors and distinctive markings. The rest of the aforementioned species tulips are tiny and many of them could easily be mistaken for crocuses.

By the end of March and into April, we start to see tulips that are more conventional in appearance. The Fosterianas (aka Emperor tulips) have large, chalice-shaped flowers in a wide range of colors, including fiery oranges and scarlet and some of the most delicate pastel shades. Screaming red 'Red Emperor' can be enjoyed at any speed or distance. Buttery yellow 'Sweetheart' is better appreciated up close. Most midseason species tulips are slightly larger than those that bloom earlier in the year. *Tulipa batalinii* comes in several named varieties in shades of gold, apricot, and red. The lady tulips *T. clusiana* have petals that are handsomely splashed with contrasting colors on their exterior. A multitude of *T. gregii* selections feature foliage distinctively mottled with lines and dashes. The latest of the species tulips continue blooming into early May.

Tall Darwin hybrids also start their show in April. Darwins include long-standing favorites

'Tangerine Beauty' tulips.

such as cherry red 'Apeldoorn' and golden yellow 'Beauty of Apeldoorn'. Of the tall tulips, the Darwins are the most likely to perennialize, that is, to multiply and come back indefinitely. Saving the best for last, May brings us the elegant lily-flowering tulips, their long, tapered petals sharply pointed at the tips. These tulips are also some of the toughest, coming back year after year. New colors preview every season, from impossible-to-ignore crimsons, scarlet, and primary yellow flamed with red, to sweet pastels.

Tulips aren't the only drought-loving bulbs. Snow iris *Iris danfordiae*, *I. histrioides*, *I.reticulata*, and *I. bucharica* are all much more likely to perennialize and grow into large clumps if kept dry in summer. Ditto many of the crocus, especially February-blooming *Crocus ancyrensis* 'Golden Bunch', *C. susianus* 'Cloth of Gold', the snow crocus *C. chrysanthus*, and Mediterranean *C. sieberi*.

The flowers of all snow irises are enormous for the size of the plant, 3 inches across on 6-inch stems. The lower petals are attractively marked with blotches of contrasting color. These intrepid bulbs live true to the postal service's rain-sleet-snow-etc. credo. Subzero temperatures may kill their first blossoms, but these plants have a plan for this eventuality—a second bud lies in reserve. Snow doesn't bother them a whit and few things are as pretty as a clump of iris blooming through a blanket of snow. After the flowers finish blooming, the irises' grasslike foliage continues to grow and lengthen for a few weeks. By May, the leaves have dried up and become brown wisps that you can either remove or ignore. Snow irises are easy and inexpensive. Perfect for the xeric garden, all they require is well-drained soil, some moisture in spring, and a location that bakes in summer. These little bulbs only need to be planted 4 inches deep—you can easily inter 100 in a half hour if you aren't overly meticulous. One hundred may sound extravagant, but it takes large numbers to make a really impressive show. Space the bulbs 4 to 5 inches apart. They look a bit sparse the first season, but eventually multiply into substantial drifts.

There's no trick to having crocuses in bloom throughout late winter and spring if you plant them in the hottest, sunniest spots in your garden. In their natural habitats, the Middle East and Central Asia, crocuses bloom as soon as the snow melts in spring. Their flowers are quite tolerant of cold, damaged only when temperatures go below zero and only then when there is no snow cover. The crocuses' propensity to close up tightly on gloomy days no doubt helps them withstand inclement weather. Crocuses (and many species tulips) are like sunbathers, who close up their beach umbrellas and head for their car the minute the sun goes behind a cloud, making these flowers useless as cut flowers—or where there is shade in the garden for any part of the day.

In my Colorado garden, sweeps of crocus start blooming in warmer microclimates not much after the first of the year. The clear yellow chalices of golden bunch crocus *Crocus ancyrensis* are the first to make their appearance, usually by the third week of January. Between snowstorms, they continue to send up nosegays of cheerful blossoms the entire month of February. A couple of weeks later, cloth of gold *C. angustifolius* joins in, its golden yellow petals brushed bronze on their undersides. Mid-February brings *C. versicolor* 'Picturatus', creamy white demitasse cups with glowing yellow throats, their exterior a soft, buttery yellow feathered with cobalt blue. At around the same time, *C. chrysanthus* 'Zwanenberg Bronze' pops up, opening first on warmer south-facing slopes, and gradually marching northward across the large central rock garden in the backyard. All of these early crocuses smell sweetly of honey and lure honeybees out of their winter slumber. *Crocus chrysanthus* and its hybrids are available in a wide selection of colors. 'Advance' is yellow with a violet exterior, 'Blue Bird' gray-blue, 'Blue Pearl' is silvery blue, 'Cream Beauty' barely yellow, 'Lady Killer' white with a purplish-blue blotch on the outside. Every one is as good as the other and ideal for brightening up the winter xeriscape.

Dutch crocus *C. vernus* varieties and the popular cultivars of *C. tommasinianus*, including

'Whitewell Purple' and 'Taplow Ruby', come from more moderate habitats—moist meadows and woodland edges in Europe. These should be sited where they will not bake during the summer months. They do better for me in the amended soil of flower beds and with weekly watering. The flowers of Dutch crocus are, as the name of the golden-yellow variety 'Yellow Mammoth' suggests, truly super-sized compared to their petite relatives. At nearly 3 inches across, they come in a wide range of colors, including: 'Pickwick', white-striped lavender; 'Flower Record', pale violet; 'Jeanne d' Arc', white; and 'Twilight', deep blue-violet. Dutch crocus generally bloom in March or April.

Lesser-Known Little Bulbs

With the emphasis on big, gaudy tulips and daffodils, many other bulbs with charming little flowers get overlooked. It's a pity because, unlike their more flamboyant counterparts, these are some of the most durable flowers for Mountain West gardeners. Planted once, these will be with you forever, the closest thing there is to a truly "maintenance-free" flower. Besides their size, the little bulbs offer other advantages. They are programmed to jump into action the minute the snow melts, which may be as early as January in a warm, protected spot. In the coldest frost pocket most will still be in their full glory by March and April, blooming unscathed through late snowstorms and all but the most frigid cold snaps.

Diminutive bulbs sport proportionately diminutive foliage, another definite plus for the garden. Inconspicuous even when green, these leaves generally ripen and disappear long before they can interfere with spring's splendor. Not even dedicated opera fans can enjoy the histrionic death scenes of the larger tulips and daffodils as their leaves dissolve—agonizingly slowly—into summer dormancy. Few pests prey on small bulbs since they are long gone by the time insects stir in spring. Voles and squirrels can be a problem. They dig up newly planted bulbs with the enthusiasm of treasure hunters going after buried gold bullion. Fortunately, they aren't usually all that accurate so most bulbs are left undiscovered.

Grecian windflower *Anemone blanda* forms colonies of dark green, ferny foliage supporting perky daisies in April. 'Blue Star' is solid lavender-blue. Naturally, 'Pink Star,' is pink. 'White Splendor' has crystalline white flowers with a yellow center. All are especially attractive planted as a ground cover beneath large tulips in either complementary or contrasting colors. The notoriously rampant grape hyacinth *Muscari armeniacum* is better behaved when grown dry, spreading slowly into a sea of blue. Mahogany and gold *Fritillaria michailovskyi* can withstand a very dry spot in the garden and still return year after year. Hyacinths are only moderately drought tolerant, daffodils even less so.

The flowers of striped squill *Puschkinia libanotica* appear turquoise from a distance, but are actually icy white with true blue stripes. Brilliant blue Siberian squill *Scilla siberica* is also available in white. *Scilla bifolia rosea* has baby pink flowers; *Scilla mischtschenkoana* is palest blue. Available in white, blue or pink, glory-of-the-snow *Chionodoxa* spp., has up-facing starry flowers. All of these are only a few inches tall, bloom in early April, and grow into large colonies in full sun or partial shade. Probably the least well known of the small bulbs is the spring starflower *Ipheion uniflorum*. Its wide-petaled stars come in white or shades of blue. Like the common grape hyacinth, it sends up foliage in the fall and blooms in mid-spring. From South America, the ipheion occasionally gets confused and blooms in autumn.

Bulbs for shade are so rarely grown that many gardeners don't even know they exist. Almost any bulb will work under deciduous trees and shrubs where light is abundant in winter and spring. True shade lovers are adapted to low light conditions year round and so can be located on the north and east side of structures and beneath evergreens. Keep in mind, though, that no bulb is likely to do well in really dense shade. One of the most shade-tolerant is Spanish bluebell *Hyacinthoides hispanica*, which comes in blues, pink or white. Each 12-inch-tall spike supports a carillon of little nodding bells. Similar is English bluebell *H. non-scripta* with fragrant

The soccer ball-sized flowers of star of Persia *Allium albopilosum.*

blue flowers on arching stems. Virginia bluebell *Mertensia virginica,* not really a bulb at all, is sold alongside bulbs as dormant roots. Its flowers, more trumpet- than bell-shaped, open pink and age to lavender blue. All three multiply rapidly in humus-enriched, moisture retentive soil and bloom in May.

Also quite shade-tolerant is the Star of Bethlehem *Ornithogalum umbellatum.* It has clusters of white star-shaped flowers in April and will carpet the ground in woodland conditions. One ornamental onion prefers shade. *Allium triquetrum* is a summer bloomer with white bellflowers on 18-inch tall triangular stems. Other woodlanders to try include checkered lily *Fritillaria meleagris* (purple and white bells in April), *F. pallidiflora* (yellow and green flowers in April), the dog's tooth violet *Erythronium* 'Pagoda' (yellow flowers in May), winter aconites *Eranthis cilicica* and *E. hyemalis* (yellow buttercups in April) and snowdrops *Galanthus* spp. (white flowers in early spring). All of the above require soil that is consistently moist, but not wet, to naturalize and come back year after year. Hardy cyclamen is the one shade-loving bulb that will reliably grow in dry shade, even under a mature spruce tree. They are spectacular both in foliage (shining green often marbled and splashed silver) and in flower (tiny versions of the florist's cyclamen). (For more shade-tolerant bulbs, see page 157.)

Additional Bulb Choices

The next group of bulbs is a mixed bag that, for no explanation, have never really caught on. Some, like *Iris bucharica,* are lesser-known members of otherwise popular tribes. Others are real oddballs or newcomers to the scene. Camassia, brodiaea, and calochortus suffer from the overlooked native syndrome common to many native wildflowers.

Of our western natives, camassia are the easiest to grow. They need moist soil, but only in the spring when they are up and about. The rest of the year they are perfectly happy sleeping among the Shasta daisies and garden phloxes, needing only occasional irrigation. All are beautiful, in shades of blue or white on plumes 15 to 30 inches tall, varying by species and variety. But *Camassia cusickii* is ethereal, its pale lavender-blue, starry flowers accented by yellow anthers. 'Blue Melody' is also particularly striking, with pale gold edges on variegated foliage. Calochortus are not always winter hardy but make magnificent annuals. *Calochortus luteus* and *C. superbus* are the toughest of the bunch. Brodieas, (syn. *Triteleia* and *Dichelostemma*), from California, are not generally hardy, but 'Starlight' has been successful in the rock alpine garden at Denver Botanic Gardens for many years. Its softball-sized umbels are luminescent yellow.

The Juno iris *Iris bucharica* was downright rare until it finally hit the big time a couple of years ago when it appeared in Martha Stewart's K-Mart bulb line-up. From Afghanistan, there is no iris better suited to our climate. The flowers are buttery-yellow and white and the spring-green foliage resembles corn stalks. One bulb quickly grows into a large clump in a sunny site that dries out and heats up in summer. An oddity that few would guess was actually a tuber is *Geranium tuberosum*, a little geranium that is also perfectly adapted to the Intermountain West. This Mediterranean native blooms lavender-pink in spring and then goes dormant during the hot, dry summer months. In other words, it likes drought.

A favorite of rock gardeners that is too seldom used in other parts of gardens is the fumewort *Corydalis solida*, a pretty little thing with lacy foliage and tubular violet-white, reddish, or pink flowers. Plant it in woodland gardens, at the edge of a path, or at the top of a wall where it can cascade down the stones. *Ixiolirion pallasii* (syn. *I. tataricum*) looks exactly like a miniature lily with long, violet-blue trumpets in May. Readily available, but too seldom seen in gardens, are the snowflakes with lovely white bells dotted green. The spring snowflake *Leucojum vernum* blooms in April, the summer snowflake *L. aestivium,* in June. Both need a moisture-retentive soil and thrive in our heaviest clay, where few other bulbs will grow.

Although a few alliums are rhizomatous, most alliums start life as bulbs and are sold alongside tulips and daffodils in the fall. However, unlike most other fall-planted bulbs, alliums don't just bloom in spring. One type or another is always in bloom from May throughout the entire summer. Of the May alliums, only *Allium karataviense* has foliage that is as attractive as its flowers. Broad, flat leaves are silvery-gray washed with overtones of purple, the dense pinkish flowers 3 to 4 inches across. Tall and stately *A. aflatunense* sends up purple flowers the size and shape of baseballs on 3-foot stems. Similar, but taller yet, is *A. rosenbachianum*, its flowers dusty pink. Most alliums form sphere-shaped flowerheads, but *A. bulgaricum* is an exception, with cascading stars of white and burgundy.

A large number of alliums bloom in June. The star of Persia *Allium albopilosum* (syn *A. christophii*) is literally the size of soccer balls, the red-violet flowers borne on sturdy 18-inch stems. Blue ping-pong balls of *A. azureum,* are carried on 2-foot-tall stems so fine they appear to float. There are several alliums with baby pink flowers, among them the nodding flowers of *A. cernuum,* the upright umbels of *A. unifolium,* and the shooter-marble sized spheres of *A. przewalskianum*. *Allium ostrowskianum* is only a few inches tall, with flowers less substantial than most alliums, but their hot pink color makes up for their size. *Allium flavum* celebrates the Fourth of July with a miniature show of fireworks, its exploding spheres of yellow flowers standing a foot tall. Also summer blooming is mountain garlic *A. senescens* 'Glaucium', with unusual foliage that twists and curls and lavender pink flowers in July and August. Drumstick allium *A. sphaerocephalon* bears purplish-red egg-shaped flowers.

Most alliums have attractive seedheads. To prevent an overwhelming amount of self-sowing, remove these once your colony is large enough. Because spring-blooming alliums tend to go dormant in summer, plant annuals in the gaps they leave. Treat bulb alliums like any other fall-planted bulb. Rhizomatous types are sold in containers—

When the handsome foliage of Turkestan onion *Allium karataviense* goes dormant in June, a ground cover of veronica fills in.

plant them like any other garden perennial. Although ornamental onions are edible, I suspect if they were palatable they would have been on our plates long ago. If you want double duty, grow chives—which are both tasty and attractive.

Fall-blooming bulbs are still mostly unheard of. Such is the colchicum's plight. A few of these "autumn crocuses" (not even remotely related to crocuses) are regularly offered for sale in autumn with tulip bulbs. There are a dozen or more varieties that do well here but are seldom used. Planting early, in late summer, when the colchicum is still fully dormant ensures flowers the same year.

The most widely available species regularly bloom on the shelf before you have a chance to get them in the ground. It's a whole lot less trouble to plant a bulb before it has produced a flower stalk that is easily snapped off.

A common complaint with fall-blooming colchicums is that they send up huge clumps of foliage in spring, which vanishes before summer heat sets in. The flowers bloom in fall "naked" (accounting for some of the more politically-incorrect common names). The shiny, dark green foliage is actually quite attractive. Just take care in siting colchicums to make assets of both flowers and foliage. Don't let the leaves smother smaller things and do allow the flowers to "borrow" leaves from other plants, if their nakedness bothers. The best known of the colchicums is the double variety 'Waterlily', though I personally prefer the chalices of the single forms. Also exceptional is *Colchicum agrippinum,* a large lilac flower that is marked by a wine-colored houndstooth pattern.

Cultural requirements vary by species, but all colchicums need well-drained soil that is not too dry when they are actively growing. Those that are happy reproduce both by division and seed to grow into large colonies. In the unlikely event you end up with too many, dig them up after the leaves die back and share them with friends. Colchicum leaves are sometimes damaged by late frosts, so treat these like the many lilies and eremerus that share the same risk—by covering emerging foliage with pine needles and evergreen boughs until the last frost date is well past.

Bulb Culture

Few things are more annoying than bulbs planted in the fall going AWOL over the winter. Of the twelve yellow snow irises I carefully interred one October, only four showed up the following spring. Presumably the rest died and turned into very expensive worm food. What went wrong? Spring bulbs are about as foolproof as a flower can be. You dig a hole, drop in a bulb, cover it with dirt, and—presto—next spring, instant flower. Without any coddling, most bulbs obligingly multiply into large, ever-expanding colonies. If all goes well. Like all living things, bulbs can be killed by all manner of natural and manmade disasters. I suspect my irises were already dead even before I brought them home. After procrastinating most of that fall, I had picked these bulbs up on a last-minute impulse. They'd likely been in a bin too long by then.

Although the bulb's best trick is its ability to spend many months out of soil, it will fare better when kept cool during its aboveground dormant

Snow iris *Iris reticulata* blooms in February in a warm microclimate. (Photo by R. Tatroe)

Shrubs and trees that have more than one season of interest are a real asset—a hawthorn in its fall finery.

stage. Temperatures comfortable for shoppers are generally too warm for bulbs. Those placed in bins in the hot sun in front of a glass window are guaranteed to cook. To be safe, buy bulbs the minute they hit store shelves in late summer. Then store them in a cool garage or basement until you can get around to planting them. If you mail-order bulbs, make sure the package isn't left on a hot porch for any length of time. Try to arrange the delivery for when someone will be home to receive it. To further increase your bulbs' likelihood of success, pick out healthy bulbs in the first place. Choosing bulbs is no more challenging than buying onions and potatoes at a grocery. The best are heavy for their size and firm, with no stem or root growth. Damaged bulbs are often shriveled and soft or have obvious signs of rot.

Other bulb killers are putting fertilizer in the planting hole, letting the soil dry out too thoroughly after planting, planting the bulbs too shallowly, choosing varieties not hardy for your region, and furry gourmands. Thoroughly mix fertilizer in the soil to keep it out of direct contact with the bulbs, or better yet, scratch fertilizer into the surface of the bed after planting. Water the beds well after planting and again whenever the soil dries out thoroughly during the winter. On the other hand, really bad drainage can cause bulbs to rot. So, other than the few exceptions previously noted, don't put bulbs where water collects. Be sure to heed planting depth recommendations. And don't accidentally plant tender bulbs like paperwhites in the garden. They are sold in the fall only for forcing indoors.

To deter burrowing bulb-eaters, line the hole with small gauge chicken wire. Bring the wire up over the bulbs after backfilling the hole with soil to form a bulb sanctuary. This, of course, won't stop deer from eating the tops and flowers. Deer and other critters generally leave untouched poisonous bulbs such as daffodils and colchicums. Sparrows and house finches start shredding crocus flowers the minute the come up. Nothing I tried discouraged them—neither strategically placing scare cat cutouts throughout the garden nor keeping the bird feeders full—until I discovered pinwheels. Now every patch of crocuses gets its own foil pinwheel. They're gaudy, true, but the flashing foil appears to work. Evidently, feathered vandals have long been the bane of the gardener. Brian Mathew, in *The Crocus*, cites C. Curtis' complaint of the "great depravations" of sparrows in 1787. Curtis' cure? Taxidermied cats amongst his crocuses. (I'm tempted to give this solution a try on days when my cats are misbehaving.)

Trees for Shade and Privacy

Trees are unquestionably the least well-adapted category of plants for most of our region, although few of us are willing to forego such a cultural icon. Where precipitation is 15 inches or less annually, trees and shrubs can have a rough time of it. For the most part, trees are temperate creatures—the rarity of hardwood forests in our region reflects this reality. If you stop cultivating the land in eastern parts of the United States, shrubs and trees are what grow back. That won't happen here. Very few trees are both drought tolerant and winter hardy. Grand old shade trees require huge amounts of water to sustain them. Palo verde and mesquite, signature trees from the warm deserts of the Southwest, can't survive our winters.

Trees also have trouble coping with our capricious weather. The heaviest snowfalls of the year often occur in early autumn when trees have not yet dropped their leaves, or in late spring after they have leafed out. The weight of even a few inches of snow can be more than a tree can withstand, breaking branches and splitting trunks. Many municipalities in other regions ban certain trees from public plantings because they are prone to breakage. But in the Intermountain West, damage is often indiscriminate. Oaks crack as readily as silver maples. It's said that overwatering trees causes weaker wood and more severe damage. But

SHADE TREES FOR THE WEST

While this may not be the best place to attempt a world-class arboretum, the selection of shade trees we can grow is still sizeable, especially when supplemental irrigation is available. Proven trees for the Intermountain West:

Common Name	Botanic Name	Height
Tartarian maple	Acer tataricum	20–25'
red horsechestnut	Aesculus x carnea	30–35'
Ohio buckeye	A. glabra	20–30'
thinleaf alder	Alnus tenuifolia	20–25'
American chestnut	Castanea dentata	to 100'
western catalpa	Catalpa speciosa	40–60'
hackberry	Celtis occidentalis	50–60'
yellowwood	Cladrastis lutea	35–50'
green ash	Fraxinus pennsylvanica	20–50'
swamp white oak	Quercus bicolor	50–60'
bur oak	Q. macrocarpa	50–80'
chinkapin oak	Q. muehlenbergii	40–50'
Purple Robe locust	Robinia pseudoacacia 'Purple Robe'	25–40'
Japanese pagoda tree	Sophora japonica	20–40'
linden	Tilia americana, T. cordata	20–40', 60–70'

unirrigated trees in the open space next to my home and in natural forests are just as prone to the occasional wrack and ruin these storms bring.

Shade and privacy are essential, and trees create both, so we continue to plant trees in spite of their fragility. Still it makes good sense to choose and place trees with care rather than, as one environmentalist put it, "cluster bombing" your property with as many trees as will fit. Shade trees get large at maturity—the average urban or suburban property has room for only one. Cottonwoods, for example, can reach 75 to 100 feet with a 50 to 75 foot spread (larger than many lots). That's more tree than most of us bargained for. At a comparably modest 60 feet, a fully-grown Marshall's ash is three times the height of a two-story house. Also keep in mind that shade trees can block out so much sunlight it can be difficult to garden beneath them. For maximum efficiency (to provide cooling for the house in summer and to let the warmth of

FLOWERING TREES WITH MORE THAN ONE SEASON OF INTEREST

Common Name	Botanic Name	Attributes	Comments
serviceberry	Amelanchier spp.	white flowers in spring; blue fruit; red fall color	
Sutherland peatree	Caragana arborescens 'Sutherland'	yellow flowers in spring; yellow fall color	
eastern redbud	Cercis canadensis	pink flowers in spring; heart-shaped leaves; yellow fall color	needs protected site
white fringe tree	Chionanthus virginicus	fragrant white flowers in spring; blue fruit; yellow fall color	
Pagoda dogwood	Cornus alternifolia	white flowers in spring; bluish berries; red fall color	
Cornelian cherry	Cornus mas	yellow flowers in spring; exfoliating bark	
hawthorn	Crataegus spp.	white flowers; fruit and fall color vary by species; 'Crimson Cloud' has pink flowers	Cratgaegus ambiguus is very drought-tolerant
golden rain tree	Koelreuteria paniculata	yellow flowers in summer; papery, lantern-shaped seedpods; yellow fall color	xeric
Amur maackia	Maackia amurensis	white flowers in summer; exfoliating bark	
crabapple	Malus spp.	flowers, fruit, and leaf color varies by species	for disease resistance, CSU recommends 'Adams', 'Centurian', 'Coralburst', 'Guinevere', 'Henning', 'Indian Summer', 'Ralph Shay', and 'Zelkirk'
Newport plum	Prunus ceracifera 'Newport'	pink flowers in spring; purple fruit; purple fall color	
Princess Kay plum	P. nigra 'Princess Kay'	white flowers in spring; red fruit; yellow fall color	
Mayday tree	P. padus	white flowers in spring; black fruit; orange fall color	
chokecherry	P. virginiana 'Canada Red' or 'Schubert'	white flowers in spring; maroon summer foliage; edible berries	suckers; best used in a lawn where the suckers can be mowed
Ussurian pear	Pyrus ussuriensis	white flowers in spring; maroon fall color	
Peking tree lilac	Syringa pekinensis	white flowers in spring; yellow fall color	
Japanese tree lilac	S. reticulata	white flowers in spring	
yellowhorn	Xanthocerus sorbifolium	white and red flowers in spring; seedpods	

the sun in winter), locate a shade tree on the southwestern corner and at least 20 feet away from the house and utility lines. (This is just a guideline—for better accuracy, observe the sun and shade patterns on your property for one season before siting a shade tree.) When siting trees in the front yard, keep in mind that ice dams can form on driveways, walks and streets, wherever the tree casts a shadow in winter. Counterintuitively, this can occur even on slopes, and even if the tree is deciduous.

Evergreens are well suited to blocking wind and creating year round privacy. For blizzard insurance you might want to try the limber pine, its flexible boughs less likely to break under snow load. 'Vanderwolf's Pyramid' is an especially nice form with long bluish needles. Spruces generally fare better than pines in unseasonable snowstorms. The columnar form of the Colorado blue spruce is more suitable than the larger species for smaller landscapes. White fir, which resembles the Colorado blue spruce (but with soft needles), is also a good option. The tradeoff is that these are thirstier than Ponderosa pines, piñons, and junipers, all better choices for drier locations, but more subject to breakage.

Small trees are good for privacy screening, to shade a patio, to make a silhouette against a bare wall, to highlight a corner, or to create a tall accent in a shrub border. Many of these trees are available either with multiple trunks or trained to a single trunk. Multitrunked trees are more casual and natural in appearance, single-trunked trees more formal and refined. To make a multitrunked tree look more like a tree rather than a large shrub, prune branches off the lower third of each trunk as it matures. For smaller ornamental trees in the 15- to 25-foot height range, the selection is vast. Why settle for a boring ginnala maple, whose one real claim to fame is red fall color, when you can have a serviceberry with white flowers in spring, bird-attracting black edible fruit in summer, and red fall color? The best ornamental trees put on multiple performances. A few, like the Russian hawthorn, manage four—fragrant white flowers in May, attractively cut leaves, golden fall color, and red berries in winter.

In extremely wet or dry conditions, year-round interest becomes secondary to survival. Alders and our native river birch tolerate wet sites where no other trees will grow. For occasionally irrigated xeriscapes, good choices are the bigtooth maple, Ohio buckeye, New Mexican privet, Gambel oak, mountain mahoganies, wafer ash, hop tree, Ponderosa pine, piñon pine, and upright juniper.

Shrubs for Irrigated Gardens

Compared to trees, we have infinitely more choices when it comes to shrubs. But be aware that, as a rule, many popular landscape shrubs from other regions—azaleas, camellias, hydrangeas, hollies, laurels, and magnolias—cannot tolerate either the alkaline soils or cold winters. Broadleaf evergreens, the most prevalent type of shrub in damper climates, present the most obvious gap in our regional plant palette. Even those that are hardy enough to endure our winters can find it difficult to deal with cold, coupled with desiccating winds, extremely bright sunlight, and lack of reliable snow cover. We are only slightly better off in regards to needled evergreen shrubs. Once again, the selection is limited by the realities of our soil and climate. All of the best conifer nurseries in the West are located in the cooler, misty climes of coastal Oregon and Washington, where conditions could hardly be more dissimilar than ours.

Lest you get the idea that we are shrub deprived, nothing could be further from the truth.

Beyond the broadleaf evergreens and true acid-lovers, just about any other cold-hardy shrub thrives in our gardens as long as supplemental irrigation can be provided. We are further blessed with a huge selection of drought-tolerant shrubs that are difficult, if not impossible, to grow in so-called "milder" climates, where abundant precipitation and humidity cause them to rot. Every region has its drawbacks. A member of my local garden club moved back to Pennsylvania after having gardened in Colorado for two decades. She had regaled us with stories of how, in Pennsylvania, "anything you stick in the ground grows." But she'd forgotten about anthracnose. Writing back to us, she described the horror of watching mature trees and shrubs turn black and die of this dreadful disease that is rare in the Intermountain West.

Shrubs are handy for making groupings with small trees, to bolster windbreaks and privacy screening, to accentuate or obscure property lines, on corners, and as foundation plantings. The tradition of planting a row of shrubs along house walls is mainly inspired by aesthetics. Shrubs soften the abrupt transition between the flat plane of the yard and the severe verticality of the house—exactly the same way a frill of parsley sets off a baked ham on a platter. Foundation plantings also disguise the bare expanse of concrete at ground level that typifies many older homes. And they do have a few unexpected benefits. Thorny shrubs growing snugly against a house wall discourage burglars from climbing through unguarded windows. Evergreen shrubs provide some insulation to the interior of the home from winter's cold and summer's heat (and give birds shelter from the same weather extremes). Dense evergreen shrubs also help cut down on street noise.

When deciding what to plant, an important consideration is protecting the structure of the house. Water from irrigation can severely damage foundation and basement walls. To be on the safe side, never irrigate next to a house wall unless you are absolutely certain your soil is fast-draining. All foundation plantings should be able to subsist on

Red large-flowered clematis 'Niobe' shares a trellis with a pink 'Morden Centennial' rose.

rainwater after they have been established by hand watering. You can plant either a uniform hedge of shrubs (the parsley look), or you can choose a mixture of shrub types (evergreen and deciduous). A mix is less formal but the decision is primarily a matter of taste. (You may also elect to skip foundation plantings altogether.)

For a regional look, consider tall western sagebrush, blue mist spirea, tall blue rabbitbrush, fernbush, mountain mahogany, cliffrose, 'Moonlight'

broom, rock spirea, clove currant, or 'Miss Kim' lilac. Because they are extremely drought-tolerant, it's no wonder junipers have become the universal foundation shrub in our region. These dense evergreens meet every criteria for a sunny site (except thorns, but it would take a really determined burglar to climb into a juniper with their reputation for tearing clothes and raising nasty welts on exposed flesh). Also prowler-proof are well-armed barberries, flowering quince, and large shrub roses. If you decide to use junipers, choose a variety that won't outgrow its allotted space. Dwarf pfitzers, yellow-tipped 'Old Gold' and 'Armstrong', both mature at 4 feet tall by 6 feet wide. All of these shrubs thrive against a hot, sunny wall.

Roses

In the past, buying a rose was always somewhat like buying a pet hamster. As with the hamster, the rose was the seductively inexpensive first step into a product care morass necessary to keep the thing alive. Specialized rose care products have always been considered essential tools of good rose husbandry. So, what explains those glorious bowers of roses growing along freeway edges in industrial parts of town, in yards of decaying homes in once prosperous neighborhoods, in historic cemeteries, and in abandoned homesteads? It's only a matter of selection. Nature played a role in the selection of these decades-old, neglected roses. Those rugged enough to fend for themselves have survived. The prima donnas are long gone.

For too long, the only standard of perfection was the rose's flower. Fungal-ridden foliage, limited winter hardiness, and a scourge of insect opponents were the price exacted for beautiful blossoms. But, no more. Rose breeders have perfected new generations of easy-care roses. Some of these are modeled after the classic hybrid tea, a rose whose exquisitely formed buds open into a huge blowsy tutu of a flower—too often carried on a scarecrow of a shrub. The improved versions have disease-resistant foliage and attractively shaped bushes. There are also rose flowers with a single row of petals reminiscent of the wild roses of hedgerows and fallow fields. Others take after old-fashioned roses, their heavy flowerheads packed with petals and redolent of musk and myrrh. Unlike many old-fashioned roses, new varieties may bloom more than once each season and huge shrubs have been transformed into a more compact size better suited to the average urban or suburban lot.

Many new roses are hardy enough that, except in the coldest parts of our region, we can skip the fall regimen of wrapping or piling mulch over tender canes. Most need only an occasional soaking from October to April to survive winter. For further insurance, choose "own-root" roses. These are more likely to resprout from their roots if a hard winter kills the top growth. Grafted roses often revert to their hardy Dr. Huey rootstock, which explains why there are so many large red spring-blooming roses across the Mountain West. A handsome rose, true, but not the 'Sheer Bliss' you planted.

The House of Meilland of Provence, France, has introduced some of the best new roses. They've brought us the carefree Meideland series, including baby pink 'Bonica', snowy white 'Alba Meideland', and traffic-stopping 'Scarlet Meideland', roses so tough they're often used in parkway median plantings and in commercial landscapes. Many of David Austin's new English roses have proven to be hardier than even their creator had hoped. Embodying all of the desirable traits of heirloom roses, but longer-blooming and smaller in size, these romantic roses come in a range of delicate shades, have powerful scents, and some of the largest petal counts of any of the modern roses. Not all of the Austin roses are as full as a square dancer's crinolines. A few are single, or like 'Belle Story', semidouble.

Not too surprisingly, the hardiest roses to date originate in Canada. The Explorer series, from the Plant Research Center in Ottawa, and the Parkland series, from the Morden Research Station in Manitoba, can withstand extremely low temperatures, even without benefit of snow cover. As a rule, the Canadian roses sacrifice fragrance for hardiness. Many, such as 'John Cabot,' are big, rangy shrubs that can be trained to cover a fence or a wall where lack of perfume is less of an issue than stamina. Fragrant 'Henry Kelsey' and 'William Baffin,' at 6 to 8 feet, are large enough to use as climbers in some situations, though they can't claim the make-you-swoon aromas of the English roses.

'John Cabot' rose in Gerry Krueger's Spokane, Washington, garden.

American rose breeders are also introducing improved roses. Jackson & Perkins, of hybrid tea fame, offers several lines of easy-care roses including their Simplicity shrub roses, ground-cover roses, and their own series of English roses. At this rate, roses are bound to lose their notoriety for being finicky hobbyist plants best enjoyed in someone else's garden, and instead earn new status as one of the easiest care plants in the landscape.

My love affair with miniature roses began, like many modern-day romances, with a chance encounter in the neighborhood supermarket. Ten years ago I was beguiled by a pot of little lavender roses all dressed up in florist's foil and a bow to celebrate Valentine's Day. When the initial flush of blossoms faded, I moved the rose to a larger pot to get it ready to go outside. That's when I discovered there were four individual cuttings in one tiny pot. I separated them, gave each its own container, and sat them in a sunny window to grow until mid-April. Once transplanted into the garden, each of these little roses developed into a handsome 24-inch by 24-inch bush. They bloomed nonstop for the rest of that summer. Over the years, these roses have accepted heavy soil without complaint, as well as shrugging off heat, hail, disease, insects, and extreme cold. They've never once been sprayed or covered in winter—all they ask is to be pruned of dead wood, fertilized in late spring, and deadheaded occasionally.

Besides that first rose, which turned out to be 'Lavender Jewel', I've also had success with other grocery store roses. Anonymous, but nevertheless pretty, red and coral varieties have done well and stay only one foot tall. Small ones like these show better when several of the same color are grouped together rather than planted singly. All of the miniatures I've tried are as tough and as floriferous as 'Lavender Jewel'. Still, buying roses in the floral department of grocery stores roses is a bit hit-and-miss. To get named varieties complete with descriptive information, check local nurseries or nursery catalogs.

EPILOGUE

It had been a mild autumn, until, for the second year in a row, an October snowstorm struck before the deciduous trees had dropped their leaves. Perennial seedheads that had, until that day, promised to enliven the garden through the coming winter lay in heaps, smashed and broken. Ornamental grasses were similarly crushed and flattened. A once magnificent Allegheny viburnum was shattered by the heavy snow, its bulk splayed across the front sidewalk. A golden raintree sapling was literally snapped in half. There would be no "winter interest" to celebrate this year.

After clearing the walkway of fallen branches, I could hardly make myself set foot out-of-doors in the weeks that followed. The cleanup could wait until spring. I was still mourning the damage, when several weeks later, Randy and I hosted a horticulturalist from Nova Scotia. Since he was interested in paleontology, we took him to see the dinosaur footprints in the Morrison formation west of Denver. As we climbed the ridge I proudly pointed out the rugged and incomparably beautiful geology and accompanying native flora. He exclaimed over the contorted and grizzled forms of the pines and junipers. It hit me then that heavy snows and constant winds are the very forces that shape the character of these evergreens, adversity sculpting their natural grace and asymmetry. In milder climates, bonsais such as these would have instead retained the cone-like symmetry of Christmas trees.

And, that would be our loss. The very forces of nature that shaped these trees shape our gardens as well. I could replace the Allegheny viburnum and the golden raintree with perfect new nursery specimens and this time try to protect them from nature's ravages, but in the end, what could this accomplish? The Intermountain West is not the place for perfect nursery specimens. While it sometimes feels like a handicap, our unpredictable weather is exactly what defines our region. Should my shrubs and trees survive they will develop a wilder sort of beauty, a beauty much more appropriate to this untamed and unpredictable place.

Although gardeners are inevitably heartsick to see their charges despoiled, nature had, once again, provided me with a not-so-gentle reminder that the high plains of Colorado is not tree country. Grasses and perennials that are much better suited to life on the prairie sustained no permanent damage from this autumn's heavy snowfall. And here is the lesson: Adapted plants survive. Occasionally we can pull one over on Mother Nature (and if we can get away with it, why not?). But ultimately, any plant that doesn't make it here is a clue to our true identity and not necessarily a reflection on our horticultural skills. Only when we stop treating nature as an adversary—and stop trying to be something we are not—can our gardens and landscapes reach their full potential.

RECOMMENDED READING

Barr, Claude A. *Jewels of the Plains: Wild Flowers of the Great Plains Grasslands and Hills.* Minneapolis, MN: University of Minnesota Press, 1983.

Ellefson, Connie Lockhart, and David Winger. *Xeriscape Colorado: The Complete Guide.* Denver, CO: Westcliffe Publishers, 2004.

Foster, H. Lincoln. *Rock Gardening: A Guide to Growing Alpines and Other Wildflowers in the American Garden.* Timber Horticultural Reprint Series. Portland, OR: Timber Press, 1968.

Hyde, Barbara. *Gardening in the Mountain West.* Boulder, CO: Johnson Printing, 1999.

Hyde, Barbara. *Gardening in the Mountain West: The Progress of a Gardener,* Vol. 2. Boulder, CO: Johnson Printing, 1995.

Knopf, Jim. *Waterwise Landscaping with Trees, Shrubs, and Vines: A Xeriscape Guide for the Rocky Mountain Region, California, and the Desert Southwest.* Boulder, CO: Chamisa Books, 1999.

Knopf, Jim. *The Xeriscape Flower Gardener: A Waterwise Guide for the Rocky Mountain Region.* Boulder, CO: Johnson Books, 1991.

Mutel, Cornelia Fleischer, and John C. Emerick. *From Grassland to Glacier: The Natural History of Colorado and the Surrounding Region.* Boulder, CO: Johnson Books, 1992.

North American Rock Garden Society. *Rock Garden Design and Construction.* Portland, OR: Timber Press, 2003.

Phillips, Judith. *Natural by Design: Beauty and Balance in Southwest Gardens.* Santa Fe, NM: Museum of New Mexico Press, 1995.

Phillips, Judith. *Plants for Natural Gardens: Southwestern Native and Adaptive Trees, Shrubs, Wildflowers and Grasses.* Santa Fe, NM: Museum of New Mexico Press, 1995.

Phillips, Judith. *Southwestern Landscaping with Native Plants.* Santa Fe, NM: Museum of New Mexico Press, 1987.

Pollan, Michael. *Second Nature: A Gardener's Education.* New York: The Atlantic Monthly Press, 1991.

Proctor, Rob. *How to Get Started in Rocky Mountain Gardening.* Nashville, TN: Cool Springs Press, 2005.

Springer, Lauren, and Rob Proctor. *Passionate Gardening: Good Advice for Challenging Climates.* Golden, CO: Fulcrum Publishing, 2000.

Springer, Lauren. *The Undaunted Gardener: Planting for Weather-Resilient Beauty.* Golden, CO: Fulcrum Publishing, 1994.

Weeds of the West. Western Society of Weed Science, the Western United States Land Grant Universities Cooperative Extension Services and the University of Wyoming, rev. 1992.

INDEX

Page numbers in **boldface** type indicate photographs